# BORDERLINES IN A GLOBALIZED WORLD

# Social Indicators Research Series

Volume 9



This new series aims to provide a public forum for single treatises and collections of papers on social indicators research that are too long to be published in our journal *Social Indicators Research*. Like the journal, the book series deals with statistical assessments of the quality of life from a broad perspective. It welcomes the research on a wide variety of substantive areas, including health, crime, housing, education, family life, leisure activities, transportation, mobility, economics, work, religion and environmental issues. These areas of research will focus on the impact of key issues such as health on the overall quality of life and vice versa. An international review board, consisting of Ruut Veenhoven, Joachim Vogel, Ed Diener, Torbjorn Moum and Wolfgang Glatzer, will ensure the high quality of the series as a whole.

*The titles published in this series are listed at the end of this volume.*

# BORDERLINES IN A GLOBALIZED WORLD

*New Perspectives in a Sociology of the World-System*

*Edited by*

G. PREYER
*J.W. Goethe Universität,*
*Frankfurt am Main*

and

M. BÖS
*Institut für Soziologie,*
*Ruprecht Karls-Universität Heidelberg*

KLUWER ACADEMIC PUBLISHERS
DORDRECHT / BOSTON / LONDON

A C.I.P. Catalogue record for this book is available from the Library of Congress.

ISBN 978-90-481-5979-6

Published by Kluwer Academic Publishers,
P.O. Box 17, 3300 AA Dordrecht, The Netherlands.

Sold and distributed in North, Central and South America
by Kluwer Academic Publishers,
101 Philip Drive, Norwell, MA 02061, U.S.A.

In all other countries, sold and distributed
by Kluwer Academic Publishers,
P.O. Box 322, 3300 AH Dordrecht, The Netherlands.

*Printed on acid-free paper*

*To Walter L. Bühl*

# CONTENTS

## III The Global and the Local: The Collapse and Reconstruction of Borderlines

GERHARD PREYER, MATHIAS BÖS

# INTRODUCTION: BORDERLINES IN TIME OF GLOBALIZATION

Scholars of different schools have extensively analyzed world-systems under the fashionable heading "globalization". Our collected new research pushes the argument one-step further. Globalization is not a homogenization of all social life on earth. It is a heterogeneous process that connects the global and the local on different levels. Furthermore, globalization is more often used as a catchall argument to pursue political goals than for sound scientific analysis. Eager followers of the concept of globalization largely overestimate its dynamics and its opponents forcefully deconstruct the concept under different perspectives. Yet, we also recognize, that globalization is a social process that leads to new forms of differentiation and thereby to an evolution of functional imperatives for all differentiated social systems, not only for the economic system, but also for the political system, for ethnic and religious communities as well as for households and families. Differentiation means distinction. Distinctions emerge on both sides: inside and outside. Analyzing the processes to bridge inside and outside, we find a set of mechanisms of selection, which produce new zones of social change but also new borderlines and new frontiers.

The world-system perspective emerged in the 1970's as a critique of the premises and practices of nineteenth century social science. One of its primary concerns was a re-conceptualization of the unit of analysis in studies of long-term, large-scale social change. This re-conceptualization took the form of a single and singular spatio-temporal unit, the Modern World-System, which emerges in Europe and parts of the Americas at the beginning of the long sixteenth century. In retrospect globalization is not at all a new phenomenon. In the development of the system of modern societies globalization is nothing that emerged from nowhere but something eagerly formed by nation states. Thus Roland Robertson, among others, argues that "globalization" is a condition of modernization. But it would be wrong to assume that the classic theory of modernization has now only another case of application. To understand contemporary developments we need new concepts, strategies of research, and explanations. This volume starts out with the concepts of *border* and *membership* to describe structural features that emerge in a global world-system. Border structures and memberships define identities traditionally associated with the nation state. Looking on different spheres of



*G. Preyer, M. Bös (eds.), Borderlines in a Globalized World, ix-xviii.*

social life we found different types of globalization that have different temporal characteristics, like large cyclical oscillations or long-term upward trends. As world-systems expand they incorporate new territories and new peoples. The processes of incorporation create new frontiers or boundaries. These frontiers or boundary zones are the locus of resistance to incorporation, ethnogenesis, ethnic transformation, and ethnocide. In a globalized world shifting borders indicate social change and new possibilities.

The word *border* has most of all a territorial connotation, often referring "to a line that separates one country, state, province etc. from another" (1996) these state lines are repeatedly established by frontiers, which move the edge of a territory or form its limits or margins. One of the few classical masters of sociological thought who tried to define the concept of borders was Georg Simmel: "The border is not a spatial fact with sociological effects, but a sociological fact, that is spatially shaped" (Simmel 1983 [1908], 467 [translation by the authors]).[1] According to Simmel borders are social meaning structures that are expressed in reference to a territory. In order to analyze borders he uses the metaphor of the line. First there is the idea of the line that finds its territorially expression in separating the plane in two parts. Human beings like mathematical points either belong to one or the other side of the line or to the line itself. The prototype of the borderline is the border of the nation state. "A society, because its space of existence is framed by conscious borders, is through that as well characterized as internally connected and vice versa: the interacting units, the functional relation of elements to each other gain there spatial expression in the framing borderline. There might be nothing else which expresses the strength of the cohesion of a state ... like that sociological centripetality which rises to the sensory-experienced picture of a stable framing borderline" (Simmel 1983 [1908], 495 [translation by the authors]).[2] In his chapter on social borders he argues that the assumed congruency of social borders with the border of the nation state is an exception. For Simmel the concept of border is important because it relates individuals and groups to each other (Simmel 1983 [1908], 467). These relations are expressed in *memberships*. Membership controls how an individual takes part in a social group. Hence membership controls which kinds of communications or actions are expected from the individual, with this control function membership regulates the relation between groups as well. Simmel carefully talks about memberships, in plural, for Simmel modernity is characterized by many overlapping social borders generating multiple sets of memberships, which in turn form the stable network of society. With the development of system theory a new metaphor of the border emerges, the border as a membrane (Luhmann 1997, 75). Like the membrane the border does not separate but connect the system with its environment. It is exactly the permeability of the border that enables the system to survive. So one of the basic performances of every system is the structuration of border crossings. The border process sustains the continuity of the system. This continuing process results often in the assumption that borders are stable and fixed, but in order to fulfill their function they have to be flexible and constantly changing. This structural feature of borderlines has again important implication for the concept of membership. Codes of membership are never fixed they are constantly changing as well, and most of all new members can be incorporated or old members excluded. Border structures are dynamic processes of connection and separation, be it the line or the membrane there is always a three-way logic of borders: borders include, exclude and connect at the same time. They characterize what it means to belong to the we-group and to belong to the they-group and, at least implicitly, the border defines what both groups have in common.

Our research project has explored how the central features of globalization the de- and re-production of borderlines and memberships can be fruitfully employed on a theoretical and empirical level. The triumph or disaster of the buzzword globalization is closely linked to the changes we faced in the world over the last decade. From the perspective of social theories in western industrialized countries – and nothing more we wish to address here – trembling borders characterized the last decade and the emergence of new border structures at all levels of social live. The notion of globalization bares the promise to capture these processes of de-bordernization and re-bordernization. The concept of border restructures our perception in order to overcome the sheer lag of useable categories to explain today's social world. The perspective of borders can be used to analyze seemingly paradoxical social processes: in a global system inclusions and exclusions, universalizations and particularizations are mutually enhancing each other, such as in economic strategies of companies like world wide mergers and particularization of interests in local communities take place together. But there is no global as such or in singular. There are many, partly connected world-systems. The global can serve as a multiple point of reference to processes that are totally different in origins, dynamics and outcomes. It is exactly the complex system of global world-systems, which has to be taken in to account in theorizing the emergent processes of particularization, fragmentation, hybridization and exclusion. World-systems form a set of border structures, partly overlapping, partly referencing to each other, but always relating the universal and the particular as well as the in and the out. Borders separate in and out, but by doing so they structure the contact and control the influence of different social systems on each other. Networks perform these mechanisms of selection. Globalization is used as a metaphor to describe the complex sets of interrelated networks within an emerging global social structure. In a time of globalization the development of networks as an increasingly important part of a new social structure means different conditions of membership as well, leading to forms of segregation and social conflicts without simple or consensual solutions. Furthermore borders do not only define in and out; they structure as well the "in between". Living "on the margin" can be a stable status as well. More often than not we find situations were memberships are not clearly defined. These aspects of borders and membership are epitomized in the metaphor of "the stranger", the immigrant, who is inside the borders but does not really belong.

It is an essential feature of social systems that they have borderlines and a code of membership. These lines of discrimination has to be produced, reproduced, and stabilized otherwise the collectivity disappears. In a time of globalization a sociology of borderlines has to emphasize the de-construction and re-construction of borderlines within global settings. Our collected studies put together bits and pieces that are useful to come to terms with these bordernization processes.

In this volume we approach world-systems from three different perspectives. The first part sets the stage in exploring the main ideas and problems in theorizing globalization processes and their relation to borderlines. The next part reconsiders the concept of borders under the dichotomy of membership / non-membership reflected in different forms of memberships as re- (or de-) bordernization processes. And the third and last part examines borderlines in the interaction of local and global processes.

In the first part "Reconceptionalizations of the Global: Borderlines in the World-System" we collect useful aspects of theorizing global processes in social sciences by introducing the concept of borders. A brief account of European history reveals, collective identity is produced by the social construction of boundaries. These boundaries divide and separate the real manifold processes of interaction and social relationships. On a global level different cultural programs of modernity were shaped by the continuous interaction between the cultural premises and repertoires of societies. Moreover, all societies continuously develop new interpretations of different dimensions of modernity – and all of them have developed different cultural agendas. *Shmuel N. Eisenstadt* employs the concept of borderlines to reconstruct the production of collective identities in European history. He argues that in discourses of identities and solidarities, the symbolic level cannot be separated from the level of social structure in structuring the allocation of entitlements and life chances. In this view modernity is a highly heterogeneous project driven by the different premises and repertoires of societies. *Christopher Chase Dunn* chooses another road to re-conceptionalize the global as a multi-layered and heterogeneous process of bordernization. Different types of globalization have different temporal characteristics. Some show long-term upward trends while others display large cyclical oscillations. The factors that explain the emergence of discourses of globalization are examined and analyzed in terms of the contradictory interests of powerful and less-powerful groups. The different trajectories of "types of globalization" let to different discourses of globalization. These discourses mirror the lags between different kinds of globalization that led to severe structural tensions within the world-system. *Thomas D. Hall* explores the potential analytical usefulness of the notion of borders within the concept of world-systems theory. "Frontier formation" within the processes of incorporation of territories and alien peoples is discussed in the light of rich examples from Europe and North America. It turns out that the image of the border, as a straight line on the map can be misleading. The process of incorporation is enacted within large frontiers or boundary zones, which are the locus of the transformation of ethnic identities, ethnogenesis and ethnocide. The theoretical discussion is illustrated with examples drawn from the interaction of European societies with the indigenous peoples of North America. This part ends with an account of the historical genesis of world-system theory and its contemporary challenges by *Richard E. Lee*. He reconstructs, how the choice in the unit of analysis improved the capacity of world-system theory to describe the long trajectories of social change. Within these processes he makes out new chances of reflexive control of processes even on a global level.

Starting from the notion of bordernization the second part "Defining Borderlines in the World-System: The Emergence of New Memberships" gives insights on how membership in different social entities could be theorized and related to empirical processes. One of the basic conditions of social systems is their "codes of membership" and the way that code is programmed. The operation of codes of membership draws the borderline between social systems and their environments. In this sense these codes of membership are constitutional for the social domain. *Gerhard Preyer* explores the evolution of membership as a basic feature of every collectivity, and distinguishes the conditions of membership on the levels of differentiated social systems, formal organizations, and elementary systems of interaction. The conditions of membership within a global setting change the structuration of solidarity and bordernization processes needed to relate the local and the global by media of electronic communication. In a global world-system social change shows new features: it is a system in which globalization and new particularization are not contrary but a result of social change. For comparative studies in the theory of social evolution the differentiation of typical codes of membership of segmentary, stratificary and functional differentiation is *one* indication of the complexity of societal systems. In modern societies the partial variability of membership and processes of inclusion are essential features. The restructuration of these "features" is *one* of the basic requirements in contemporary social development of solidarity and bordernization in different communities. The emergence of a global world-system, today, leads to new conditions of membership and role sets on the basis of social implementation of new media. *Barrie Axford* undertakes a close examination on what membership means in a globalized world. The notion of network, exemplified in transnational networks, is used to describe the dialectical relationships between bordernization and globalization. *Axford* examines the role of transnational networks of actors in the de-territorialization of social relationships in a globalized world. He adopts a modified structuralist perspective on the ways in which actors both reproduce and transform the conditions for action. Considering the applicability of the "network metaphor" to understand some of the dynamics of globalization, leads to a critique of the activities of transnational networks and of their "thickness" or "thinness" as contexts for identity formation. Finally, three different areas of network practice are discussed to exemplify the argument. The empirical analysis is structured around the question how actors relate themselves within these global settings. Increasing immigration, poly-ethnicity, and stabilization of ethnic identities is a common trait for all western societies. Increasing poly-ethnicity forces the political system of the open society to give rules who belongs to society and who does not. With the implementation of these policies different paradoxes arise. The paradoxes of external border-structures are of special importance because they blur the member/non-member distinction of the open society. Other paradoxes arise when we look at the normative definitions of membership within the open society. These paradoxes can be interpreted as a product of the interaction between the collectivity of the open society and its political system. Talcott Parsons calls this collectivity 'societal community'. *Mathias Bös* systematizes the paradoxes within the normative patterns of membership introduced by immigration in open societies. Nationally constituted societies are conceptionalized as sets of internal and external border structures institutionalized in a setting of three different policies of membership: immigration policies, nationality laws and citizenship policies. In this context the example of refugees in Germany after World War II serves *Uta Gerhardt* and *Birgitta Hohenester* as the basis to explore the chances of phenomenological sociology in reframing membership processes as processes of typification. Re-typification is shown as embedded in institutional settings of citizenship that can be – and in fact were – highly influenced by political actors. Integration by social equality accompanied by cultural diversity transformed the entire German society from dictatorship to democracy. Following Schütz, it is argued that a "formula of transformation" is needed that could help merge two realms of typifications – that of foreigners as the formerly out-group and that of inhabitants as the formerly in-group – into one. Citizenship as a set of legal entitlements has become a more inclusive category. However, the domain of politics has gone through fundamental changes as well.

The last part "The Global and the Local: The Collapse and Reconstruction of Borderlines" is committed to the dichotomy of the global and the local and its relation to borderlines in a time of globalization. *Christie Davies* and *Eugene Trivizas* talk about what they call "the imposition of liberty". They analyze the erosion of particularistic moral standards in Ireland in 1980s and 1990s due to powerful de-bordernization processes, which replaced these standards by the universalistic values of the legal and political institutions of the European center. As international European institutional structures displaced those of the Irish nation state and enforced unwanted civil rights on Irish territory, a de-bordernization in law and morality took place. The Irish nation state has been made subordinate to regional moral, legal and political institutional structures and been forced to uphold an external and universalistic set of rules in place of a particular Irish moral tradition. The individual citizens of Ireland enjoy now more freedom but the collective identity of Ireland has been eroded. With the fall of communism across Eastern Europe in 1989 and the official end of the USSR in 1991, the fundamental borderline that divided both Europe and the world after the Second World War, the line that defined "East" and "West", has ceased to exist. *F. Peter Wagner* surveys one of the most important publicly recognized de-bordernization processes: the collapse of the communist world. In reconstructing the historical cleavages between the "East" and "West" Wagner lays out the issues of development in regard to spatial displacement and representation that influences "western" ways of imagining the "East". Today, virtually the whole world population is immersed in a global context. From a society, which existed above all at a state-nation level, we have passed into another that operates economically, institutionally and socio-culturally on a planetary scale. This situation brings about socio-economic restructurings of local settings, which can be seen in de-territorialization processes and attempts at their re-territorialization. Here de-territorialization refers to the tendencies of these settings to break down socio-economically or culturally due to the fact that the processes and decisions over their organization and processing, taken on a world wide scale, become ever more out of control of the people who live within them. *Francisco Entrena* explores the de- and re-territorialization patterns of local settings in an era of globalization. The restructuring of border structures along the distinction of the global and the local manifest themselves in the stressing of local particularisms and group social bonds, which become strongly territorialized and localized.

The presented studies explore the concept of border in respect to sociological theory, membership and locality. The notion of globalization is used but anchored either in reference to a specific theoretical construct or in reference to an empirical process. By doing so the concept of globalization loses much of its ambiguity. Which does of course not mean that the processes the word describes are not ambiguous and paradox, they comprise the entangled aspects of the universal and the particular of the global and the local. Nevertheless the different contributions show that the concept of borderlines within the world-systems is a useful starting point for theoretical or empirical consideration on today's social world. The concepts of border and membership are capable to pinpoint globalization as a process with its own "heterogeneous" evolution, discarding the picture of globalization as a development to a homogenous global system. The theoretical and empirical research on economies, cultures, and politics in global world-system is only at its beginning. But some conclusions could be made.

In the *economic* sphere one has to notice that global strategies of production lead to ongoing evaluations of the comparative advantages of locations. Globalization does not mean that all are winner. On the contrary we have to face the development of large new region of exclusion in South-America, Asia, and Africa. Yet, also in western societies such regions of exclusion may emerge, the so-called processes of "Brasilanization". Furthermore new technologies and overpopulation effects the ecological environment, this also leads to conflicts within and fragmentation of societies. These "effects" are not limited to a local level; they are global in their very nature. We have to assume that the success of global and regional economic and political problem solving differs highly. The question is what are the effects of these differences. It is the task of further research to study the role of nation-states in the networks of a global world-system, most of all in the changed constellation between the political and the economic system. Important is to keep in mind that there will be no inclusion of all human beings as members in one "global community" or one "global culture". But there will be many global communities and networks in which people are members: The home of the employees of Siemens, which operates in 152 states at present, is not a global community as such but their local firms which process in reference to the whole trust. Concerning *socio-cultural* aspects of globalization, we recognize that in a global world-system the cultural traditions of the world regions overlap mainly in the interactions of the political, scientific and economic elites, and it is appropriate to presume that the mutual interests are fragile. Traveling and worldwide tourism are only weak mechanisms of global social integration because they are structured by luxurized ghettonization. It is unlikely that the world-system leads to a universal lifestyle and homogenous identities in classic sense. In the system of religion and culture new "fashions" emerge together with different kinds of fundamentalisms. The concept of "hybridization" might serve as a reference point to approach the problem from a different angel. Not in theorizing difference and separation but in theorizing mixture and creativity. Perhaps many phenomena can be explained not only by diffusion of cultural traits but also by their adaptation to multi-functional conditions of membership. Collective identities and their borders are heterogeneous projects still largely driven by premises and resources of the different societies, which constantly adapt to the evolution of different codes of membership. Some sobering remarks are as well at place concerning the *political realm*. It is doubtful that powerful global political regimes will emerge. In this context it is not at all sure if there is an increasing differentiation between political and juridical praxis in all parts of Asia, Africa or South-America. The same is true for the influence of private networks in business and politics. A global world-system cannot be regulated as a whole by norms and directives. There is no hegemon. In this sense it is the end of the universalistic claims of modernity, yet not of generalized "cognitive orientations" like Niklas Luhmann has called it. Especially within the political realm these "cognitive orientations" towards general principals within world society may serve as a reference for discourses of legitimization. But they will only lead to highly selective attempts to control codes of conduct on a world scale. World society is a chaotic and heterachic system without any center or regulation of the whole system. One of the key questions is, which structures and networks of exchange between the economic system and the political system are to be expected. The restructuring of the political membership - non-membership distinction, which means citizenship, is constantly at hand in order to cope with refugee flows or regional integration.

In respect to progress in *sociological theory*, this volume shows that the concepts of border and membership set forward by Simmel to analyze modern society about 100 years ago can be fruitfully employed to analyze the emerging structures within world-systems. The contributions in this volume supply arguments to deconstruct two myths of sociological theorizing on border structures and memberships: the assumption of continuity and the assumption of congruency. Border structures and memberships are highly flexible and changing over time furthermore they are overlapping and crosscutting. One of the dominant *assumptions of continuity* is often made in respect to borders and memberships of nation states. We have shown that the assumption of continuity is neither true in the territorial aspect of national constituted societies or world regions nor in respect to codes of memberships which are constantly changed and re-typified. Even processes seen as basic to the continuous existence of the nation state like moral or legal border structures are constantly changing and permeable. The same is true for the *assumption of congruency*; especially the borders of national constituted societies were never congruent. Subsystems of society, like businesses or households, always formed crosscutting networks. Full membership in a society might be important to determine life chance for each individual, but it was never a unified singular "meta"-status encompassing all other status. The different codes of membership forming different units of border structures are more and more oriented towards their own functional imperatives than towards any supposed "national unity". This inherent multiplexety of social systems blends easily into the multilayered structure of world-systems. Generally speaking: Social change in time of *globalization* is a heterogeneous development driven by premises and resources of different social systems. Therefore it is to expect that different forms of globalization produce tensions and a-synchronicities within the world-system. It is a chaotic and heterachic system. World-systems have borders zones, but there are no coherent regulations of border processes in such systems. Therefore there is no general control of border operations. Theorizing the complex picture sketched here is surly no easy task. But like this volume hopefully shows there are promising ideas and approaches which can and should be explored. Our research has shown that social systems are mainly determined by their codes of membership in respect to participation in communication, employment and decision-making, and that continuously re-programming these codes of membership is a functional imperative. Further research has to show the consequences of these processes in respect to the restructuration of social systems in time of globalization.

Our research was initiated and planned by the project Protosociology[3] and the periodical *Protosociology* An International Journal of Interdisciplinary Research, Johann Wolfgang Goethe-University Frankfurt am Main, Germany, *www.rz.uni-frankfurt.de/protosociology*. The editors would like to thank the contributors and in particular Immanuel Wallerstein and Shmuel Eisenstadt for help and encouragement.

We also like to mention Georg Peter who gives helpful arguments to incorporate the different aspects of the whole project.

## NOTES

[1] "Die Grenze ist nicht eine räumliche Tatsache mit soziologischen Wirkungen, sondern eine soziologische Tatsache, die sich räumlich formt" Simmel, Georg. 1983 [1908]. *Soziologie - Untersuchungen über die Formen der Vergesellschaftung*. Berlin: Dunker & Humblot.

[2] "So ist eine Gesellschaft dadurch, dass ihr Existenzraum von scharf bewußten Grenzen eingefaßt ist, als eine auch innerlich zusammengehörige charakterisiert, und umgekehrt: die wechselwirkende Einheit, die funktionelle Beziehung jedes Elementes zu jedem gewinnt ihren räumlichen Ausdruck in der einrahmenden Grenze. Es gibt vielleicht nichts, was die Kraft insbesondere des staatlichen Zusammenhaltens so stark erweist, als dass diese soziologische Zentripetalität, ... zu einem wie sinnlich empfundenen Bilde einer fest umschließenden Grenzlinie aufwächst." Ibid.

[3] From the project "Protosociology" are published on globalization and structural evolution: G. Preyer (Hrs.). *Strukturelle Evolution und das Weltsystem.* Theorien, Sozialstruktur und evolutionäre Entwicklungen. Frankfurt am Main: Suhrkamp Verlag STW 1998, G. Preyer *Die globale Herausforderung*. Wie Deutschland an die Weltspitze zurückkehren kann. Frankfurt am Main: Frankfurter Allgemeine Zeitung/Gabler Edition 1998. G. Preyer, J. Schissler. *Integriertes Management*. Was kommt nach der Lean-Production. Frankfurt am Main: Frankfurter Allgemeine - Buch 1996.

## REFERENCES

(1996). *Webster's new universal unabridged dictionary*. New York: Barnes & Noble Books.

Luhmann, Niklas (1997). *Die Gesellschaft der Gesellschaft*. Frankfurt am Main: Suhrkamp.

Simmel, Georg (1983 [1908]). *Soziologie - Untersuchungen über die Formen der Vergesellschaftung*. Berlin: Dunker & Humblot.

# Reconceptionalizations of the Global: Borderlines in the World-system

SHMUEL NOAH EISENSTADT

# THE CONTINUAL RECONSTRUCTION OF MULTIPLE MODERN CIVILIZATIONS AND COLLECTIVE IDENTITIES

## 1 CONSTRUCTIONS OF COLLECTIVE IDENTITY

The starting point of this analysis is the recognition that the major patterns of social interaction and social structure which crystallize in any population are always structured on multiple levels, in different arenas of social and cultural activities, in different contexts of action and they also tend to exhibit systemic tendencies.

The populations which live within the confines of what has been designated as a "society" or a macro-societal order are not usually organized into one "system," but rather into several frameworks or "systems," including political systems, economic formations, different ascriptive collectivities, and civilizational frameworks seemingly naturally given.

In every such continuous pattern of social interaction, there develop tendencies to some systemic qualities, with the concomitant construction of boundaries of the different patterns of interaction. However, these are very fragile. But being fragile does not mean that they are non-existent. It does mean, however, that special mechanisms of control and integration, special regulative mechanisms – above all, those of the institutionalization and reproduction of the general prerequisites of social interaction – are needed to overcome the inherent instability and fragility of their boundaries in order to maintain and assure their reproduction.

Such integrative mechanisms and processes of control become more important and autonomous and hence also more fragile – as manifest for instance in the connection of bureaucracies of general systems of social law – as different social and political systems and civilizational frameworks become more complex. It was Herbert Simon's signal contribution to point out that the mechanisms of control are autonomous analytical dimensions, and that every such mechanism of control has an in-built second order of stability and instability.[1] These mechanisms of control, these integrative mechanisms may acquire an autonomy of their own in the construction and maintenance of systemic boundaries.



*G. Preyer, M. Bös (eds.), Borderlines in a Globalized World, 3-12.*

However, whatever the strengths of the systemic tendencies of patterns of social interaction, such patterns never develop as entirely self-enclosed systems, nor are they naturally given. The processes of the construction of collectivities, social systems and civilizational frameworks constitute processes of continuous struggle in which ideological, "material" and power elements are continuously interwoven. These processes are structured, articulated and carried by different social actors, above all by different coalitions of elites and contra-elites and influentials in interactions with the broader sectors of the society. Each "system" with its flexible boundaries is carried by different coalitions of such carriers. These different structures and patterns – these "systems" – evince different patterns of organization, continuity and change. They may change within the "same" society to different degrees and in different ways in various areas of social life.

These differences in the settings and contexts of various activities are not random or accidental. They are closely related to the specific organizational exigencies and to the basic symbolic problematique of each type and level of activity. These different types of problematiques are often combined and recombined in various concrete situations, according to the definitions of the settings of such situations.

Needless to say, not all components or themes or tropes which can be found in the cultural repertoire of a society are relevant to and activated in all such activities and situations. There is continual selection, reconstruction, reinterpretation, and invention of themes, tropes, parameters, models and codes, as well as of the modes of semiotic mediation employed in their presentation. Such selection, recomposition, and reinterpretation emphasize the distinctiveness and autonomy of each sphere or arena of activity, as well as its connection with the more general frameworks or meta-contexts. Yet, to whatever extent they are interconnected, they are never fully integrated in a closed system and they are always subject to continuous reinterpretation, and each one of them necessarily evinces strong tendencies to some, albeit limited, autonomy. Thus, the different arenas of human activity do not lose their partial autonomy or the possibility of innovation within and across them.

## 2 BOUNDARIES OF SOCIAL SYSTEMS

The construction of the boundaries of social systems, collectivities and organizations, necessarily delineates their relations with their environment. It is wrong, however, to assume that there is a natural environment of any society, of any pattern of social interaction. There is no such thing as the "natural" environment "out there". Rather, each pattern of social interaction, each society constructs its own environment, continuously highlighted. It is the construction of such multiple environments in different ecological settings, which highlights the distinct features of the construction of the human environment. Any environment is, within very broad limits, constructed by society and can be understood only in relation to that society or pattern of social interaction. Of course, in the construction of an environment, any society has some material to base itself on.

Each "natural" environment provides several possible institutional choices, and one of these choices is being chosen by the respective social actors. Once such choices have been made, they set the limits or the boundaries of the system and generate the systemic sensitivity to environmental changes. These sensitivities are created not by the environment as such, nor by technology as such, but by society – in reconstructing the environment by using different technologies.

The concretization of these institutional tendencies takes place in different political-ecological settings. Two aspects of these settings are of special importance. One, emphasized strongly in recent research, is the importance of international political and economic systems in general, including the place of societies within them, and different types of relations of hegemony and dependency in particular. The second is the great variety of the political-ecological settings of societies, such as differences between large and small societies, and their respective dependence on internal or external markets. Both of these aspects greatly affect the ways in which institutional contours and dynamics tend to develop.

The fact that any setting of social interaction in general, and macro-societal orders in particular, are always acting in some inter-societal, "international" setting – makes them vulnerable to forces and change which may activate the various potentialities of protest and conflict that develop within them. Changes in various parts of the respective international system or systems of any society may impinge more directly on different groups and they may become more vulnerable to such impingements. Changeability and conflict are also inherent in the constitution of any social order because, as we have seen, such patterns of social interaction, however strong their systemic tendencies, never develop as entirely self-enclosed entities.

## 3 CONSTITUTIONS OF SYMBOLIC BOUNDARIES

Thus, indeed, collective identities and boundaries are also continually constituted, constructed and reconstructed. Truly enough in classical sociology and anthropology collectivities, collective identities were conceived, often implicitly, as quasi naturally given, almost as a non-social basis for social action, as a stable, unchanging, basically premodern counterpart to the fragile and alienating structure of modern social order.

As against these implicit assumptions of the classical approaches we propose that collective identity is not naturally generated but socially constructed: it is the intentional or non-intentional consequence of interactions which in their turn are socially patterned and structured.[2]

Collective identity is produced by the social construction of boundaries. These boundaries divide and separate the real manifold processes of interaction and social relationships; they establish a demarcation between inside and outside, strangers and familiars, kin and akin, friends and foes, culture and nature, enlightenment and superstition, civilization and barbary. Such a distinction does also pose the problem of crossing the boundaries: the stranger can become a member, and a member can become an outsider or a stranger. Religious conversion and excommunication represent obvious illustrations of this process of crossing the boundaries.

Collective identity depends on special processes of induction of the members in the collectivity, ranging from various rites of initiation to various collective rituals, in which the attribute of "similarity" among its members, as against the strangeness, the differences, the distinction of the other, is symbolically constructed and defined. Constructing boundaries and constructing a basis for trust solidarity and communal equality are two aspects of such processes.

The major codes of the construction of collective identity are those of primordiality, civility, and transcendental or sacredness. These codes have to be seen as ideal types, while real codings always combine different elements of these ideal types. Therefore concrete historical codings of collective identity are not homogeneous. They contain various components, the importance of which varies in different situations.

The construction of boundaries and solidarity is not, however, a purely "symbolic" affair, unrelated to the divisions of labor, to the control over resources and to social differentiation. Obviously solidarity entails consequences for the allocation of resources, above all for structuring the entitlements of the members of the collectivity as against the outsiders, and for different institutions within the collectivity. Such combination of constitution of "symbolic" boundaries together with the structuring of access to resources entails continuous struggle – and such struggle always takes place in specific historical contexts in which different combinations of primordial, civil and sacred orientations or "codes" come together.

## 4 THE COMPONENTS OF EUROPEAN HISTORICAL EXPERIENCE

I shall illustrate some of these processes by the analysis of the modern (European) nation states against the background of the historical experience of European Civilization.

The starting point of such analysis are some general characteristics of European civilization as it crystallized in the Medieval period[3] – the most important of which is the structural and cultural ideological pluralism that constituted one of the major components of the European historical experience. The structural pluralism that developed in Europe was characterized above all by a strong combination of low, but continuously increasing levels of structural differentiation with the continuously changing boundaries of different collectivities and frameworks. Parallelly there developed in Europe a multiplicity of prevalent cultural orientations which developed out of several traditions – the Judeo-Christian, the Greek and the various tribal ones; and a closely related multiplicity and complexity of ways to resolve the tensions between the transcendental and mundane orders, through either worldly (political and economic) or other-worldly activities. This multiplicity of orientations was rooted in the fact that the European civilization developed out of the continuous interaction between, on the one hand, the secondary breakthrough of two major Axial civilizations – the Jewish and the Greek one and on the other hand numerous "pagan" tribal traditions and society.

The combination of such multiple cultural traditions, with pluralistic structural and political-ecological conditions, explains the fact that in Western and Central Europe there developed – more than in other Christian civilizations – continuous tensions between hierarchy and equality, as the basic dimensions of participation of different sectors of the society in the political and religious arenas; and between the strong commitment and autonomous access of different groups and strata to the religious and political orders, on the one hand, and the emphasis on the mediation of such access by the Church or by political powers, on the other. At the same time there developed a strong tendency to define the respective institutional arenas or collectivities or strata as distinct social spaces with relatively sharply defined boundaries.

A second major repercussion of these ideological and structural dimensions is the fact that the mode of change that has developed in Western Europe, from at least the late Middle Ages on, was characterized by a relatively high degree of symbolic and ideological articulation of the political struggle and of movements of protest; by a high degree of coalescence of changes in different institutional arenas; by a very close relationship between such changes and the restructuring of political centers and regimes. Changes within various institutional arenas in Western Europe – such as the economic or the cultural arenas – impinged very intensely on one another and above all on the political sphere. These changes gave rise to a continuous process of restructuration of the boundaries of these different arenas, which did not however obliterate their respective autonomies.

The various centers and collectivities that developed in Europe did not simply coexist in a sort of adaptive symbiosis. The multiple centers and subcenters, as well as the different collectivities, which developed in Europe tended to become arranged in a complicated but never unified rigid hierarchy, in which no center was clearly predominant – but in which many of them aspired not only to actual but also to ideological predominance and hegemony.

All these collectivities and central institutions were legitimized in a variety of terms – in terms of primordial attachments and traditions, of transcendental criteria, as well as in terms of criteria of civic traditions. The continuous restructuring of centers and collectivities that took place in Europe was closely connected with the continuous oscillation and tension between the sacred, primordial, and civil dimensions of the legitimation of these centers and as components of these collectivities. While, for instance, many collectivities were defined mainly in primordial terms and the Church was seemingly defined mainly in sacred ones, yet at the same time, however, each collectivity and center also attempted to arrogate all the other symbols of legitimation to itself.

One of the major characteristics of the reconstruction of centers and of collectivities in Europe was that the very frequent attempts at such reconstruction were closely connected, first with very strong ideological struggles, which focused on the relative symbolic importance of the various collectivities and centers; second with attempts to combine the structuring of the boundaries of these centers and collectivities with the reconstruction of the bases of their legitimation; and third with a very strong consciousness of discontinuity between different stages or periods of their development.

## 5 NEW TYPES OF COLLECTIVITIES

The processes of constitution of collectivities was taken up anew in Europe from the sixteenth century or in close relation to several distinct historical processes. The most important of these processes were formations of the modern states – the absolutist states which later were transformed in the wake of the Great Revolutions into modern constitutional, later democratic states – often into nation-states; the development of new state-society relations most fully manifest in the emergence of a distinct type or types of civil society; the concomitant transformation of political processes; and last but certainly not least the development of capitalist, later industrial-capitalist types of political economy. The processes of construction of new types of collectivities, of collective identity or consciousness developed within modern European societies in conjunction with the processes of constitution of the new states and of legitimation of the new political regimes.

As in preceding historical periods, the different concrete types of collective identity or consciousness that developed in Europe combined primordial, civil and cultural-religious components or orientations and continually oscillated between these components, but there developed some far-reaching changes in the contents of these components and in their concrete constellations – leading to the crystallization of the nation-state as an ideal and as a reality alike.

Among the most important of such changes was the development of the very strong emphasis on territorial boundaries as the main loci of the institutionalization of collective identity; of new, above all secular definitions of each of the components of collective identity; the growing importance of the civil and procedural components thereof; and a continual tension between such different components. Closely related was the strong tendency to the ideologization of these components of construction of collective identities, and the concomitant tendency to the charismatization of the newly constructed collectivities and centers.

The emphasis on the territorial components of collective identity entailed the development of a very strong connection between the construction of states and that of the major "encompassing" collectivities – a connection which became epitomized in the tendency to the construction of what was to be called the nation state. The crystallization of the conceptions of nation state entailed development of a very strong tendency to the congruence between the cultural and political identities of the territorial population; the promulgation, by the center, of strong symbolic and affective commitments to the center; and of a close relationship between the centers and the more primordial dimensions of human existence and of social life.

Within these centers and collectivites there continually developed a high degree of tension between the ideals and premises of hierarchy and equality especially with regard to access to the center and the construction of the collective goals as articulated and propagated by the center, and the contestation or confrontation between equality and hierarchy constituted a continual focus of political struggle.

The concrete mode of interweaving of the construction of states with that of new types of collective consciousness and boundaries was, as Lipset and Rokkan have shown, in different European societies, the outcome of the resolution of the religious cleavages which arose in the Reformation and Counter-Reformation. Such resolution entailed the reconstruction and redefinition of components of collective identity in different patterns of primordial, civil, and cultural orientations – giving rise to different types of nation-states.[4]

## 6 THE VARIOUS CULTURAL PROGRAMMES OF MODERNITY

The European nation-state model has spread, with the expansion of modernity, far beyond Europe or "the West". But although this model served as such a semi-universal model – and some of its components such as emphasis on national boundaries of states; on the center's permeation of its peripheries, according to some culture programme, yet the concrete contours of these different modes of state has greatly varied among different societies in Asia and Africa – just as they varied also among European societies and between them and the United States and Latin America.

Thus, just to mention only a few obvious illustrations – India certainly could be described as a nation-state in the European sense – in different modes this is also true of many contemporary "islamic" or "Confucian" states. Even Japan which may be seen as the epitome of the pristine nation-state does yet in fact greatly differ, with its denial of being a part of universalistic civilization from the original European nation state model. Such variations have been shaped among others by the historical experience of their respective ancestors or setting – which certainly differed greatly from the European historical experience.

The very existence of these differences bears on one central problem of sociological analysis, namely the nature of modernization, of modernity. These differences signal a very far-reaching shift or change from the understanding which developed either in the period of the Enlightenment in the nineteenth century or, and above all, from the understanding of modernity that developed in the first decade or so after the Second World War and which were epitomized in the studies of modernization and of the convergence of industrial societies. These studies assumed, or were seen as assuming, that with growing modernization or industrialization the basic institutional and cultural aspects of modern society have become very similar. Or, in greater detail, these studies have assumed: (1) that the very process of modernization or industrialization generates not only relatively similar institutional problems, but also (2) that similar institutional solutions, or at least a very limited range of such solutions, will develop in most of these societies; and (3) that the dynamics of modern societies will therefore be shaped, above all, by the crystallization of such institutional solutions to these problems. Behind these theories loomed the conviction that progress toward modernity – be it political, industrial, or cultural – is almost inevitable. While, truly enough with the passing of time, there developed in all these studies a growing recognition of the possible diversity of transitional societies, it was still assumed that such diversity would disappear, as it were, at the end-stage of modernity.

But, as is well known, and as has been abundantly analyzed in the literature, the ideological and institutional developments in the contemporary world have not upheld this vision. The fact of the great institutional variability of different modern and modernizing societies – not only among the "transitional," but also among the more developed, even highly industrialized societies – became continuously more and more apparent.[5]

It is not that in many central aspects of their institutional structure – be it in occupational and industrial structure, in the structure of education or of cities – very strong convergence have not developed in different modern societies. But these convergences were above all manifest in the development of common or similar problems – the symbolic and institutional modes of "coping" as it were with these problems and the institutional and cultural dynamics and cultural discourse that developed in conjunction with them, differed greatly between different societies.

The growing recognition of these facts called for the development of a new perspective on the understanding of modernity and modernisation. Such perspective entails a far-reaching reappraisal of the vision of modernization, of modern civilizations – it calls for a reconception of modernity which bears also directly on the problems of shifting boundaries and changing solidarities. The focal point of such new perspective is the fact that the differences in the institutional dynamics and in the discourse that have been continuously developing in different modern societies are due not only, as has been often assumed in the seventies and early eighties, to various historical contingencies, such as for instance the historical timing of the incorporation of different societies into the emerging international systems, but that they all are above all rooted in different, distinct, cultural programmes of modernity that developed in these societies.

The various cultural programmes of modernity that developed in these societies have been continuously crystallized through the process of a highly selective incorporation and transformation in these civilizations of the various premises of Western modernity. These cultural programmes entailed, among others, different emphases on the various components of the "original" Western programme of modernity – such as man's active role in the universe; the relation between Wertrationalitat and Zweckrationalitat; the conceptions of cosmological time and its relation to historical time; the belief in progress; the relation of progress to history as the process through which the programme of progress develops; the relations to the major utopian visions; and the relation between the individual and the collectivity, between reason and emotions, and between the rational and the romantic and emotive, could be realized.[6]

While modernity was, within many of the non-Western societies, conceived as growing participation on the international scene – as well as in their internal discourse in terms derived from the ideas of equality and participation, other dimensions – especially those of individual liberty, of social and individual emancipation and individual autonomy as closely related to the historical unfolding of reason, which were constitutive of the Western European discourse on modernity from the Enlightenment on, were not necessarily always accepted.

These differences are not purely cultural or academic. They are closely related to basic institutional processes. Thus, to give only one illustration, in the political realm, they are closely related to the relations between the utopian and the civil components in the construction of modern politics; between "revolutionary" and "normal" politics, or between the general will and the will of all; between civil society and the state, between individual and collectivity. They entailed also different conceptions of authority and of its accountability, different modes of protest and of political activity, and also of different models of nation-states.

These different cultural programmes of modernity were not shaped by what has been sometimes designated as the natural evolutionary potentialities of these societies; by the natural unfolding of their respective traditions, nor by their placement in the new international settings. Rather they were shaped by the continuous interaction between the cultural premises and repertoires of these societies; the conceptions of social and political orders of authority, hierarchy and equality that were prevalent in them; their historical experience; and the mode of impingement of the different on them and of their incorporation into the modern political, economic, ideological world frameworks;

and by the structure of the elites and counter-elites, especially heterodoxies and movements of protest, which were predominant then; and by the themes promulgated and articulated by different counter-elites and movements of protest in different sectors of the society. The conceptions of modernity and the cultural agendas that developed in different societies differed greatly in different societies. Moreover, within all societies continuously developed new questionings and reinterpretations of different dimensions of modernity – and in all of them there have been developing different cultural agendas.

All these attested to the growing diversification of the visions and understanding of modernity, of the basic cultural agendas of the elites of different societies – far beyond the homogenic and hegemonic visions of modernity that were prevalent in the fifties. Yet at the same time while such diversity has certainly undermined the old hegemonies, yet it was closely connected – perhaps paradoxically – with the development of new multiple common reference points and networks, with a globalization of cultural networks and channels of communication far beyond what existed before, and they all entailed continuous struggles over shifting boundaries and changing solidarities.

## NOTES

1 H. Simon (1965): *The Architecture of Complexity.* Yearbook of the Society for General Systems Research, 10:63-76. Idem, *The Complexity*, Second 4. Idem (1977): *Models of Discovery and Other Topics in the Methods of Science* (Boston: D. Reidel) pp. 175-265.

2 This section is based on S. N. Eisenstadt and B. Sussman, "The Construction of Collective Identity," *European Journal of Sociology*, forthcoming.

3 See S.N. Eisenstadt (1987): *European Civilisation in a Comparative Perspective*, (Oslo, Norwegian University Press), ch. I.

4 See S.N. Eisenstadt (1988): *Fundamentalism, Revolutions and Modernity* (Cambridge, Cambridge University Press), forthcoming, ch. II.

5 S.N. Eisenstadt (1966): *Modernization: Protest and Change*, Englewood Cliffs, Prentice Hall, 1966; idem. (1973): *Tradition, Change and Modernity*, (New York, John Wiley and Sons); J.H. Goldthorpe (1971): "Theories of Industrial Society. Reflections on the Recrudescence on Historicism and the Future of Futurology," *Archives Européennes de sociologie*, Vol. 12, No. 2; S.N. Eisenstadt (1977): "Convergence and Divergence in Modern and Modernizing Societies," *International Journal of Middle East Studies*, Vol. 8, No. 1, 1977.

6 See S.N. Eisenstadt, *Tradition, Change and Modernity*, op. cit.; idem., *Fundamentalism, Revolution and Modernity*, op. cit.

CHRISTOPHER CHASE-DUNN

# GLOBALIZATION: A WORLD-SYSTEMS PERSPECTIVE REFLECTING ON SOME NON-RHETORICAL QUESTIONS

The discourse on globalization has become a flood. What are the trends and processes that are alleged to constitute globalization? How do they correspond with actual recent and long-term changes in the world economy and the world polity? What are the interests of different groups in the political programs implied by the notions of globalization? And what should be the response of those peoples who are likely to be left out of the grand project of world economic deregulation and the free reign of global capital?

These questions are addressed from the world-systems perspective, an historically oriented analysis of cycles, trends and long-run structural features of the world-economy. The recent explosion of awareness of transnational, international and global processes is set in the historical perspective of the last 600 years of the emergence of a capitalist intersocietal system in Europe and its expansion to the whole globe.

International economic integration has been a long-term trend since the great chartered companies of the seventeenth century, but this trend also reveals a cycle in the rise and fall of the proportion of all economic exchange that crosses state boundaries. Political globalization also has a long history in the emergence of international organizations over the last 200 years. Most of the many versions of globalization discourse focus on a recent qualitative transformation and emphasize the unique qualities of the new stage, while the longer view sees recent changes as part of a much older process of capitalist development and expansion in which there are important continuities as well as changes.

The trends and cycles reveal important continuities and imply that future struggles for economic justice and democracy need to base themselves on an analysis of how earlier struggles changed the scale and nature of development in the world-system. While some populists have suggested that progressive movements should employ the tools of economic nationalism to counter world market forces (e.g. Moore 1995), it is here submitted that political globalization of popular movements will be required in order to create a democratic and collectively rational global system.



*G. Preyer, M. Bös (eds.), Borderlines in a Globalized World, 13-34.*

## 1 THE WORLD-SYSTEMS PERSPECTIVE

Today the terms "world economy," "world market," and "globalization" are commonplace, appearing in the sound-bites of politicians, media commentators, and unemployed workers alike. But few know that the most important source for these phrases lies with work started by sociologists in the early Seventies. At a time when the mainstream assumption of accepted social, political, and economic science held that the "wealth of nations" reflected mainly on the cultural developments within those nations, a growing group of social scientists recognized that national "development" could be best understood as the complex outcome of local interactions with an aggressively expanding Europe-centered "world-system" (Wallerstein 1974; Frank 1978).[1] Not only did these scientists perceive the global nature of economic networks 20 years before they entered popular discourse, but they also saw that many of these networks extend back at least 600 years. Over this time, the peoples of the globe became linked into one integrated unit: the modern world-system.

Now, 20 years on, social scientists working in the area are trying to understand the history and evolution of the whole system, as well as how local, national and regional entities have been integrated into it. This current research has required broadening our perspective to include deeper temporal and larger spatial frameworks. For example, some recent research has compared the modern Europe-centered world-system of the last five hundred years with earlier, smaller intersocietal networks that have existed for millennia (Frank and Gills 1993; Chase-Dunn and Hall 1997). Other work uses the knowledge of cycles and trends that has grown out of world-systems research to anticipate likely future events with a precision impossible before the advent of the theory. This is still a new field and much remains to be done, but enough has already been achieved to provide a valuable understanding of the phenomenon of globalization.

The discourse about globalization has emerged mainly in the last decade. The term means many different things, and there are many reasons for its emergence as a popular concept. The usage of this term generally implies that a recent change (within the last decade or two) has occurred in technology and in the size of the arena of economic competition. The general idea is that information technology has created a context in which the global market, rather than separate national markets, is the relevant arena for economic competition. It then follows that economic competitiveness needs to be assessed in the global context, rather than in a national or local context. These notions have been used to justify the adoption of new practices by firms and governments all over the world and these developments have altered the political balances among states, firms, unions and other interest groups.

The first task is to put this development into historical context. The world-systems perspective has shown that intersocietal geopolitics and geoeconomics has been the relevant arena of competition for national-states, firms and classes for hundreds of years. The degree of international connectedness of economic and political/military networks was already important in the fourteenth and fifteenth centuries. The first "transnational corporations" (TNCs) were the great chartered companies of the seventeenth century. They organized both production and exchange on an intercontinental scale. The rise and fall of hegemonic core powers, which continues today with the relative decline of the United States hegemony, was already in full operation in the seventeenth century rise and fall of Dutch hegemony (see Arrighi 1994; Modelski and Thompson 1996; Taylor 1996).

The capitalist world-economy has experienced cyclical processes and secular trends for hundreds of years (Chase-Dunn 1989:Chapter 2). The cyclical processes include the rise and fall of hegemons, the Kondratieff wave (a forty to sixty year business cycle)[2], a cycle of warfare among core states (Goldstein 1988), and cycles of colonization and decolonization (Bergesen and Schoenberg 1980). The world-system has also experienced several secular trends including a long-term proletarianization of the world work force, growing concentration of capital into larger and larger firms, increasing internationalization of capital investment and of trade, and accelerating internationalization of political structures.

In this perspective, globalization is a long-term upward trend of political and economic change that is affected by cyclical processes. The most recent technological changes, and the expansions of international trade and investment, are part of these long-run changes. One question is exactly how the most recent changes compare with the long-run trends? And what are the important continuities as well as the qualitative differences that accompany these changes? These are the questions that I propose to explore.

## 2 TYPES OF GLOBALIZATION

There are at least five different dimensions of globalization that need to be distinguished. There are also several misunderstandings and misinterpretations that need to be clarified. Let us evaluate five different meanings of globalization:

### *2.1 Common ecological constraints*

This aspect of globalization involves global threats due to our fragile ecosystem and the globalization of ecological risks. Anthropogenic causes of ecological degradation have long operated, and these in turn have affected human social evolution. But ecological degradation has only recently begun to operate on a global scale. This fact creates a set of systemic constraints that require global collective action.

### *2.2 Cultural globalization*

This aspect of globalization relates to the diffusion of two sets of cultural phenomena:

(i) the proliferation of individualized values, originally of Western origin, to ever larger parts of the world population. These values are expressed in social constitutions that recognize individual rights and identities and transnational and international efforts to protect "human rights".

(ii) the adoption of originally Western institutional practices. Bureaucratic organization and rationality, belief in a law-like natural universe, the values of economic efficiency and political democracy have been spreading throughout the world since they were propagated in the European Enlightenment (Meyer 1996; Markoff 1996).

Whereas some of the discussions of the world polity assume that cultural components have been a central aspect of the modern world-system from the start (e.g. Meyer 1989; Mann 1986), I would emphasize the comparatively non-normative nature of the modern world-system (Chase-Dunn 1989: Chapter 5). But I would certainly acknowledge the growing salience of cultural consensus in the last 100 years. Whereas the modern world-system has always been, and is still, multicultural, the growing influence and acceptance of Western values of rationality, individualism, equality, and efficiency is an important trend of the twentieth century.

### *2.3 Globalization of communication*

Another meaning of globalization is connected with the new era of telematics. What does "technological" globalization mean? For media of communication another aspect of globalization seems relevant, one on which Anthony Giddens (1996) insists. Social space comes to acquire new qualities with telematics, albeit only in the networked parts of the social world. In terms of accessibility, cost and velocity, the hitherto known political and geographic parameters that structured social relationships are much less relevant.

One may well argue that time-space compression (Harvey 1989) by new information technologies is simply an extension and acceleration of the very long-term trend toward technological development over the last ten millenia (Chase-Dunn 1994). Yet, the rapid decrease in the cost of communications may have qualitatively altered the relationship between states and consciousness. Global communication facilities have the power to move things visible and invisible from one part of the globe to another whether any nation-state likes it or not. This does not only apply to economically relevant exchange, but also to ideas, to gather support for issues worldwide and to form lines of opposition. How, and to what extent, will this undermine the power of states to structure social relationships?

### *2.4 Economic globalization*

Economic globalization means globe-spanning economic relationships. The interrelationships of markets – finance, goods and services – and the networks created by transnational corporations are the most important manifestations of this. Though the capitalist world-system has been international in essence for centuries, the extent and degree of of trade and investment globalization has increased greatly in recent decades. Economic globalization has been accelerated by what telematics has done to the movement of money. It is commonly claimed that the market's ability to shift money from one part of the globe to another by a push of a button has changed the rules of policy-making, putting economic decisions much more at the mercy of market forces than before.

### *2.5 Political globalization*

Political globalization consists of the institutionalization of international political structures. The Europe-centered world-system has been primarily constituted as an interstate system – a system of conflicting and allying states and empires. Earlier world-systems, in which accumulation was mainly accomplished by means of institutionalized coercive power, experienced an oscillation between multicentric interstate systems and core-wide world empires in which a single "universal" state conquered all or most of the core states in a region. The Europe-centered system has also experienced a cyclical alternation between political centralization and decentralization, but this has taken the form of the rise and fall of hegemonic core states that do not conquer the other core states. Hence the modern world-system has remained multicentric in the core, and this is due mainly to the shift toward a form of accumulation based more on the production and profitable sale of commodities–capitalism. The hegemons have been the most thoroughly capitalist states and they have preferred to follow a strategy of controlling trade and access to raw material imports from the periphery rather than conquering other core states to extract tribute or taxes.

Power competition in an interstate system does not require much in the way of cross-state cultural consensus to operate systemically. But since the early nineteenth century the European interstate system has been developing both an increasingly consensual international normative order and a set of international political structures that regulate all sorts of interaction. This phenomenon has been termed "global governance" by Craig Murphy (1994) and others. It refers to the growth of both specialized and general international organizations. The general organizations that have emerged are the Concert of Europe, the League of Nations and the United Nations. The sequence of these "proto-world-states" constitutes a process of institution-building, but unlike earlier "universal states" this one is slowly emerging by means of condominium among core states rather than conquest. This is the trend of political globalization. It is yet a weak, but persistent, concentration of sovereignty in international institutions. If it continues it will eventuate in a single global state that could effectively outlaw warfare and enforce its illegality.

## 3 MEASURING ECONOMIC GLOBALIZATION

The brief discussion above of economic globalization implies that it is a long-run upward trend. The idea is that international economic competition as well as geopolitical competition were already important in the fourteenth century and that they became increasingly important as more and more international trade and international investment occurred. In its simplest form this would posit a linear upward trend of economic globalization. An extreme alternative hypothesis about economic globalization would posit a completely unintegrated world composed of autarchic national economies until some point (perhaps in the last few decades) at which a completely global market for commodities and capital suddenly emerged.

Let us examine data that can tell us more about the temporal emergence of economic globalization. There are potentially a large number of different indicators of economic globalization and they may or may not exhibit similar patterns with respect to change over time. Trade globalization can be operationalized as the proportion of all world production that crosses international boundaries. Investment globalization would be the proportion of all invested capital in the world that is owned by non-nationals (i.e. "foreigners"). And we could also investigate the degree of economic integration of countries by determining the extent to which national economic growth rates are correlated across countries.[3]

It would be ideal to have these measures over several centuries, but comparable figures are not available before the nineteenth century, and indeed even these are sparse and probably unrepresentative of the whole system until well into the twentieth century. Nevertheless we can learn some important things by examining those comparable data that are available.

Figure 1 shows trade and investment globalization. Trade globalization is the ratio of estimated total world exports (the sum of the value of exports of all countries) divided by an estimate of total world product (the sum of all the national GDPs). Investment globalization is the total book value of all foreign direct investment divided by the total world product.

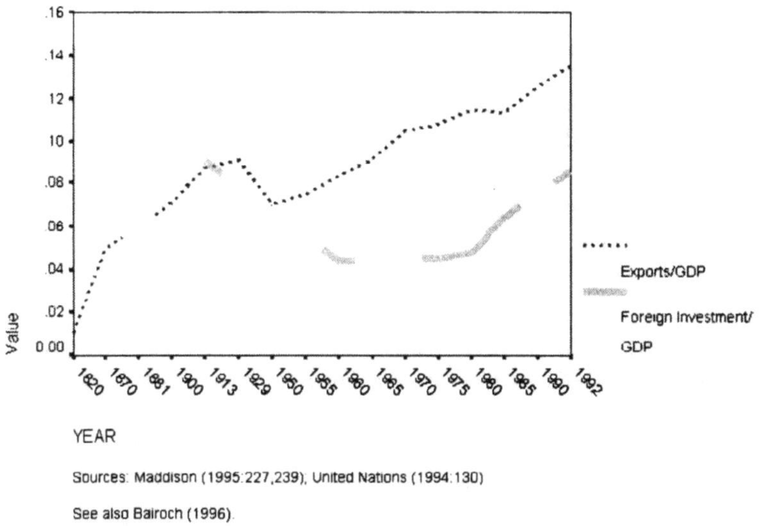


*Figure 1: Economic Globalization: Trade and Investment*

The trade globalization figures show the hypothesized upward trend as well as a downturn that occurred between 1929 and 1950. Note that the time scale in Figure 1 is distorted by the paucity of datum points before 1950. It is possible that important changes in trade globalization are not visible in this series because of the wide temporal gaps in the data. Figure 1 also shows that the trade indicator differs in some ways from the investment indicator. Investment globalization was higher (or as high) in 1913 as it was in 1991, while trade globalization was considerably lower in 1913 than it was in 1992. We have fewer time points for the investment data, so we cannot tell for sure about the shape of the changes that took place, but these two series imply that different indicators of economic globalization may show somewhat different trajectories.

A third indicator of economic globalization is the correlation of national GDP growth rates (Grimes 1993). This shows the extent to which periods of national economic growth and stagnation have been synchronized across countries. In a fully integrated global economy it would be expected that growth and stagnation periods would be synchronized across countries and so there would be a high correlation of national growth rates. Grimes shows that, contrary to the hypothesis of a secular upward trend toward increasing global integration, the correlation among national growth rates fluctuates cyclically over the past two centuries. In a data series from 1860 to 1988 Grimes found two periods in which national economic growth-decline sequences are highly correlated across countries: 1913-1927; and after 1970. Before and in between these peaks are periods of very low synchronization.

Further research needs to be done to determine the temporal patterns of different sorts of economic globalization. At this point we can say that the step-function version of a sudden recent leap to globalization can be rejected. The evidence we have indicates that there are both long-term secular trends and huge cyclical oscillations. Trade globalization shows a long-term trend with a big dip during the depression of the 1930s. The investment globalization indicates a cycle with at least two peaks, one before World War I and one after 1980. Grimes's indicator of synchronous economic growth indicates a cyclical fluctuation with one peak in the 1920s and another since 1970.

These results, especially those that imply cycles, indicate that change occurs relatively quickly and that the most recent period of globalization shares important features with earlier periods of intense international economic interaction. The question of the similarities and differences between the most recent wave and earlier waves of globalization is clearly an important one.

## 4 SYSTEMIC CYCLES OF ACCUMULATION

Giovanni Arrighi (1994) shows how hegemony in the modern world-system has evolved in a series of "systemic cycles of accumulation" (SCAs) in which finance capital has employed different forms of organization and different relationships with organized state power. These qualitative organizational changes have accompanied the secular increase in the power of money and markets as regulatory forces in the modern world-system. The SCAs have been occurring in the Europe-centered world-system since at least the fourteenth century.

Arrighi's model shows both the similarities and the differences in the relationships that obtain between financial capital and states within the different systemic cycles of accumulation. The British SCA and the American SCA had both similarities and important differences. The main differences that Arrighi emphasizes are the "internalization of transaction costs" (represented by the vertical integration of TNCs) and the extent to which the U.S. tried to create "organized capitalism" on a global scale. The British SCA had fewer global firms and pushed hard for international free trade. The U.S. SCA is characterized by a much heavier focus on global firms and by a more structured approach to "global governance" possibly intended to produce economic growth in other core regions, especially those that are geopolitically strategic.

Arrighi argues that President Roosevelt used the power of the hegemonic state to try to create a balanced world of capitalist growth. This sometimes meant going against the preferences of finance capital and U.S. corporations. For example, the Japanese miracle was made possible because the U.S. government prevented U.S. corporations from turning Japan (and Korea) into just one more dependent and peripheralized country. This policy of enlightened global Keynesianism was continued in a somewhat constrained form under later presidents, albeit in the guise of domestic "military Keynesianism" justified by the Soviet threat.

In this interpretation the big companies and the finance capitalists returned to power with the decline in competitiveness of the U.S. economy. The rise of the Eurodollar market forced Nixon to abandon the Bretton Woods financial structure, and this was followed by Reaganism-Thatcherism, IMF structural adjustment, streamlining, deregulation and the delegitimation of anything that constrained the desires of global capital investment. The idea that we are all subject to the forces of a global market-place, and that any constraint on the freedom to invest will result in a deficit of "competitiveness," is a powerful justification for destroying the institutions of the "Second Wave" (e.g. labor unions, welfare, agricultural subsidies, etc.).[4]

Under conditions of increased economic globalization the ability of national states to protect their citizens from world market forces decreases. This results increasing inequalities within countries, and increasing levels of dis-satisfaction compared to the relative harmony of national integration achieved under the Keynesian regimes. It is also produces political reactions, especially national-populist movements.[5] Indeed Philip McMichael (1996) attributes the anti-government movements now occurring in the U.S. West, including the bombing of the Federal Building in Oklahoma City, to the frustrations caused by the deregulation of U.S. agriculture.

It would also be useful to investigate the temporal patterns of the other types of globalization: cultural[6], political, technological and ecological. Of interest too are the relationships between these and economic globalization. Much empirical work needs to be done to operationalize these concepts and to assemble the relevant information. Here, for now, I will hypothesize that all these types exhibit both long-run secular and cyclical features. I will also surmise that cultural and political globalization are lagged behind the secular upward trend of economic globalization.

## 5 THE POLITICS OF GLOBALIZATION

This last hypothesis bears on the question of adjustments of political and social institutions to increases in economic and technological globalization. I would submit that the current period of economic globalization has occurred in part due to technological changes that are linked to Kondratieff waves, and in part because of the profit squeezes and declining hegemony of the U.S. economy in the larger world market.[7]

The financial aspects of the current period of economic globalization began when President Nixon canceled the Bretton Woods agreement in response to pressures on the value of the U.S. dollar coming from the rapidly growing Eurodollar market (Harvey

1995). This occurred in 1967, and this date is used by many to mark the beginning of a K-wave downturn.

The saturation of the world market demand for the products of the post-World War II upswing, the constraints on capital accumulation posed by business unionism and the political entitlements of the welfare states in core countries caused a profit squeeze that motivated large firms and investors and their political helpers to try to break out of these constraints. The possibilities for global investment opened up by new communications and information technology created new maneuverability for capital. The demise of the Soviet Union[8] added legitimacy to the revitalized ideology of the free market and this ideology swept the Earth. Not only Reagan and Thatcher, but Eurocommunists and labor governments in both the core and the periphery, adopted the ideology of the "lean state," deregulation, privatization and the notion that everything must be evaluated in terms of global efficiency and competitiveness.

Cultural globalization has been a very long-term upward trend since the emergence of the world religions in which any person could become a member of the moral community by confessing faith in the "universal" god. But moral and political cosmography has usually encompassed a smaller realm than the real dimensions of the objective trade and political/military networks in which people have been involved. What has occurred at the end of the twentieth century is a near-convergence between subjective cosmography and objective networks. The main cause of this is probably the practical limitation of human habitation to the planet Earth. But the long-run declining costs of transportation and communications are also an important element. Whatever the causes, the emergent reality is one in which consciousness embraces (or goes beyond) the real systemic networks of interaction. This geographical feature of the global system is one of its uniquenesses, and it makes possible for the future a level of normative order that has not existed since human societies were very small and egalitarian (Chase-Dunn and Hall 1997).

The ideology of globalization has undercut the support and the rationale behind all sorts of so-called Second Wave institutions – labor unions, socialist parties, welfare programs, and communist states. While these institutions have not been destroyed everywhere, the politicians of the right (e.g. Newt Gingrich in the U.S.) have explicitly argued for their elimination.

At the same time, the very technologies that made capitalist economic globalization possible also have the potential to allow those who do not benefit from the free reign of capital to organize new forms of resistance, or to revitalize old forms. It is now widely agreed by many, even in the financial community, that the honeymoon of neo-liberalism will eventually end and that the rough edges of global capitalism will need to be buffed. Patrick Buchanan, a conservative candidate for the U.S. presidency in 1996, tried to capitalize on popular resentment of corporate downsizing. The Wall Street Journal has reported that stock analysts worry about the "lean and mean" philosophy becoming a fad that has the potential to delegitimate the business system and to create political backlashes. This was expressed in the context of a discussion of the announcement of huge bonuses for AT&T executives following another round of downsizing.

I already mentioned the difficulties that states are having in controlling communications on the Internet. I do not believe the warnings of those who predict a massive disruption of civilization by hordes of sociopaths waging "cyberwar".[9] But I do think that the new communications technologies provide new opportunities for the less powerful to organize themselves to respond should global capitalism run them over or leave them out.

The important question is what are the most useful organizational forms for resistance? What we already see are all sorts of nutty localisms, nationalisms and a proliferation of identity politics. The militias of the U.S. West are ordering large amounts of fertilizer with which to resist the coming of the "Blue Helmets" – a fantasized world state that is going to take away their pistols and deer rifles.[10]

Localisms and specialized identities are the postmodern political forms that are supposedly produced by infomatics, flexible specialization, and global capitalism (Harvey 1989). I think that at least some of this trend is a result of desperation and the demise of plausible alternatives in the face of the ideological hegemony of neoliberalism and the much-touted triumph of efficiency over justice. Be that as it may, a historical perspective on the latest phase of globalization allows us to see the long-run patterns of interaction between capitalist expansion and the movements of opposition that have tried to protect people from the negative aspects of market forces and exploitation. And this perspective has implications for going beyond the impasse of the present to build a more cooperative and humane global system (Boswell and Chase-Dunn, forthcoming).

## 6 THE SPIRAL OF CAPITALISM AND SOCIALISM

The interaction between expansive commodification and resistance movements can be denoted as "the spiral of capitalism and socialism". The world-systems perspective provides a view of the long-term interaction between the expansion and deepening of capitalism and the efforts of people to protect themselves from exploitation and domination. The historical development of the communist states is explained as part of a long-run spiraling interaction between expanding capitalism and socialist counter-responses. The history and developmental trajectory of the communist states can be explained as socialist movements in the semiperiphery that attempted to transform the basic logic of capitalism, but which ended up using socialist ideology to mobilize industrialization for the purpose of catching up with core capitalism.

The spiraling interaction between capitalist development and socialist movements can be seen in the history of labor movements, socialist parties and communist states over the last 200 years. This long-run comparative perspective enables one to see recent events in China, Russia and Eastern Europe in a framework that has implications for the future of social democracy. The metaphor of the spiral means this: both capitalism and socialism affect one another's growth and organizational forms. Capitalism spurs socialist responses by exploiting and dominating peoples, and socialism spurs capitalism to expand its scale of production and market integration and to revolutionize technology.

Defined broadly, socialist movements are those political and organizational means by which people try to protect themselves from market forces, exploitation and domination, and to build more cooperative institutions. The sequence of industrial revolutions, by which capitalism has restructured production and taken control of labor, have stimulated a series of political organizations and institutions created by workers to protect their livelihoods. This happened differently under different political and economic conditions in different parts of the world-system. Skilled workers created guilds and craft unions. Less skilled workers created industrial unions. Sometimes these coalesced into labor parties that played important roles in supporting the development of political democracies, mass education and welfare states (Rueschemeyer, Stephens and Stephens 1992). In other regions workers were less politically successful, but managed at least to protect access to rural areas or subsistence plots for a fall-back or hedge against the insecurities of employment in capitalist enterprises. To some extent the burgeoning contemporary "informal sector" in both core and peripheral societies provides such a fall-back.

The mixed success of workers' organizations also had an impact on the further development of capitalism. In some areas workers or communities were successful at raising the wage bill or protecting the environment in ways that raised the costs of production for capital. When this happened capitalists either displaced workers by automating them out of jobs or capital migrated to where fewer constraints allowed cheaper production. The process of capital flight is not a new feature of the world-system. It has been an important force behind the uneven development of capitalism and the spreading scale of market integration for centuries. Labor unions and socialist parties were able to obtain some power in certain states, but capitalism became yet more international. Firm size increased. International markets became more and more important to successful capitalist competition. Fordism, the employment of large numbers of easily-organizable workers in centralized production locations, has been supplanted by "flexible accumulation" (small firms producing small customized products) and global sourcing (the use of substitutable components from broadly dispersed competing producers), are all production strategies that make traditional labor organizing approaches much less viable.

## 7 COMMUNIST STATES IN THE WORLD-SYSTEM

Socialists were able to gain state power in certain semiperipheral states and use this power to create political mechanisms of protection against competition with core capital. This was not a wholly new phenomenon. As discussed below, capitalist semiperipheral states had done and were doing similar things. But, the communist states claimed a fundamentally oppositional ideology in which socialism was allegedly a superior system that would eventually replace capitalism. Ideological opposition is a phenomenon which the capitalist world-economy has seen before. The geopolitical and economic battles of the Thirty Years War were fought in the name of Protestantism against Catholicism. The content of the ideology may make some difference for the internal organization of states and parties, but every contender must be able to legitimate itself in the eyes and hearts of its cadre. The claim to represent a qualitatively different and superior socio-economic system is not evidence that the communist states were indeed structurally autonomous from world capitalism.

The communist states severely restricted the access of core capitalist firms to their internal markets and raw materials, and this constraint on the mobility of capital was an important force behind the post-World War II upsurge in the spatial scale of market integration and a new revolution of technology. In certain areas capitalism was driven to further revolutionize technology or to improve living conditions for workers and peasants because of the demonstration effect of propinquity to a communist state. U.S. support for state-led industrialization of Japan and Korea (in contrast to U.S. policy in Latin America) is only understandable as a geopolitical response to the Chinese revolution. The existence of "two superpowers" – one capitalist and one communist – in the period since World War II provided a fertile context for the success of international liberalism within the "capitalist" bloc. This was the political/military basis of the rapid growth of transnational corporations and the latest revolutionary "time-space compression" (Harvey 1989). This technological revolution has once again restructured the international division of labor and created a new regime of labor regulation called "flexible accumulation". The process by which the communist states have become reintegrated into the capitalist world-system has been long, as described below. But, the final phase of reintegration was provoked by the inability to be competitive with the new form of capitalist regulation. Thus, capitalism spurs socialism, which spurs capitalism, which spurs socialism again in a wheel that turns and turns while getting larger.

The economic reincorporation of the communist states into the capitalist world-economy did not occur recently and suddenly. It began with the mobilization toward autarchic industrialization using socialist ideology, an effort that was quite successful in terms of standard measures of economic development. Most of the communist states were increasing their percentage of world product and energy consumption up until the 1980s.

The economic reincorporation of the communist states moved to a new stage of integration with the world market and foreign firms in the 1970s. Andre Gunder Frank (1980: chapter 4) documented a trend toward reintegration in which the communist states increased their exports for sale on the world market, increased imports from the avowedly capitalist countries, and made deals with transnational firms for investments within their borders. The economic crisis in Eastern Europe and the Soviet Union was not much worse than the economic crisis in the rest of the world during the global economic downturn that began in the late 1960s (see Boswell and Peters 1990, Table 1). Data presented by World Bank analysts indicates that GDP growth rates were positive in most of the "historically planned economies" in Europe until 1989 or 1990 (Marer et al, 1991: Table 7a).

Put simply, the big transformations that occurred in the Soviet Union and China after 1989 were part of a process that had long been underway since the 1970s. The big socio-political changes were a matter of the superstructure catching up with the economic base. The democratization of these societies is, of course, a welcome trend, but democratic political forms do not automatically lead to a society without exploitation or domination. The outcomes of current political struggles are rather uncertain in most of the ex-communist countries. New types of authoritarian regimes seem at least as likely as real democratization.

As trends in the last two decades have shown, austerity regimes, deregulation and marketization within nearly all of the communist states occurred during the same period as similar phenomena in non-communist states. The synchronicity and broad similarities between Reagan/Thatcher deregulation and attacks on the welfare state, austerity socialism in most of the rest of the world, and increasing pressures for marketization in the Soviet Union and China are all related to the B-phase downturn of the Kondratieff wave, as are the current moves toward austerity and privatization in many semiperipheral and peripheral states. The trend toward privatization, deregulation and market-based solutions among parties of the Left in almost every country is thoroughly documented by Lipset (1991). Nearly all socialists with access to political power have abandoned the idea of doing more than buffing off the rough edges of capitalism. The way in which the pressures of a stagnating world economy impact upon national policies certainly varies from country to country, but the ability of any single national society to construct collective rationality is limited by its interaction within the larger system. The most recent expansion of capitalist integration, termed "globalization of the economy," has made autarchic national economic planning seem anachronistic. Yet, a political reaction against economic globalization is now under way in the form of revived ex-communist parties, economic nationalism (e.g., Pat Buchanan, the Brazilian military) and a coalition of oppositional forces who are critiquing the ideological hegemony of neo-liberalism (e.g., Ralph Nader, environmentalists, populists of the right, etc.).

## 8 POLITICAL IMPLICATIONS OF THE WORLD-SYSTEM PERSPECTIVE

The age of U.S. hegemonic decline and the rise of post-modernist philosophy have cast the liberal ideology of the European Enlightenment (science, progress, rationality, liberty, democracy and equality) into the dustbin of totalizing universalisms. It is alleged that these values have been the basis of imperialism, domination and exploitation and, thus, they should be cast out in favor of each group asserting its own set of values. Note that self-determination and a considerable dose of multiculturalism (especially regarding religion) were already central elements in Enlightenment liberalism.

The structuralist and historical materialist world-systems approach poses this problem of values in a different way. The problem with the capitalist world-system has not been with its values. The philosophy of liberalism is fine. It has quite often been an embarrassment to the pragmatics of imperial power and has frequently provided justifications for resistance to domination and exploitation. The philosophy of the enlightenment has never been a major cause of exploitation and domination. Rather, it was the military and economic power generated by capitalism that made European hegemony possible.

To humanize the world-system we may need to construct a new philosophy of democratic and egalitarian liberation. Of course, many of the principle ideals that have been the core of the Left's critique of capitalism are shared by non-European philosophies. Democracy in the sense of popular control over collective decision-making was not invented in Greece. It was a characteristic of all non-hierarchical human societies on every continent before the emergence of complex chiefdoms and states. My point is that a new egalitarian universalism can usefully incorporate quite a lot from the old universalisms. It is not liberal ideology that caused so much exploitation and domination. It was the failure of real capitalism to live up to its own ideals (liberty and equality) in most of the world. That is the problem that progressives must solve.

A central question for any strategy of transformation is the question of agency. Who are the actors who will most vigorously and effectively resist capitalism and construct democratic socialism? Where is the most favorable terrain, the weak link, where concerted action could bear the most fruit? Samir Amin (1992) contends that the agents of socialism have been most heavily concentrated in the periphery. It is there that the capitalist world-system is most oppressive, and thus peripheral workers and peasants, the vast majority of the world proletariat, have the most to win and the least to lose.

On the other hand, Marx and many contemporary Marxists have argued that socialism will be most effectively built by the action of core proletarians. Since core areas have already attained a high level of technological development, the establishment of socialized production and distribution should be easiest in the core. And, organized core workers have had the longest experience with industrial capitalism and the most opportunity to create socialist social relations.

I submit that both "workerist" and "Third Worldist" positions have important elements of truth, but there is another alternative which is suggested by the structural theory of the world-system: the semiperiphery as the weak link.

Core workers may have experience and opportunity, but a sizable segment of the core working classes lack motivation because they have benefited from a non-confrontational relationship with core capital. The existence of a labor aristocracy has divided the working class in the core and, in combination with a large middle strata, has undermined political challenges to capitalism. Also, the "long experience" in which business unionism and social democracy have been the outcome of a series of struggles between radical workers and the labor aristocracy has created a residue of trade union practices, party structures, legal and governmental institutions, and ideological heritages which act as barriers to new socialist challenges. These conditions have changed to some extent during the last two decades as hyper-mobile capital has attacked organized labor, dismantled welfare states and down-sized middle class work forces. These create new possibilities for popular movements within the core, and we can expect more confrontational popular movements to emerge as workers devise new forms of organization (or revitalize old forms). Economic globalization makes labor internationalism a necessity, and so we can expect to see the old idea take new forms and become more organizationally real. Even small victories in the core have important effects on peripheral and semiperipheral areas because of demonstration effects and the power of core states.

The main problem with "Third Worldism" is not motivation, but opportunity. Democratic socialist movements that take state power in the periphery are soon beset by powerful external forces which either overthrow them or force them to abandon most of their socialist program. Popular movements in the periphery are most usually anti-imperialist class alliances which succeed in establishing at least the trappings of national sovereignty, but not socialism. The low level of the development of the productive forces also makes it harder to establish socialist forms of accumulation, although this is not impossible in principle. It is simply harder to share power and wealth when there are very little of either. But, the emergence of democratic regimes in the periphery will facilitate new forms of mutual aid, cooperative development and popular movements once the current ideological hegemony of neoliberalism has broken down.

## 9 SEMIPERIPHERAL DEMOCRATIC SOCIALISM

In the semiperiphery both motivation and opportunity exist. Semiperipheral areas, especially those in which the territorial state is large, have sufficient resources to be able to stave off core attempts at overthrow and to provide some protection to socialist institutions if the political conditions for their emergence should arise. Semiperipheral regions (e.g., Russia and China) have experienced more militant class-based socialist revolutions and movements because of their intermediate position in the core/periphery hierarchy. While core exploitation of the periphery creates and sustains alliances among classes in both the core and the periphery, in the semiperiphery an intermediate world-system position undermines class alliances and provides a fruitful terrain for strong challenges to capitalism. Semiperipheral revolutions and movements are not always socialist in character, as we have seen in Iran. But, when socialist intentions are strong there are greater possibilities for real transformation than in the core or the periphery. Thus, the semiperiphery is the weak link in the capitalist world-system. It is the terrain upon which the strongest efforts to establish socialism have been made, and this is likely to be true of the future as well.

On the other hand, the results of the efforts so far, while they have undoubtedly been important experiments with the logic of socialism, have left much to be desired. The tendency for authoritarian regimes to emerge in the communist states betrayed Marx's idea of a freely constituted association of direct producers. And, the imperial control of Eastern Europe by the Russians was an insult to the idea of proletarian internationalism. Democracy within and between nations must be a constituent element of true socialism.

It does not follow that efforts to build socialism in the semiperiphery will always be so constrained and thwarted. The revolutions in the Soviet Union and the Peoples' Republic of China have increased our collective knowledge about how to build socialism despite their only partial successes and their obvious failures. It is important for all of us who want to build a more humane and peaceful world-system to understand the lessons of socialist movements in the semiperiphery, and the potential for future, more successful, forms of socialism there.

Once again the core has developed new lead industries – computers and biotechnology – and much of large scale heavy industry, the classical terrain of strong labor movements and socialist parties, has been moved to the semiperiphery. This means that new socialist bids for state power in the semiperiphery (e.g., South Africa, Brazil, Mexico, perhaps Korea) will be much more based on an urbanized and organized proletariat in large scale industry than the earlier semiperipheral socialist revolutions were. This should have happy consequences for the nature of new socialist states in the semiperiphery because the relationship between the city and the countryside within these countries should be less antagonistic. Less internal conflict will make more democratic socialist regimes possible, and will lessen the likelihood of core interference. The global expansion of communications has increased the salience of events in the semiperiphery for audiences in the core and this may serve to dampen core state intervention into the affairs of democratic socialist semiperipheral states.

Some critics of the world-system perspective have argued that emphasis on the structural importance of global relations leads to political do-nothingism while we wait for socialism to emerge at the world level. The world-system perspective does indeed encourage us to examine global level constraints (and opportunities), and to allocate our political energies in ways which will be most productive when these structural constraints are taken into account. It does not follow that building socialism at the local or national level is futile, but we must expend resources on transorganizational, transnational and international socialist relations. The environmental and feminist movements are now in the lead and labor needs to follow their example.

A simple domino theory of transformation to democratic socialism is misleading and inadequate. Suppose that all firms or all nation-states adopted socialist relations internally but continued to relate to one another through competitive commodity production and political/military conflict. Such a hypothetical world-system would still be dominated by the logic of capitalism, and that logic would be likely to repenetrate the "socialist" firms and states. This cautionary tale advises us to invest political resources in the construction of multilevel (transorganizational, transnational and international) socialist relations lest we simply repeat the process of driving capitalism to once again perform an end run by operating on a yet larger scale.

## 10 A DEMOCRATIC SOCIALIST WORLD-SYSTEM

These considerations lead us to a discussion of socialist relations at the level of the whole world-system. The emergence of democratic collective rationality (socialism) at the world-system level is likely to be a slow process. What might such a world-system look like and how might it emerge? It is obvious that such a system would require a democratically-controlled world federation that can effectively adjudicate disputes among nation-states and eliminate warfare (Goldstein 1988). This is a bare minimum. There are many other problems that badly need to be coordinated at the global level: ecologically sustainable development, a more balanced and egalitarian approach to economic growth, and the lowering of population growth rates.

The idea of global democracy is important for this struggle. The movement needs to push toward a kind of popular democracy that goes beyond the election of representatives to include popular participation in decision-making at every level. Global democracy can only be real if it is composed of civil societies and national states that are themselves truly democratic (Robinson 1996). And global democracy is probably the best way to lower the probability of another way among core states. For that reason it is in everyone's interest.

How might such a global social democracy come into existence? The process of the growth of international organizations which has been going on for at least 200 years will eventually result in a world state if we are not blown up first. Even international capitalists have some uses for global regulation, as is attested by the International Monetary Fund and the World Bank. Capitalists do not want the massive economic and political upheavals that would likely accompany collapse of the world monetary system, and so they support efforts to regulate "ruinous" competition and beggar-thy-neighborism. Some of these same capitalists also fear nuclear holocaust, and so they may support a strengthened global government which can effectively adjudicate conflicts among nation-states.

Of course, capitalists know as well as others that effective adjudication means the establishment of a global monopoly of legitimate violence. The process of state formation has a long history, and the king's army needs to be bigger than any combination of private armies which might be brought against him. While the idea of a world state may be a frightening specter to some, I am optimistic about it for several reasons. First, a world state is probably the most direct and stable way to prevent nuclear holocaust, a desideratum which must be at the top of everyone's list. Secondly, the creation of a global state which can peacefully adjudicate disputes among nations will transform the existing interstate system. The interstate system is the political structure which stands behind the maneuverability of capital and its ability to escape organized workers and other social constraints on profitable accumulation. While a world state may at first be dominated by capitalists, the very existence of such a state will provide a single focus for struggles to socially regulate investment decisions and to create a more balanced, egalitarian and ecologically sound form of production and distribution.

The progressive response to neoliberalism needs to be organized at national, international and global levels if it is to succeed. Democratic socialists should be wary of strategies that focus only on economic nationalism and national autarchy as a response to economic globalization. Socialism in one country has never worked in the past and it certainly will not work in a world that is more interlinked than ever before. The old forms of progressive internationalism were somewhat premature, but internationalism has finally become not only desirable but necessary. This does not mean that local, regional and national-level struggles are irrelevant. They are just as relevant as they always have been. But, they need to also have a global strategy and global-level cooperation lest they be isolated and defeated. Communications technology can certainly be an important tool for the kinds of long-distance interactions that will be required for truly international cooperation and coordination among popular movements. It would be a mistake to pit global strategies against national or local ones. All fronts should be the focus of a coordinated effort.

W. Warren Wagar (1996) has proposed the formation of a "World Party" as an instrument of "mundialization" – the creation of a global socialist commonwealth. His proposal has been critiqued from many angles – as a throw-back to the Third International, and etc. I suggest that Wagar's idea is a good one, and that a party of the sort he is advocating will indeed emerge and that it will contribute a great deal toward bringing about a more humane world-system. Self-doubt and post-modern reticence may make such a direct approach appear Kantian or Napoleonic. It is certainly necessary to learn from past mistakes, but this should not prevent us debating the pros and cons of positive action.

The international segment of the world capitalist class is indeed moving slowly toward global state formation. The World Trade Organization is only the latest element in this process. Rather than simply oppose this move with a return to nationalism, progressives should make every effort to organize social and political globalization, and to democratize the emerging global state. We need to prevent the normal operation of the interstate system and future hegemonic rivalry from causing another war among core powers (e.g, Wagar 1992; see also Chase-Dunn and Bornschier 1998). And, we need to shape the emerging world society into a global democratic commonwealth based on collective rationality, liberty and equality. This possibility is present in existing and evolving structures. The agents are all those who are tired of wars and hatred and who desire a humane, sustainable and fair world-system. This is certainly a majority of the people of the Earth.

## NOTES

1 For a useful introduction see Shannon (1996).

2 It has become conventional to refer to the expansion phase of the K-wave as the "A-phase," while the contraction or stagnation period is called the "B-phase".

3 We could also examine changes in the degree of multilateralization of trade by looking at the average of degree of export partner concentration across all the nation-states (and over time). Export partner concentration is the ratio of the value of the exports to the largest trade partner to the total exports of a country. A related indicator of the degree of average national specialization could be measured by using commodity concentration, the proportion of national exports that are composed of the single largest export. At present I do not have access to these numbers.

4 The "Second wave" means industrialism in Alvin Toffler's terminology, now adopted by Newt Gingrich.

5 A recent debate on WSN, the world-system network, focused on nationalist vs. internationalist popular responses to globalization and downsizing.
See "gopher://csf.Colorado.EDU:70/00/wsystems/praxis/globprax".

6 One long-run indicator of cultural globalization would be linguistic diversity, a distributional measure of the proportions of the world's population that speak the various languages. It is obvious that linguistic diversity has decreased greatly over the past centuries, but it would be interesting to see the temporal shape of this trend. Have recent movements to revitalize and legitimate indigenous cultures slowed the long-term decrease in linguistic diversity?

7 For evidence of relative U.S. economic decline see Chase-Dunn 1989:p.266, Table 12.3. This shows that U.S. proportion of world GNP declined from 32.1% in 1960 to 26.9% in 1980. See also Bergesen and Fernandez (1998).

8 The world-systems literature on the reintegration of state communism in the capitalist world-economy is substantial. See Chase-Dunn (1980), Boswell and Peters (1989) and Frank (1980).

9 Barbara Belejack says, "Another concern to activists and NGOs is the growing body of 'cyberwar' and 'netwar' literature pioneered by Rand Corporation analyst David Ronfeldt, who along with David Arquilla of the U.S. Naval Postgraduate School in Monterey, California, coined the terms in a 1993 article 'CyberWar is Coming!' In 1993, Ronfeldt was thinking along the lines of a potential threat from an updated version of the Mongol hordes that would upset the established hierarchy of institutions. He

predicted that communication would be increasing organizing 'into cross-border networks and coalitions, identifying more with the development of civil society (even global civil society) than with nation-states, and using advanced information and communictions technologies to strengthen their activities'. By 1995 Ronfeldt was characterizing the Zapatista activists as highly successful in limiting the government's maneuverability, and warning that 'the country that produced the prototype social revolution of the 20th century may now be giving rise to the prototype social netwar of the 21st century'". From "Cyberculture Comes to the Americas" by Barbara Belejack (102334.201@CompuServe.COM) available at http://csf.colorado.edu/mail/wsn/sp97/ 0021.html

[10] The same solid citizens of the West who were quite willing to grant the experts back in Washington the benefit of the doubt on Vietnam are, twenty-five years later, doubting the moral and ethical foundations of the U.S. federal government.

## REFERENCES


Arrighi, Giovanni (1994): *The Long Twentieth Century*, (New York: Verso).

Bairoch, Paul (1996): "Globalization Myths and Realities: One Century of External Trade and Foreign Investment," Robert Boyer and Daniel Drache (eds.) , *States Against Markets: The Limits of Globalization*, (London and New York: Routledge).

Bergesen, Albert and Ronald Schoenberg (1980): "Long waves of colonial expansion and contraction, 1415-1969," pp. 231-278, Albert J. Bergesen (ed.) *Studies of the Modern World-System*, (New York: Academic Press).

— and Roberto Fernandez (1998): "Who has the most Fortune 500 firms?: a network analysis of global economic competition, 1956-1989," Christopher Chase-Dunn and Volker Bornschier (eds.) *The Future of Hegemonic Rivalry*, (London: Sage).

Boli, John and George M. Thomas (1997): "World culture in the world polity," *American Sociological Review* 62, 2:171-190 (April).

Boswell, Terry and Peters, Ralph (1990): "State socialism and the industrial divide in the world-economy: a comparative essay on the rebellions in Poland and China," *Critical Sociology*.

Boswell, Terry and Christopher Chase-Dunn. Forthcoming. *The Spiral of Capitalism and Socialism*.

Chase-Dunn, Christopher (ed.) (1980): Socialist States in the World-System, (Beverly Hills, CA.: Sage).

— (1998): *Global Formation: Structures of the World-Economy*, (Lanham, MD.: Rowman and Littlefield).

— (1994): "Technology and the changing logic of world-systems," pp. 85-106 Ronen Palan and Barry Gills (eds.) *The State-Global Divide: a Neostructural Agenda in International Relations*. Boulder, (CO.: Lynne Rienner).

— and Volker Bornschier (eds.) (1998): *The Future of Hegemonic Rivalry*, (London: Sage).

— and Thomas D. Hall (1997): *Rise and Demise: The Comparative Study of World-Systems*, (Boulder, CO.: Westview).

Frank, Andre Gunder (1978): *World Accumulation 1492-1789*, (New York: Monthly Review Press).

— (1980): *Crisis: In the World Economy*, (New York: Holmes and Meier).

— and Barry Gills (eds.) (1993): *The World System: Five Hundred Years or Five Thousand?* (London: Routledge).

Giddens, Anthony (1996): *Introduction to Sociology*, (New York: Norton).

Goldstein, Joshua (1988): *Long Cycles: Prosperity and War in the Modern Age*, (New Haven: Yale University Press).

Grimes, Peter (1993): "Harmonic convergence?: frequency of economic cycles and global integration, 1790-1990," A paper presented at the annual meeting of the Social Science History Association, Baltimore, November 4.

Harvey, David (1989): *The Condition of Postmodernity*, (Cambridge, MA.: Blackwell).

— (1995): "Globalization in question," *Rethinking Marxism* 8,4: pp, 1-17 (Winter).

Lipset, Seymour Martin (1991): "No third way: a comparative perspective on the Left," pp 183-232, Daniel Chirot (ed.) *The Crisis of Leninism and the Decline of the Left*: The Revolution of 1989, (Seattle: University of Washington Press).

Maddison, Angus (1995): *Monitoring the World Economy, 1820-1992*, (Paris: OECD).

Mann, Michael (1986): *Sources of Social Power*, Vol. 1, (Cambridge: Cambridge University Press).

Marer, Paul, Janos Arvay, John O'Connor and Dan Swenson (1991): "Historically planned economies: a guide to the data," *I.B.R.D.* (World Bank), Socioeconomic Data Division and Socialist Economies Reform Unit.

Markoff, John (1996): *Waves of Democracy: Social Movements and Political Change*. Thousand Oaks, CA.: Pine Forge Press.

McMichael, Philip (1996): *Development and Social Change: A Global Perspective*, (Thousand Oaks, CA.: Pine Forge).

Meyer, John W. (1989): "Conceptions of Christendom: notes on the distinctivenes of the West," pp. 395-413, Melvin L. Kohn (ed.) Cross-national Research in Sociology, (Newbury Park, CA.: Sage).

— (1996): "The changing cultural content of the nation-state: a world society perspective," George Steinmetz (ed.) *New Approaches to the State in the Social Sciences*, (Ithaca: Cornell University Press).

Modelski, George and William R. Thompson (1996): *Leading Sectors and World Powers*: The Coevolution of Global Politics and Economics, (Columbia, SC: University of South Carolina Press).

Moore, Richard K. (1995): "On saving democracy," a contribution to a conversation about global praxis on the World-SystemsNetwork (WSN)gopher://csf.Colorado.EDU:70/00/ wsystems/praxis/globprax

Murphy, Craig (1994): *International Organization and Industrial Change: Global Governance since 1850*, (New York: Oxford).

Robinson, William (1996) *Promoting Polyarchy*, (Cambridge: Cambridge University Press).

Rueschemeyer, Dietrich, Evelyne Huber Stephens and John Stephens 1992 *Capitalist Development and Democracy*, (Chicago: University of Chicago Press).

Shannon, Thomas R (1996): *An Introduction to the World-Systems Perspective*, (Boulder,CO.: Westview).

Taylor, Peter J. (1996): *The Way the Modern World Works: World Hegemony to World Impasse*, (New York: John Wiley).

Toffler, Alvin (1980): *The Third Wave*, (New York: Morrow).

United Nations (1994): *World Investment Report 1994*: Transnational Corporations, Employment and the Workplace, New York .

Wagar, W. Warren (1992): *A Short History of the Future*. Chicago: University of Chicago Press.

— (1996): "Toward a praxis of world integration," *Journal of World-Systems Research* 2, 2 (http://csf.colorado.edu/wsystems/jwsr.html)

Wallerstein, Immanuel (1974): *The Modern World-System*, Vol. 1, (New York: Academic Press).

THOMAS D. HALL

# WORLD-SYSTEMS, FRONTIERS, AND ETHNOGENESIS:

*Incorporation and Resistance to State Expansion**

## 1 INTRODUCTION

The expansion of the European world-system necessarily entailed incorporation of new areas and peoples. In the process it created borderlines, boundaries zones, or frontiers between its various components and the external world. World-system analysis, which was developed to explain the dynamic expansion of the European based modern world-system, has paid insufficient attention to how local forces and actors shape the process. In particular, the study of the roles of gender, race, ethnicity, and interactions with nonstate peoples have been somewhat neglected (K. Ward 1993; Hall 1989a, 1989b, 1996a, 1996b).

Recently, several writers have extended world-systems analysis into the distant, precapitalist, past (Abu-Lughod 1989, 1993; Chase-Dunn and Hall 1991, 1997a; Frank and Gills 1993; Peregrine and Feinman 1996). While disagreeing on many points, all agree that systematic intersocietal relations preceded the formation of the modern world-system in the long sixteenth century (1450-1640 C. E.), and all world-systems tend to expand and absorb new areas, and often new peoples. Thus, the role of world-systemic processes in the formation, transformation, fossilization, and obliteration of borderlines, boundary zones, or frontiers is also ancient. These processes remain relatively understudied and undertheorized.

Our understanding, our ability to theorize and explain, past patterns is severely curtailed by such slighting of the study of frontiers. In the language of statistical research, our sampling of the relevant "universe" has been systematically biased. Thus, we have not been able to understand "core" processes due to underattention to those occurring on the far peripheries and in ancient times. World-system structure and dynamics must be studied in all places and all times if we are to understand the evolutionary dynamics of the system itself, and understand what is truly new at the turn of the second millennium of the common era. That is, far peripheries are as relevant as the



*G. Preyer, M. Bös (eds.), Borderlines in a Globalized World, 35-66.*

core. This is not a matter of political correctness or humane inclusiveness – though they are important – but a matter of valid theory-building.

I have argued many times (especially 1989a, 1989b) that some processes can be best, or maybe only, studied on the far peripheries for the simple reason that is where they occur most often and most visibly. Peter Sahlins begins his masterful study of the French-Spanish "fossilized" boundary with an epigraph from Pierre Vilar which is particularly useful here: "The history of the world is best observed from the frontier" (1989, p. xv). Hence the study of borderlines and frontiers is indispensable to understanding the modern world.

My goal in this paper is to begin to develop a world-system analysis based account of frontiers. I summarize much of the work done from this perspective, illustrate the points with various examples, and suggest many issues and topics for further discussion. I hope to persuade readers that a comparative world-systems perspective on the formation, transformation, fossilization, and obliteration of borderlines, boundary zones, or frontiers is vital to our understanding of them. I do not, however, claim that a comparative world-systems perspective can explain everything. In short, a comparative, historical world-system perspective is a necessary, but not sufficient requirement to understand the dynamics of borderlines, boundary zones, or frontiers.

I begin the account with thumbnail sketch of world-system analysis, a brief recapitulation of the major findings of its extension into the ancient world, and the elaboration of the analysis of world-system incorporation. I then turn to an account of frontier dynamics, illustrated with various examples. I conclude with a discussion of theoretical and empirical problems which need further study.

## 2 COMPARATIVE WORLD-SYSTEMS ANALYSIS

According to Immanuel Wallerstein, a world-system is an intersocietal system which has a self-contained division of labor. Thus it is a "world," but not necessarily global. It has some degree of internal coherence, and is a key unit of analysis within which all other social structures and processes should be analyzed (Chase-Dunn 1989; Shannon 1996; and So 1990; Wallerstein 1974a, 1974b, 1979, 1980, 1983, 1984, 1989, 1991, 1993, 1995).

A world-system must be studied as a whole. Thus, the study of social, political, economic, or cultural change in any component of the system must begin by understanding that component's role within the system, whether it be a nation, state, region, ethnic group, class, gender role, or nonstate society. World-systems analysis has a dual research agenda: (1) how do the processes of the system affect the internal dynamics and social structures of its components; and (2) how do changes in its components affect the entire system? (Bach 1980).

A world-system has three components: (1) a core which employs advanced industrial production and distribution, has strong states, a strong bourgeoisie, and a large working class; (2) a periphery which specializes in raw materials production and has weak states, a small bourgeoisie, and many peasants; and (3) a semiperiphery which is intermediate between core and periphery, in its economic, social, and political roles and its own internal social structure. Core capitalists use various sorts of coercion to promote unequal exchange and accumulate capital which leads simultaneously to core development and peripheral impoverishment.

By the 1980s archaeologists found that world-system analysis, while suggestive, could not be used without major modifications (Hall and Chase-Dunn 1993; Peregrine 1996). This led to the extension of world-systems analysis to precapitalist settings. Christopher Chase-Dunn and I (1991, 1995, 1997a, 1998a, 1998b) have argued that such extension requires that many of the assumptions of the theory of the modern world-system must be transformed into empirical questions.

Several findings of this work are germane to the discussion of borderlines, boundary zones, or frontiers. First, world-systems, or core/periphery structures, date back at least to the neolithic revolution (approximately 10,000 to 12,000 years ago). Second, these core/periphery structures are a major locus of social change. Not all change can be explained from the world-system level, but system processes are a crucial part of all social change. Fourth, these world-systems, have themselves, evolved.

Fifth, world-systems have several types of dynamic cycles. All world-systems pulsate, that is expand and contract, or expand rapidly, then more slowly. All state-based world-systems (that is since about 3,000 B.C.E.) have cycles of rise and fall of core states. A typical, but not universal process is the displacement or conquest of the dominant core state by a semiperipheral marcher state (Chase-Dunn and Hall, Ch. 5). In the capitalist world-system this becomes the hegemonic cycle wherein one core power displaces others in succession: the Dutch, followed by British, followed by United States. State-based systems also seem to oscillate between public and private dominant forms of capital accumulation (Arrighi 1994). (Capital accumulation refers to amassing wealth in any form; capitalist accumulation to "the amassing of wealth by means of the making of profits from commodity production" (Chase-Dunn and Hall 1997a, 271)). Precapitalist tributary systems, range from very private forms of accumulation, feudal systems to very centralized forms, a centralized empire. The modern capitalist system ranges from accumulation sponsored or fostered by states to accumulation concentrated in private holdings. We are currently in the more private phase of this cycle.

The sixth finding is most relevant here. World-systems typically have four sets of non-coterminous boundaries (Chase-Dunn and Hall 1997a, Ch. 3). The narrowest is the bulk goods exchange network. Somewhat larger is the network of political/military interactions. Larger still are the network of prestige or luxury goods exchange and a network of information exchange (See Figure 1). Only on isolated island systems or in the late 20th century have these four boundaries coincide. Indeed, what is often discussed as "globalization" is, in this view, the convergence of these four boundaries with the limits of planet earth. The ways in which these networks are nested and overlap is a matter of continuing empirical and theoretical research.

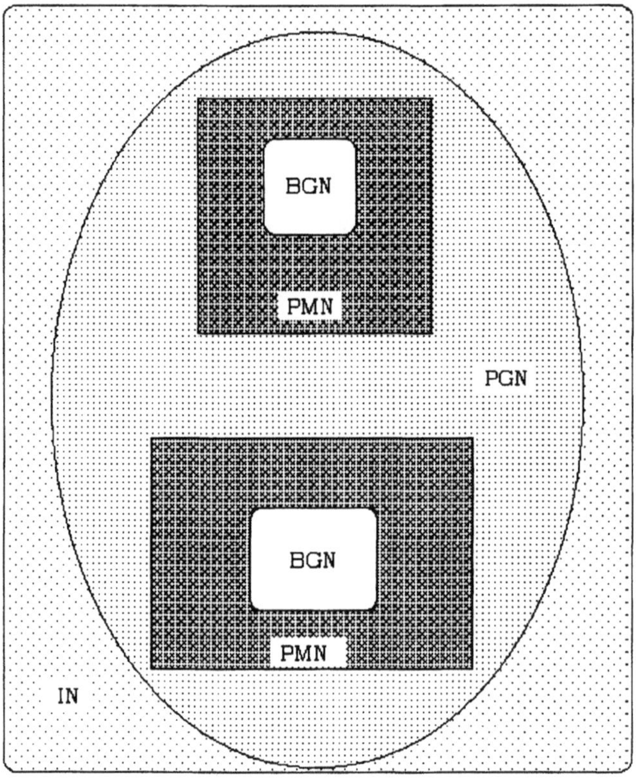


*Figure 1: Spatial Boundaries of World Systems*

## 3 WORLD-SYSTEM INCORPORATION AND GROUP (TRANS)FORMATIONS

When a world-system expands new areas are incorporated and borderlines or boundary zones, in short frontiers, are formed and transformed (Wallerstein 1974b; Hall 1996b; Hopkins, et al 1987; Markoff 1994). Here Richard Slatta's metaphor of frontiers as membranes is quite useful (1990, 1997, 1998). Viewed from a global perspective a frontier is relatively narrow and sharp. Viewed more closely it is a broad zone with considerable internal differentiation both spatially and temporally. In either case, the permeability of the membrane varies with respect to the types of goods, groups, and individuals and the direction of their flow through it. In this sense, a borderline, or boundary is, as Peter Sahlins argues (1989), the result of often long, complex, and highly politicized process of negotiation. Furthermore, the tonal quality often persists long after a precise boundary line has been accepted.

In the history of the western United States frontier has often been used to refer to areas with a population density under two persons per square mile. Donna Guy and Thomas Sheridan define frontiers "as zones of historical interaction where, in the brutally direct phrase of Baretta and Markoff (1978:590), 'no one has an enduring monopoly on violence'". They continue, "Frontiers were, in a most basic sense, contested ground" (1998b, 10). They go on to recap the history of controversy about this term. My own definition is, "a region or zone where two or more distinct cultures, societies, ethnic groups, or modes of production come into contact," and I would add, often conflict (Hall 1997, 208). Borderlines, for me, are the political markings around which such frontiers, or boundary zones form. Following Peter Sahlins (1989) the boundary, or borderline marks a politically negotiated delimiting of state sovereignty, which typically is surrounded by a zone of interaction that persists long after the line has been drawn. For purposes of this essay I will use the term "frontier" because as Guy and Sheridan say, "no other term suffices" (p. 10).

Incorporated areas and peoples often experienced profound effects from incorporation, and occasionally devastating ones, even when the extent of incorporation was relatively limited. They also react against and resist these effects to whatever degree possible. This resistance rebounds back to the overall system and often shapes its policies and actions. These interactions also reshape the ethnic landscape. Frontiers are zones where ethnogenesis, ethnocide, and genocide are common. To concentrate solely on one set of actors and ignore the others is to misunderstand fundamentally these processes. Thus, the study of incorporation entails close attention to local conditions, actors, and actions. To explore this more fully it is useful to summarize the analysis of world-system incorporation.

## 4 WORLD-SYSTEM INCORPORATION

Because my studies of the region that became Southwestern United States demonstrated that the effects of incorporation have important, interactive effects long before colonization is complete, I extended Wallerstein's dichotomous concept of incorporation to a continuum that ranges from weak to strong (Hall 1986a, Hall 1987, 1989a). I also argued that changes in the degree of incorporation affect those incorporated, and conversely their reactions shape the incorporation process.[1] At the weakest extreme of incorporation are areas external to a world-system. With slight contact an external arenas becomes a contact periphery. With somewhat stronger incorporation these become marginal peripheries. Marginal peripheries are analogous to what Aguirre Beltran called a "region of refuge," an area that is only partially incorporated into a state system (1979). Marginal incorporation can freeze social change within such areas. This "preserves" the area in two ways. First, it sets it aside for future development by the state. Second, it "preserves" older, "traditional," social forms, and hence is a "refuge" for social forms that have been destroyed elsewhere in the system. At the strongest extreme of incorporation such areas become full-blown or dependent peripheries. Most studies of the modern world-system focus primarily only on dependent peripheries. To label this entire range an undifferentiated "incorporation" masks important variations and makes it more difficult to understand world-system processes and effects on frontiers of a world-system (See Figure 2).

| **Continuum of Incorporation** | **none** | **weak** | **moderate** | **strong** |
|---|---|---|---|---|
| Impact of Core on Peripheral Area | none | strong | stronger | strongest |
| Impact of Peripheral on Core | none | low | moderate | strong |

| **Sources** | **Labels for Segments of the Range** | | | |
|---|---|---|---|---|
| Hall 1989b, Chase-Dunn and Hall 1997a | External Arena | Contact | Marginal or Region of Refuge | Full-blown or Dependent |
| Wallerstein 1983 | none | External Arena | Incorporation | Periperalization |
| Arrighi 1979 | none | Nominal for N A L or M A L | | Effective or Real |
| Sherratt 1993 | none | Margin | | Periphery |
| Frank & Gills 1993 | none | Hinterland | | Periphery |

*Figure 2: The Continuation of Incorporation*

Some important aspects of incorporation are the amount of goods exchanged, the type of goods (e.g., the amount of labor involved in their production and whether they are raw products, manufactured goods, or prestige goods), degree of centralization of the exchange process, and relative importance of the transfer to each economy. At the weak pole of the continuum the primary influence will be from core areas to peripheral areas.

For instance, furs from northern North America were not vital to European economies, yet the trade produced major social and economic changes among indigenous groups (Wolf 1982: Chap. 6; Kardulias 1990; Abler 1992). Difference in size of economies is important. Often trade with one peripheral region has no major impact on the core, whereas trade with all peripheral areas combined may have significant impact.

The fur trade brought several dramatic changes to indigenous social organization. Most dramatic was a dependency on European goods, as metal pots and cutting implements replaced more frangible pots, baskets, and stone tools. As the desire for European goods turned into a need, more furs were required to acquire European goods. This led to over-harvesting of game and a chain reaction of expansion in search of new hunting grounds, which in turn heightened warfare and depleted the environment.

Heightened competition for hunting grounds transformed warfare from line fighting to what we would today call guerrilla fighting, and transformed guns from luxuries to necessities. The intensified harvesting of furs led families to scatter in the winter to pursue fur bearing animals (Abler 1992; Kardulias 1990; Meyer 1994). This left women in charge of home camps while men were absent for long periods. Intensified conflict encouraged stronger fortifications. Finally, increased travel, contact, and migration helped spread diseases, often long before direct contact with Europeans. The impacts of disease often were devastating to the maintenance of local social structures (Reff 1991; Thornton 1987; Thornton et al. 1991).

Wallerstein (1989: Chap. 3) argues that in the modern world-system, even when an area has been plundered by a core power, it has not been incorporated and peripheralized until local production has become integrally linked into the commodity chains of the larger world-system. However, plunder can have profound consequences for local groups. Thus I include regularized plunder as a form of incorporation. This is not to deny that peripheralized production is more stable since it typically is not as disruptive to a peripheral region as plundering, nor does it exhaust resources as rapidly.

In this view, West Africa was incorporated into the European world-system when slave raiding became regularized, rather than, as Wallerstein would have it, after the development of colonial agriculture in Africa. If trade in bullion is the criteria for incorporation, then West Africa has been linked to the Mediterranean and Near Eastern core regions since at least the ninth century CE when the importation of gold for coins minted in Byzantium and Egypt began (Curtin 1984: 32). These coins played an important part in the Eurasian world-system (Abu-Lughod 1989; Moseley 1992; and Willard 1993).

Similarly, Peru, Mexico, and what is now southeastern United States became incorporated – albeit weakly – into the European world-system at first contact with Spanish explorers. A key aspect of incorporation is its reversibility. Changes in the world-system, or in the specific incorporating state, or in local resistance to incorporation, or any combination of these often change the weakening of the degree of incorporation. Although weakening of degree of incorporation is not all that unusual historically, the net tendency is for regions and peoples to become incorporated more and more strongly into expanding world-systems. That is, strengthening of incorporation typically is easier than weakening incorporation. Hence, incorporation has a grain or direction to it like wood or corduroy.

Because of this tendency, weakened incorporation does not return automatically to the status quo ante. Indeed, a lowered degree of incorporation can produce nearly opposite effects in specific settings. For example, taking slaves from a region often undermines the prosperity of the raided groups. If the degree of incorporation decreases, typically slave raiding also will decrease, and local prosperity may often increase. Conversely, if the core supplies goods that have no local substitutes, prosperity that depended on those goods would decrease as the flow declined. The loss of trade connections to Mesoamerica undermined the entire Chacoan economy (Mathien and McGuire 1986). According to So (1984) the lessening of incorporation of Canton in the 1840s gave rise to unemployment, peasant uprisings, and rebellions.

The volatility of local changes, is, if anything, greater in weakly incorporated areas than in more strongly incorporated areas. Thus, weakly incorporated areas tend to vary more widely through time, and hence are vital objects of study to discern the detailed mechanisms of incorporation-induced social changes (Hall 1989b). This, among other reasons, is why frontier regions always seem to bear a superficial resemblance to each other even while exhibiting tremendous differences. For detailed examples see Guy and Sheridan (1998a), Hall (1989a, 1998a), Slatta (1997), Weber and Rausch (1994).

Finally, because of the volatility and reversibility of incorporation processes frontiers have a tendency to move, or shift through time. Any one area, or people, may follow a complex trajectory of incorporation with successive strengthening and weakening phases. It may well be the final, or at least contemporary, consequences of long historical sequences of incorporation are best studied and explained by examination of the entire trajectory of incorporation, not just its degree at any one point in time.

## 4 INCORPORATION AND ETHNOGENESIS, TRANSFORMATION, AND ETHNOCIDE

Incorporation also can have major effects on individuals and groups. Many of the American Indian groups we know today were built from an aboriginal base of loosely connected bands during the process of incorporation, e.g., the Diné (Navajo) [Hall 1989a.] While language, customs, and a vague sense of being the same "people" predate the arrival of Europeans, Diné-wide institutions such as the Navajo Tribal Council were developed, among other things, to deal with incorporation into American society.

These effects are wide spread. Brian Ferguson and Neil Whitehead have collected studies of "tribal zone," a region along state borders where contact with nonstate groups is common (1992a, 1992b). They purposely use the vague term "tribe" to refer to a range of nonstate societies from the simplest band groups to sprawling chiefdoms. They are well aware of the vagueness and misuses of the term "tribe" (Ferguson 1997, 475-476). They argue four fallacies underpin the common Hobbesian image of "tribal" peoples. First, that post-contact conditions and relations are a continuation of precontact conditions and relations. Second, that ethnic divisions are survivals of precontact divisions. Third, that "tribal" warfare is unreasoned hostility. An implicit fourth fallacy is that ethnographers, ethnohistorians, and historians typically have an adequate understanding to the relevant context of contact.

Studies of many regions show that both state-nonstate and inter-nonstate warfare increased substantially after state contact. That is, contact and even weak incorporation increase violence. Ferguson and Whitehead do not claim that all was idyllic prior to initial incorporation. Only that state contact intensified violence, and sometimes transformed it into more virulent forms. These accounts also illustrate how groups are transformed or created through interactions that can either amalgamate or fragment previously existing groups. The transformation from an autonomous nonstate society to a subordinate ethnic group is a complex process in which identities, cultures, and social organizations are transformed. Thus, the Navajo example cited above is typical, not unusual.

"Tribal" warfare is not "unreasoned hostility," but typically conflict over access to state supplied goods and the uses of local resources controlled or produced by the contacting state. These goods and resources may be used for very different political ends by leaders in nonstate societies, often to enhance prestige and to gain followers. Thus, local leaders not only need access to trade goods and local resources, but also must block the access of their rivals. These needs are a source of inter-, and sometimes intra-, group warfare.

Because leaders in kin-ordered prestige hierarchies used goods differently, state officials often did not understand this origin of conflict, and called it "unreasoned hostility". This conclusion was all too easy to draw, given the ethnocentric assumption by state officials that nonstate peoples are "barbarians," "backward" and "inferior". Interestingly enough, officials who actually understood the customs of nonstate societies were not rare. Typically these officials had been born in the contact zone or they had spent a long time there. Equally typically, central state officials did not listen to their advice. For detailed examples see Barfield (1989) or Hall (1989a).

Reconstruction of precontact social conditions is frequently very difficult because all these effects occur nearly simultaneously with contact period. That a representative of a literate society is present to record events and conditions means that change already may be extensive. To avoid such ethnographic upstreaming (reading the present into the past, Sheridan (1992), critical and cautious combinations of archaeological data with reports of the earliest observers must serve to temper these distortions. David Anderson's (1994) reconstruction of Savannah River chiefdoms is an excellent example of such work. He combines archaeological data with careful, critical reading of the reports of the De Soto expedition. He shows how conditions can change very rapidly. Sometimes, however, there is little change and aboriginal conditions and organization persist. The point is neither change nor persistence should be assumed, but should be determined empirically. Christopher Chase-Dunn and I have sketched some of the precontact world-systems in North America (1998a).

Incorporation can also have divisive effects. For the White Earth Anishinaabeg (Chippewa or Ojibwa) increasing incorporation fractured old clan and band distinctions and created a new division between more and less assimilated Anishinaabeg, or in local parlance, between full- and mixed-bloods (Meyer 1994). Sandra Faiman-Siva (1997) finds much the same processes among the Mississippi Choctaw. Indeed, the full-blood/mixed-blood distinction is an important consequence of incorporation into the European world-system with far-reaching legal consequences.

Gender roles and gender relations are also reshaped by incorporation. Women are often harmed by incorporation even while men may benefit. There are gender and class differentials in contraception (Bradley 1996), fertility (Ward 1984), labor force participation (Ward 1990; Ward and Pyle 1995; Bose and Acosta-Belen 1995), and household structure and function (Smith et al. 1988). The key process here seems to be that new resources are differentially accessible by gender, giving increased power to men, and decreasing social power and changing the social roles of women. Both Dunaway (1996a, 1997, 1999) and Faiman-Siva (1997) find this holds for Cherokee and Choctaw. It remains unclear, however, whether the direction of this differential is a direct result of incorporation into a capitalist system, or an indirect result of the strong patriarchy of the British, Spanish, and French states. Maria Mies (1986) and Vandana Shiva (1993) have addressed the general issue of patriarchy and capitalism in considerable detail. Still, the affects of incorporation on gender differentials and gender roles is an area in need of further empirical and theoretical development (Ward 1993).

These examples make a compelling case for why special care is needed in dealing with the labels we apply to groups, especially nonstate groups that have experienced some degree of incorporation. Sometimes a shared identity of a group is the product of incorporation. Conversely, unified groups can become divided internally, or even shattered by incorporation. These examples also make a compelling case for viewing zones of incorporation, frontiers, or zone surrounding borderlines as regions where ethnogenesis, ethnic transformation and transmutation, culturicide, and genocide are common (Chappell 1993a, 1993b, Fenelon 1997, 1998). This is one reason why they are so important to study: this is where these processes occur with the greatest variety.

## 5 INCORPORATION IN PRECAPITALIST CONTEXTS

The extension of world-systems analysis into precapitalist settings suggests refinements to the analysis of incorporation. First, incorporation is not unidimensional, but multidimensional along the four types of world-system boundaries. Incorporation can be economic (for either bulk goods or luxury goods), political/military, or be cultural, which includes all types of information and symbols. Second, incorporation creates multiple frontiers, corresponding to each of the boundaries. Third, ceteris paribus, incorporation will begin at the furthest boundaries, cultural, symbolic, informational, or luxury goods, and proceed to narrower, more intense forms along the political-military boundary and finally along the bulk goods dimension. Fourth, relations among the dimensions of incorporation and the resulting frontiers is complex theoretically and empirically.

Studies of the interactions between the Near Eastern and Mediterranean urbanized core region and peripheral regions in Europe during the Bronze Age by Andrew Sherratt support this analysis (1993a, 1993b, 1993c, 1994, 1995). He argues that beyond what he calls the periphery is a margin whose characteristics include "that it is dominated by time-lag phenomena – 'escapes' – rather than structural interdependence with the core" (Sherratt 1993a: 43). According to Sherratt goods followed long chains from the Near Eastern core through the periphery and then into northern Europe. He notes that the nodal points of connection to Europe in the Bronze Age eventually became important centers in their own right (shown in his Fig. 12, pg. 44). He uses these distinctions to divide the Bronze Age world-system into zones of core, periphery, and margin (his Fig. 13, p. 44 and Fig. 14, p. 45).

Sherratt's "margin" approximates the range of incorporation from contact through marginal peripheries. The alternative label for this range, regions of refuge, highlights that his "escapes" are regions where older social forms may be preserved. In short, they "escape" pressures for change exerted in more strongly incorporated areas. His "structural interdependence" and "periphery" correspond to full-blown peripheral and semiperipheral regions. Similarly, the concept of "hinterland" used by Frank and Gills

(1993), Gills and Frank (1991) and by Collins (1978, 1981) also corresponds roughly to the weaker range of incorporation.

## 6 FURTHER ANALYSIS OF FRONTIERS: REFINEMENTS AND COUNTERFACTUALS

I begin with a return to the fur trade. In the southeast Cherokees became extensively involved in what Dunaway (1994, 1996a, 1996b) calls "a putting-out system financed by foreign merchant-entrepreneurs" (1994:237). Incorporation via the fur trade transformed both techniques of production and associated culture:

As export production became entrenched, new hunting and warfare techniques emerged.These changes altered division of labor within the household and within the village, and a reformed relationship with precolonial society toward secular and national governance, eventually created the "tribal half-government" that permitted the Europeans to treat the Cherokees as a unified corporate entity (Dunaway 1994: 237).

The export of 100,000s of deer hides transformed a luxury trade into a bulk goods trade and constituted full-blown or dependent incorporation. This trade played an important role in European economies and vastly disrupted local relations, changing gender relations and roles, local political organization, and cultural values. Increased incorporation promoted changes along all world-system boundary criteria: information/culture, luxury trade, political/military interaction, and bulk goods trade.

The spread of horses from colonies in New Mexico to various foraging groups illustrates a much weaker form of incorporation. Horses dramatically transformed production techniques, political and social organization, and the cultures of all groups who acquired them (Secoy 1953; Mishkin 1940). Horses differ from most other European goods because they can reproduce without human intervention. Horses transformed the buffalo hunt from a rare and dangerous task into a far more successful enterprise. It allowed both concentration and dispersal of populations and transformed erstwhile sedentary (or sometimes semisedentary) horticulturalists into full-time nomadic hunters. Groups who continued occasional gardening could now congregate in larger base camps because they could hunt over larger territories. Conversely, groups who were, or became, entirely nomadic could use a greater range of territory (Secoy (1953). The access to a high quality protein[2] source allowed population efflorescence, and attracted migrants to the plains, especially those from eastern forested areas who were losing territory to better armed fur gatherers. Competition and warfare increased.

As horses were spreading from the northwestern New Spain toward the north and east, guns were spreading from the northeast, primarily from French fur traders, to the southwest. These two frontiers crossed in the mid- to late eighteenth century, giving the groups in that region nearly equal access to guns and horses. This coincidence gave rise to the celebrated Plains cultures, and gave Comanche bands the tools to dominate the

South Plains (Secoy 1953; Hall 1989a). Indeed, Comanches actually sold guns to Spanish peasants in New Mexico where the government tried to maintain a monopoly on weapons.

Elsewhere in Latin America the spread of feral horses and cattle also vastly disrupted indigenous world-systems (Baretta and Markoff 1978), and in the Pampas region of southern South America gave rise to a whole new type of society: the Gauchos (Slatta 1983, 1997). Access to horses produced some of the most dramatic social transformations that came from the mildest degree incorporation into the European world-economy.

Both examples illustrate why incorporation can be so hard to reverse. Short of removing horses, Plains Indians groups could not have returned to the status quo ante. Indeed, their incorporation was so weak that many would consider them to have remained outside the world-system, in the external arena, especially after horses became feral in the west. This highlights the inherent fuzziness of the lower limits of incorporation. The point is not to draw some arbitrary line, but rather to emphasize that the lower limits of incorporation are empirically and theoretically problematic.

What if the fur trade had ceased? The source of metal goods would have been lost. In time, as animal and human populations might have recovered from epidemics and excessive predation, social relations and organization might have returned to previous conditions. But this would have been unlikely because epidemics frequently undermine the very basis of culture and social structure, especially if too many of those who possess special knowledge die. When population did recover, people might have discovered new solutions to old problems. Thus, new social structures and organization typically would not have been identical to those predating initial incorporation.

Once the source of useful goods (e.g., metals) was lost, attempts would have been made to acquire them through alternative channels, or to develop substitutes. Here, we should not lose sight of the impact of basic knowledge. Once a group has seen a technology, they at least know that it exists. Depending on resources and fundamental skills they may, or may not, be able to reconstruct it. Even where they cannot reconstruct it, knowledge of its existence might precipitate quests to acquire it that would not otherwise have occurred. Thus, even minimal contact can lead to vast disruptions through the spread of new knowledge.

The history of what is now the Southwest of the United States suggests another example. In the late eighteenth century, toward the end of the era of Spanish control, incorporation increased and frontier warfare declined. When incorporation decreased during the unrest which accompanied the rebellion of Mexico from Spain (1810-1821) fighting with nomads increased on the frontier as state resources used for rations to guarantee the peace became scarce (Griffen 1988a, 1988b; Hall 1989a). This illustrates how even relatively small shifts in degree of incorporation can cause significant social, political, and cultural changes.

As we have seen, when goods obtained from state peoples significantly affect survival, as with metal tools in North America, or guns nearly everywhere, these goods become necessities. For the recipients luxury trade becomes bulk goods trade, and incorporation has increased. In west Africa, members of a group without guns often found themselves on a one-way voyage to the Americas. When there was no legitimate way to acquire state controlled goods – whether due to a ban on trade, or a lack of suitable goods to trade, raiding could become an alternative means of acquisition. Thus, trading and raiding frequently alternate in frontier settings. This is was one source of the nearly constant warfare between nomadic and sedentary peoples on the frontiers of the Spanish empire (Guy and Sheridan 1998a; Hall 1989a; Hall 1998a; Slatta 1997, 1998; Jones 1998). Similar processes occur almost everywhere nomadic peoples confront sedentary peoples (Lattimore 1951, 1962a, 1962b, 1962c; Barfield 1989, 1990, 1991; Hall 1991a, 1991b; Chase-Dunn and Hall 1997a, espec. ch. 8). Many factors shape the interactions, but they are all processes with spatial dimensions.

## 7 SPATIAL ASPECTS OF INCORPORATION AND FRONTIER (TRANS)FORMATION

As Slatta's metaphor of the frontier as membrane suggested, some of the complexity of the effects of incorporation on frontier formation and transformation stems from problems of scale of analysis. Incorporation occurs at multiple geographical scales – local, regional, global – simultaneously and recursively. The world-system serves as the largest, though not fully determinative context for broad regional processes. In turn, regional (or state) processes serve as a context for subregional (or substate) processes. These all serve as contexts for the most local processes. Furthermore, all these levels of change interact, simultaneously and recursively, with class, ethnic, gender, economic, and political processes. Seeking a key factor for these processes is a fool's errand. Rather, interactions among all these factors shape social processes on frontiers and along borderlines.

At times the different levels and different factors may counteract each other. Sometimes the counter forces may be so well balanced that no changes occur. In this case situations that appear "static" may, in fact be dynamic, but temporarily balanced. One of the key insights of Peter Sahlins' analysis in *Boundaries* is that the French-Spanish border bisecting Cerdanya was not fossilized, but in dynamic balance.

## 8 PHYSICAL AND SOCIAL GEOGRAPHY

The effects of interaction between peoples living in different ecological zones are also shaped by world-systemic processes. Many observers, especially Owen Lattimore (1940, 1962a) and William McNeill (1964), have highlighted the salience of the boundary between the steppe and the sown, that is between nonarable grasslands and arable lands. This boundary is actually a zone where regular rainfall drops below the limit for agriculture. Nomads live on the steppe side, whereas farmers live on the sown side. Small changes in the drought resistance of crops, or slight changes in climate may cause the boundary zone to shift, but it is relatively fixed. While the farmer-nomad difference typically seen as racial, ethnic, or cultural, it is most often a matter of adaptation. People on opposite sides of the zone differed culturally and ethnically, but not physiologically. Frederick Barth and Gunnar Haaland (1969) report many cases in which individuals or families switched modes of adaptation. Usually, they changed identities at the same time. Ecological borders often produce interesting cross-border interactions that alter the social structure and organization of groups on both sides.

There are analogous differences between plains (or valleys) and mountainous regions. Because of their low level of differentiation, plains facilitate gradients, continua, and general similarity in adaptations and cultures. Highly differentiated mountainous areas, like the Basin and Range Province or Great Basin in western United States (D'Azevedo 1986) or mountainous regions of California (Heizer 1978), encourage sharper boundaries, and close grained local differentiation. On the one hand, American Indian Plains cultures on the Great Plains in the United States exhibited considerable cultural convergence, especially after adoption of horses (Lowie 1954; Hoebel 1982). On the other hand, Apachean groups, many of whom dwelt in the Basin and Range Province, were highly differentiated (see Hall 1989, 1996a; Melody 1977; Ortiz 1979, 1983).

Clearly, the natural environment and society interact. That interaction defines the land usage and limits the social organization of those who exploit it. For instance, Rudi Lindner argues that the Huns abandoned the use of horses after moving west of the Carpathians. Forested areas made horses a liability, hampered a nomadic lifestyle, and promoted sedentary living (1981, 1983).

The interaction between valley people and hill people is perhaps the earliest form of world-system formation (see Chase-Dunn and Hall 1997a, Ch. 7 and Chase-Dunn and Mann 1998). Ecological borders (a point stressed by Lattimore) are fertile locations to study intergroup interactions. Such interactions typically transform the social organization and structure of the participating groups and precipitate the formation of systems composed of very different kinds of peoples. Thus, many frontiers areas have a high degree of geographical differentiation.

## 9 GEOPOLITICS

The geopolitical role of incorporated groups also shapes frontier dynamics. Their location relative to world-system expansion is a major factor in determining whether they function as buffers or barriers. A group that occupies a region in the path of expansion is typically treated as a barrier to be pacified, displaced, or destroyed. A group that occupies a region between the expanding system and its other adversaries is typically treated as a geopolitical buffer. Spanish officials in northern New Spain incessantly sought the settlement and or removal of Apache bands because they blocked internal communication, whereas they allied with Comanche bands (after 1786) in order to buffer intrusion by European adversaries. After the war with Mexico (1846-1848) the situation reversed, as Comanches became an internal barrier and Apaches at most a border nuisance. This reversal accounts for the relatively strong survival of Apachean groups and the near annihilation of Comanches, whose population reached a low of approximately 1000 at the turn of the twentieth century (Hall 1986, 1989a, 1998a).

The distinction between buffer and barrier is close to, but distinct from, the distinction between internal and external frontiers. This distinction is very close the Marvin Mikesell's (1960) differentiation between frontiers of inclusion and frontiers of exclusion. An external frontier exists along the edges of an expanding world-system. A group that lives on an external frontier is more likely to serve as a buffer than a barrier. In contrast, an internal frontier is encapsulated within an expanding system: for example, the interior of North America, which Europeans settled after settling the coastal regions. This internal frontier was the setting of most of the last battles with Native Americans.

These distinctions clarify the varied responses of nonstate peoples to world-system encroachment. If an expanding world-system needs territory, conquest and removal of indigenous populations is highly likely. Conversely, if the world-system needs people, often for slaves or other coerced workers, retreat to an external arena by indigenous populations is likely, and constitutes defeat for the system, and escape from incorporation. This is why the same action – leaving traditionally occupied territory – can be either a defeat or a victory, depending on the goals of the expanding world-system (see Gunawardana 1992).

Geopolitical considerations also illuminate processes of marginal incorporation. If incorporation is weak the incorporating agency's concern with frontier groups will diminish if these groups retreat beyond the frontier zone into less desirable environments. The retreat affords these "marginal" groups a respite and time and space to adapt to new circumstances.This may determine whether they survive or are destroyed by the encounter. Thus, the degree of incorporation shapes the probability of survival for indigenous groups as much as their tenacity and skills of resistance. Inversely, a group with great cultural tenacity and strong resistance might survive weak incorporation, while a less tenacious or weaker group might not.

There is one other type of buffer zone, an "empty zone" (Upham 1992). There are two types of empty zones. First are emptied frontiers. That is, a zone from which indigenous populations have been driven by invasion, warfare, disease, or other disaster (Dunaway 1996a). Empty zones might be confused with neutral zones that develop between competing groups and which buffer unwanted contacts. In some areas of California ethnographers have reported the existence of "neutral territories" that no group claimed. These areas were available for exploitation by any group that chose to do so (Heizer and Treganza 1956: 356). Johnston (1978) surmises that there was a "no man's land" along the east side of the Sacramento River between Central Wintun (Nomlaki) and Yana settlements, and that this served as a buffer zone between the two groups (Chase-Dunn and Hall 1997a, Ch. 7; Chase-Dunn and Mann 1998). Meyer (1994) reports a similar buffer between the Anishinaabe and Lakota peoples in what is now the Dakotas and Minnesota.

Anderson (1994) reports the existence of such zones in precontact southeastern United States. Indeed, these zones were so effective that when De Soto crossed them he actually "surprised" the people on the other side. That is, these zones so effectively cut communications, that people on the far side had no advanced warning of De Soto's impending arrival, in contrast to his experiences in populated areas, where runners spread word of his presence in advance of his arrival.

Neutral territory implies a more pacific and cooperative system. The existence of such empty buffer zones or neutral grounds provides an unoccupied territory between competing groups that reduces the likelihood of destructive encounters. These zones might also serve as barriers to incorporation by obviating contact between groups. They also served as ecological recuperation zones where game and vegetative matter that had been over harvested might recover.

Geographical location, technology, and environment significantly shape the process of incorporation. Incorporation is likely to remain weak, in the marginal range, if the frontier area contains few valuable resources and if it does not block expansion. When this is the case indigenous groups have a higher likelihood of survival with some degree of social and cultural integrity. This accounts, in part, for the continued survival of Native American groups in Arizona, New Mexico, and much of the interior western United States (Hall 1989a). Conversely, it also explains much of the drive for their removal in eastern United States.

Changes in definitions of what constitutes resources by expanding systems or changes in dominant technologies typically change the degree of incorporation. After World War II when water, uranium, oil, and coal increased in value more serious attempts were made to incorporate energy resource owning groups more fully into the United States political-economy in order to exploit those resources. It is important to note that this move toward dependent peripheralization did little to benefit those groups (Snipp 1988).

Much of this discussion has emphasized economic, or at least material conditions, and early phases of incorporation. It is worthwhile to turn some attention to cultural and political aspects of incorporation, especially in more recent times.

## 10 POLITICAL AND CULTURAL INCORPORATION

Several writers have treated political aspects of incorporation, most notably Stephen Cornell (1988) and Duane Champagne (1989, 1992) (see, too Meyer 1994; Dunaway 1996a; Faiman-Silva 1997). Cornell and Champagne emphasize the ways in which political organization has changed and adapted to inclusion within the American political system. Cornell in particular has emphasized changing relations of tribal, factional, and national or pan-Indian identities as the political context has changed. Meyer, through a detailed examination of the White Earth Anishinaabeg has examined how increasing involvement in farming and timber industries has led to a split between full-bloods and mixed bloods. I should note here that the full- mixed-blood distinction is more of a cultural metaphor that a true indication of biological heritage. Like race in the Caribbean or Brazil, perceptions are strongly shaped by social characteristics. She explicitly critiques my earlier concept of incorporation for failure to address such issues. Dunaway, as we have seen, describes political and cultural changes which emanated from involvement in the fur trade. Sandra Faiman-Silva (1997) has extended and synthesized Cornell's approach to political incorporation with my work in her analysis of Choctaw history. She examines in considerable detail the effects of involvement with Weyerhauser corporation and the timber industry in Eastern Oklahoma in the last several decades.

Faiman-Silva's synthesis is rich and complex. She sees the Choctaw moving from "nation" to "tribe" to "ethnic minority" (1997, p. 23). She also notes that these relationships "connote asymmetrical political realities and cultural dominance relationships" (p. 24) in addition to economic relationships. Specifically, Americans sought to undermine traditional clan relations in favor of more centralized chiefly roles. By the 1820s most Choctaws remained small-scale subsistence agriculturists, but a small group of capitalist oriented planters was emerging (p. 30.) New factions emerged around these class relationships, often expressed in the idiom of full and mixed-blood differences. "Progressives drafted a constitution in 1826 that dispensed with many ancient Choctaw practices, including hereditary chiefs, traditional burial practices, infanticide, polygyny, and matrilineal inheritance" (p. 33). Elected leaders were increasingly mixed bloods. By the late 20th century Choctaws were much more heavily involved in the capitalist economy: directly through participation capitalist enterprises, notably Weyerhauser, and indirectly by administering their own affairs, albeit with federal money.

Faiman-Silva emphasizes that tribal economic development "remains foremost a problem that is simultaneously structural and political-economic, rooted in historic and contemporary indigenous sovereignty issues and class exploitation" (p. 214). She argues that three obstacles to full Choctaw sovereignty, remain formidable. First, the asymmetry between Native American ethnicities and the U.S. political economy. Second is the volatile nature of high-stakes bingo. Local opposition centers on the moral issue of gambling, the regressive nature of the business, and low skill and low pay of service employment it generates. Third are the continuing high rates of unemployment. She asks, "As the twenty-first century looms, will Choctaw culture survive as more than a distant memory played out at the annual Labor Day tribal gathering?" (p. 218). Much the same question arises with respect to the Miamis in Indiana (Rafert 1996). Indeed, they have been unable to convince the federal government that they remain Indians.

One may ask along with Choctaw Chief Roberts whether tribalism is becoming extinct, "as Choctaws transform into a rural ethnic minority community". Indeed, one may turn Faiman-Silva's closing sentence into a key question, is it true that "Tribal culture persists as a superstructural bas relief over a base driven by world economic forces in a global market place" (p. 224)? I should note here, that several Choctaws disagree with Faiman-Silva's analysis, but it is clear that even they see Choctaw identity as problematic, albeit for different reasons.

Here Joane Nagel's (1996) discussion of symbolic ethnicity is singularly germane. Symbolic ethnicity is "a source of personal meaning, and the benefits of ethnic identity involve mainly emotional fulfillment, social connectedness, or, sometimes recreational pleasure" (p. 25). For Native Americans, this is much more problematic because of the legacy of a biological, racialist, rooting of American concepts of ethnicity. This, in turn, is overlain by the competing levels of Native American identity, as a member of clan and/or tribal faction, as member of a native nation, and as an American Indian. Since acceptance by the federal government often carries important economic consequences, the drive for recognition further politicizes ethnic identity.

These issues become prominent in discussions of who is an authentic "Indian," and who can produce authentic American Indian art (Nagel 1996: Ch. 2; Churchill 1994, pp. 89-113; 1996, pp. 483-499; Durham 1992). Again, these "symbolic issues" are tightly intertwined with important economic issues: making a living as an artist and/or the right to collect fees from tourists. Given the circumstances of high unemployment rates, these are far from trivial issues. They are vital issues.

Thus, we may ask if one of the late 20th century aspects of incorporation is a transformation of identity from something that "just is" into a resource around which political and cultural mobilization can crystallize? If so, can we still speak of incorporation? This question raises, in turn, three other, closely intertwined issues: gender roles, spirituality, and legal relations.

## 11 GENDER ROLES, SPIRITUALITY, CULTURE, AND LAW

As we have seen gender roles have been transformed time and again during incorporation. Yet maintenance of gender roles, can itself be a form of resistance to incorporation. This may be in the form of persisting matrilineal traditions, or in different allocations of gender roles in political processes, or in gender differentials in political participation (Jaimes and Halsey 1992), or in the use of indigenous spirituality to resist alcohol and drug abuse (C. Ward, et al. 1999). Following the prescriptions of Kathryn Ward (1993), this question might best be inverted to ask what can we learn about incorporation by examining gender role changes, rather than asking what does degree of incorporation tell us about gender roles?

In early colonial La Plata and Northern New Spain captives taken from indigenous populations by Spaniards seem to have been predominantly women and children (Hall 1989a; Socolow 1992; Jones 1994, 1998). Adult males were seen as problematic captives. First, the obligation to participate in warfare, defense, and resistance made them particularly intractable and hazardous. Second, they were much harder to resocialize than children – although this applies to adult females as well. Third, captives taken from foraging societies were not very useful as coerced laborers in agricultural settings. Spaniards all over the western hemisphere complained of this, as did American farmers (Knack 1987; Hurtado 1988). Conversely, adult males taken from sedentary societies may not be useful in nomadic societies because the costs of supervision surpass the value of any work they could be forced to do.

The situation is different for women and children. When infant mortality rates are high, as was true for all societies before the mid-nineteenth century, the reproductive capacity of women is especially valuable. In cultural settings where polygyny was accepted, captive women could become secondary wives who could do menial labor under the supervision of the primary wife. At times, this labor was a major motive for capturing women. Ties of affection for children born in captivity may have tempered any desires to flee. According to Susan Socolow (1992) this is one reason why many European women often chose to stay with Indian captors rather than return to Spanish society.

Captured Indian women presented an significantly different problem to European societies. They could be forced to become servants and/or concubines, but they had no acceptable role. Their children took on a lower caste status, even on extreme frontiers where such distinctions were sometimes not so tightly drawn (Gutíerrez 1991). Again, attachment to children could temper desires to flee.

Children of captured Spanish women were accepted more readily into the Indian society. This differential acceptance of their children also encouraged them to remain in Indian societies. The same differential acceptance was accorded captured children. Among most nomadic foragers a child raised in captivity often was adopted and became a full fledged member of the group. The best a captured Indian child raised in Spanish society could hope for (in New Mexico at least) was to beconsidered *genízaro* (Horvath 1977, 1979; Hall 1989a, 1989b).

Children raised in captivity could not return to their native group. They would have been socialized for life in the capturing group, typically inappropriate for their native group. Furthermore, their emotional ties would have been to their captors who had raised them. The general acceptance of such children within Indian societies obviated the pressure to form distinctive communities. These differences are relative; they are "rules of thumb," not absolutes.

Indian women continue to play different roles in modern times (Jaimes and Halsey 1992). Ward et al's (1999) analysis is instructive here. They suggest that Native women, drawing on indigenous traditions, are developing ways to resist some of the most debilitating consequences of conquest. In doing so, they build upon traditional female roles, but simultaneously reconstruct Native ethnicities and identities. That is, their resistance to cultural incorporation, or cultural dominance, is, in itself, a form of ethnogenesis.

Similarly, Native spirituality has become highly politicized. Many writers have vociferously opposed to the (mis)use of Indian culture and spirituality. Wendy Rose (1992) and Ward Churchill (1992, 1994, 1996) have protested mightily against White Shamanism, calling it a "new hucksterism". Their complaint is that Euroamericans, who long since have given up their own pre-modern religious practices and beliefs are trying to regain them through [mis]appropriating practices of various Native American groups. They both note the irony of Euroamericans trying to co-opt what they spent so many years attempting to destroy during the allotment era (Hoxie 1984). Vine Deloria (1995) and Elizabeth Cook-Lynn (1996) have echoed this same complaint.

All these differences carry important legal implications. As noted earlier, Native American groups, and indigenous peoples throughout the world, have had considerable success in manipulating European notions of sovereignty to their own benefit (Wilmer 1993, 1995). By putting European derived states in the position of denying their own bases of sovereignty when they deny the claims of Native groups, indigenous peoples have been able to retain some degree of sovereignty. European states have found the ideological havoc wreaked by outright denial of Native sovereignty too dear a price to pay for the few resources they have sought from Native Peoples. Again, with important exceptions.

This, of course, has not stopped them from trying, as both Carol Ward (1997) and David Wilson (1997) argue (see too, Gedicks, 1993). This has meant that Europeans have had to resort to different sources of justifications such as: promises of economic development, jobs, increased access to industrial goods and services, education and health care chief among them in order to justify claims on Native resources.

Although, Native peoples have met with some success in this arena they have had to fight on European grounds – within European law (for detailed examples from northern New Spain see Cutter 1995a, 1995b, 1995c). Recently, one of the more outstanding successes has been to use the doctrine of sovereignty to set up various gaming operations. By exploiting the contradictory desires for access to gambling and desire to forbid it, Indians have begun to turn considerable profits. But as noted for the

Choctaw, this success is fragile and volatile and subject to redefinition by the federal Congress.

The question remains, how much they have had to give up to win these victories. By fighting European civilization on its own turf, they had to accept some of the premises of that turf. Thomas Biolsi persuasively argues that the law is "a fundamental constituting axis of modern social life – not just a political resource or an institution but a constituent of all social relations of domination" (Biolsi 1995, p. 543; 1992, in press). That is, political incorporation has entailed major changes driven by European legal traditions. In other words, incorporation has, and continues to massively disrupt Native American traditions. This is shown most dramatically and forcefully in the works of contemporary Native American writers (Alexie 1993, 1996; Erdrich 1984, 1988; Power 1994; Seals 1979, 1992; Silko 1977, 1991; and many more).

## 12 CONCLUDING DISCUSSION

This type of exploratory and explicative paper does not call for conclusions, but rather a concluding discussion which relates to the general themes of the paper and the entire collection. If each of the four boundaries a world-system generates its own zone of incorporation, and if only two broad types of world-system are considered, tributary and capitalist, and if the range of nonstate societies is lumped into three broad categories of bands, tribes, and chiefdoms (see Hall 1989: chap. 3 for a discussion of these distinctions), there are at least 24 potential types zones of incorporation, frontiers, or border regions. When the buffer/barrier and internal/external frontier distinctions are added, the types of frontiers proliferate enormously. This, in itself is revealing. It helps explain why so many scholars have found frontiers at once fascinating objects of study, yet tremendously intractable in terms of developing parsimonious theories of their processes and changes.

Though complex, the preceding analysis provides conceptual tools for much broader, multi-tiered comparisons among frontiers. It also provides a means of rendering more intelligible comparisons of say, the Chinese frontier, the Roman frontier, and the Spanish frontiers in northern New Spain and southern La Plata. By attending to such factors as the type of world-system doing the incorporating, the motives behind the incorporation, including especially the types of resources sought, the roles of the incorporated regions and peoples in the larger system, and the pre-incorporation social organization of the incorporated groups analysts can not only understand the incorporation process better, but also highlight the complex ways in which incorporated peoples have resisted, and continue to resist, incorporation.

As Wilma Dunaway (1996b) observes, the resistance may not always be effective, but it often gives incorporated peoples a marginal degree of autonomy. In this light, many of the actions of Native American groups, whether they were attempts to flee a jurisdiction, like that of Chief Joseph, the myriad cases of armed resistance, legal attempts to preserve and enhance tribal autonomy, and the pursuit of some new economic opportunities such as gambling facilities, or the rejection of others like strip mining of coal, or insisting on writing their own histories, become readily understandable. More importantly, these are clearly not haphazard or irrational resistance to change, but rather intelligent, often well-chosen attempts to control and resist the processes of incorporation.

As was seen earlier, same action, flight, may have precisely opposite consequences depending on the specific constellation of conditions under which it occurs. The lens of incorporation also helps highlight and clarify the differences between the incorporation of indigenous peoples and the "assimilation" of migrants. Although both groups come to be seen as ethnic minorities, their origins and goals are often quite different. Incorporated indigenous peoples most often are concerned with preservation of autonomy and distinctiveness. Sovereignty is a vital issue, as Franke Wilmer (1993) has argued. For migrants, fair treatment and economic opportunities are more often the most salient issues. Often the two interact and compete, as David Chappell has shown to be the case in contemporary New Caldonia (1993b) and Kevin Mulroy has shown for the Seminole maroons (Mulroy 1993). These differences, like so many discussed in this paper, are matters of degree, not absolutes.

Most indigenous groups have experienced several waves of incorporation. The results of incorporation range from genocide, through culturicide (Fenelon 1997, 1998), to assimilation, or to transformation into a minority group. Some of these ethnic minorities, may, like some Native American groups, retain a degree of political and cultural autonomy within the larger system. The interplay of world-systemic, national, regional, and local factors that shape these consequences remains complex and poorly understood. However, it is not only the degree of incorporation, but entire history of the incorporation process, the trajectory of incorporation, that shapes the final result. How and the degree to which this is so is far from clear because such trajectories have seldom been studied, and even less frequently been compared (Hall 1989a is an elementary attempt).

But incorporation into a world-system, itself, is changing. By the late twentieth century there are virtually no nonstate societies that have not already experienced at least some degree of incorporation. One of the important emergent constraints on the modern world-system is that there are no more new territories or peoples to incorporate. One the one hand repeated incorporations have reduced human cultural diversity. On the other hand, frontiers have long been regions of human creativity, and zones of ethnogenesis. Often in adapting to volatile conditions and repeated interactions new forms of social organization and identities have grown with frontiers. But incorporation and the consequent formation of frontiers has not stopped, only changed forms. Now internal frontiers are far more common than external frontiers, especially frontiers between zones of the world-system itself, as where the core meets the periphery (or semiperiphery in the view of some) along the United States-Mexico border.

As the discussion of political and cultural incorporation indicates, new zones of change, new borderlines, new frontiers are forming along the edges of, and within, the modern world-system. As world-system penetrates deeper into social processes, as more relations are commodified, new zones of change are created. What is highly problematic is how these will manifest themselves spatially. Roland Robertson has observed that globalization is accompanied by glocalization, the localized flavoring of global processes (1995). This too, however, is an ancient process, long predating the modern world-system. Incorporated groups have always resisted, and often modified the system that incorporated them (e.g., Miller 1993).

World-systems are simultaneously homogenizing and heterogenizing forces. Only those seduced by modernization theory, or the "end of history," have been surprised by the continuous creation and maintenance of ethnic and cultural differences. How and why this occurs varies with type of world-system, the type of region being incorporated, and the specific context of the incorporation process. While the specific mechanisms and the particular raw materials upon which these forces impinge are new at the end of the second millennium of the common era, the underlying dialectic is ancient indeed.

I have argued elsewhere (Hall 1998b), as have David Chappell (1993a) and Anthony D. Smith (1986, 1991), that ethnic diversity among states is the modal, or normal (in the statistical sense) condition of states, not ethnic homogeneity. Why anyone thought otherwise is, itself, a complex problem that while not discussed here, warrants investigation. A major conclusion of those arguments, one that is most relevant here, is that there is much to be learned about our contemporary, "modern" world from the study of ancient worlds. Similarly, we can learn much about modern frontiers and borderlines by studying how older, even ancient, frontiers and borderlines were formed, transformed, and transcended.

Clearly, a world-system analysis approach to incorporation of new regions and peoples as a fundamental creator and transformer of frontiers cannot answer all our questions. But I hope it is equally clear, that most of our questions cannot be answered without such an approach. To paraphrase Vilar, to understand the center, go to the frontier.

***Acknowledgements**
I have presented many parts and versions of this paper in a variety of venues: Political Economy of the World-System Roundtables at the American Sociological Association meetings in 1992, 1997; Association of American Geographers 1994; Social Science History meetings in 1995 and 1996; International Society for the Comparative Study of Civilizations in 1997; International Studies Association in 1997 and 1998; at the American History Association in 1998; and Political Economy of the World-System meeting 1998. I thank the many commentators, discussants, and listeners for useful comments. As always, they are not to be held

accountable for my failures to heed their often sage advice. I would also like to thank the Faculty Development Committee and the John and Janice Fisher Fund for faculty development at DePauw University for support to attend these meetings. I wish to thank Regents of University of California to reproduce Figure 1 from my article with Christopher Chase-Dunn in American Indian and Culture Research Journal.

## NOTES

[1] For fuller explication of the conventional world-system analysis of incorporation see Chase-Dunn and Hall (1997a, Ch. 4) or Dunaway (1996, Chs. 1 and 2).

[2] Meat from the American Bison has higher protein content than beef or chicken, but lower fat, cholesterol, and calories than beef, chicken, or pork.

## REFERENCES

Abler, Thomas S. (1992): "Beavers and Muskets: Iroquois Military Fortunes in the Face of European Colonization," R. Brian Ferguson and Neil L. Whitehead, eds., *War in the Tribal Zone* (School of American Research Press, Santa Fe, New Mexico), pp. 151-174.

Abu-Lughod, Janet (1989): *Before European Hegemony*: The World System A.D. 1250-1350, (Oxford University Press, New York).

— (1993): "Discontinuities and Persistence: One World System or A Succession of World Systems?" Andre Gunder Frank and Barry K. Gills, eds., *The World System*: Five Hundred Years of Five Thousand? (Routledge, London), pp. 278-290.

Aguirre Beltran, Gonzalo, (1979): *Regions of Refuge*, (Society for Applied Anthropology, Monograph No. 12, Washington, D.C.), Originally, (1967): *Regiones de Refugio*, (Ediciones Especiales, No. 46, Instituto Indigenista Interamericano, Mexico City.

Alexie, Sherman (1993): *Tonto and Lone Ranger and Tonto FistFight in Heaven*, (Atlantic Monthly Press, New York).

— (1996): *Indian Killer*, Atlantic Monthly Press, New York.

Anderson, David G. (1994): *The Savannah River Chiefdoms*: *Political Change in the Late Prehistoric Southeast*, (University of Alabama Press, Tuscaloosa).

Arrighi, Giovanni (1979):"Peripheralization of Southern Africa, I: Changes in Production Processes," *Review* 3: pp. 161-191.

— (1994): *The Long Twentieth Century*, (Verso, London).

Bach, Robert L. (1980): "On the Holism of a World-System Perspective," pp. 289-318 T.K. Hopkins and I. Wallerstein, eds., *Processes of the World-System*, (Sage, Beverly Hills).

Baretta, Silvio R. D. and John Markoff (1978): "Civilization and Barbarism: Cattle Frontiers in Latin America," *Comparative Studies in Society and History* 20: pp. 587-620.

Barfield, Thomas J. (1989): *The Perilous Frontier*, (Blackwell, London).

— (1990): "Tribe and State Relations: The Inner Asian Perspective," Philip S. Khoury and Joseph Kostiner, eds., *Tribe and State Formation in the Middle East*, University of California Press, Berkeley), pp. 153-182.

— (1991): "Inner Asia and Cycles of Power in China's Imperial Dynastic History," Gary Seaman and Daniel Marks, eds., *Rulers from the Steppe*: State Formation on the Eurasian Periphery, Ethnographics Press, Center for Visual Anthropology, University of Southern California, Los Angeles), pp. 21-62.

Barth, Frederick (1969): *Ethnic Groups and Boundaries*, (Little Brown, Boston), especially editor's "Introduction".

Biolsi, Thomas (1992): *Organizing the Lakota: The Political Economy of the New Deal on the Pine Ridge and Rosebud Reservations*, (University of Arizona Press, Tucson, AZ).

— (1995): "Bringing the Law Back In: Legal Rights and the Regulation of Indian-White Relations on the Rosebud Reservation," *Current Anthropology* 36: pp. 543-571.

—: *Law and the Production of Race Relations*: Indian and White On and Off Rosebud Reservation, (unpublished Ms).

Bose, Christine E. and Edna Acosta-Belen, eds. (1995): *Women in the Latin American Development Process*, Temple University Press, Philadelphia).

Bradley, Candice (1997): "Fertility in Maragoli: The Global and the Local," *Economic Analysis Beyond the Local System*, edited by Richard Blanton, Peter Peregrine, Deborah Winslow, and Thomas D. Hall, (University Press of America, Lanham, MD), pp. 121-138.

Champagne, Duane, *American Indian Societies: Strategies and Conditions of Political and Cultural Survival*, (Cultural Survival, Cambridge, MA, 1989).

— (1992): *Social Order and Political Change: Constitutional Governmnts Among the Cherokee, the Choctaw, the Chickasaw, and the Creek*, (Stanford University Press, Stanford).

Chappell, David A. (1993 a): "Ethnogenesis and Frontiers," *Journal of World History* 4: pp. 267-275.

— (1993b) "Frontier Ethnogenesis: The Case of New Caldonia," *Journal of World History* 4: pp.307-324.

Chase-Dunn, Christopher (1998): *Global Formation: Structures of the World-Economy*, (Basil Blackwell, London).

Chase-Dunn, Christopher and Thomas D. Hall, eds. (1991): *Core/Periphery Relations in Precapitalist Worlds*, (Westview Press, Boulder, CO, 1991).

— (1995): "The Historical Evolution of World-Systems," *Protosociology* 7: pp. 23-34, pp. 301-303.

— (1997a): *Rise and Demise: Comparing World-Systems*, (Westview Press, Boulder, CO).

_____ (1997 b): "Ecological Degredation and the Evolution of World-Systems," *Journal of World-Systems Research* 3:403-431, (*electronic journal*: http://csf.colorado.edu/wsystems/jwsr.html)

— (1998a): "World-Systems in North America: Networks, Rise and Fall and Pulsations of Trade in Stateless Systems," *American Indian Culture and Research Journal* 2: pp. 23-72.

— (1998): "The Historical Evolution of World-Systems: Iterations and Transformations," Gerhard Preyer, ed., *Strukturelle Evolution und das Weltsystem. Theorien, Sozialstrukturen und Evolutionare Entwicklungen*, (Suhrkamp Taschenbuch Wissenschaft Nr. 1346. Frankfurt am Main: Suhrkamp Verlag), pp. 316-338.

Chase-Dunn, Christopher and Kelly M. Mann (1998): *The Wintu and Their Neighbors: A Very Small World-System in Northern California*, (University of Arizona Press, Tucson).

Churchill, Ward (1992): *Fantasies of the Master Race: Literature, Cinema and the Colonization of American Indians*, edited by M. Annette Jaimes, (Common Courage Press, Monroe, ME).

— (1994): Indians R Us: *Culture and Genocide in Native North America*, (Common Courage Press, Monroe, ME).

— (1996): *From A Native Son: Selected Essays on Indigenism*, 1985-1995, (South End Press, Boston).

Collins, Randal (1978): "Some Principles of Long-term Social Change: The Territorial Power of States," Louis Kriesberg, ed., *Research in Social Movements, Conflicts, and Change*, (JAI Press, Greenwich, CT), pp. 1-34.

— (1981): "Long-term Social Change and The Territorial Power of States," pp. 71-106 Randall Collins, ed., *Sociology Since Midcentury*, (Academic Press, New York).

Cook-Lynn, Elizabeth (1996): *Why I Can't Read wallace Stegner and other Essays: A Tribal Voice*, (University of Wisconsin Press, Madison).

Cornell, Stephen (1988): *The Return of the Native: American Indian Political Resurgence*, (Oxford University Press, New York).

Curtin, Philip D. (1984): *Cross-Cultural Trade in World History*, (Cambridge University Press, Cambridge).

Cutter, Charles R. (1995a): "Judicial Punishment in Colonial New Mexico," *Western Legal History* 8: pp. 115-129.

— (1995b): "Indians As Litigants in Colonial Mexico," *Paper presented at Social Science History Association meeting*, Chicago, IL, Nov.

— (1995c): *The Legal Culture of Northern New Spain, 1700-1810*, (University of New Mexico Press, Albuquerque).

D'Azevedo, Warren L. (1986): *Handbook of North American Indians*, Volume 11: Great Basin, (Smithsonian, Washington, D.C.).

Deloria, Vine, Red Earth (1995): *White Lies: Native Americans and the Myth of Scientific Fact*, (Scribners, New York).

Dunaway, Wilma (1994): "The Southern Fur Trade and the Incorporation of Southern Appalachia into the World-Economy, 1690-1763," *Review* 18: pp. 215-242.

— (1996a): *The First American Frontier: Transition to Capitalism in Southern Appalachia, 1700-1860*, (University of North Carolina Press, Chapel Hill).

— (1996b): "Incorporation as an Interactive Process: Cherokee Resistance to Expansion of the Capitalist World System, 1560-1763," *Sociololgical Inquiry* 66: pp. 445-470.

— (1997): "Rethinking Cherokee Acculturation: Women's Resistance to Agrarian Capitalism and Cultural Change, 1800-1838," *American Indian Culture and Research Journal* 21: pp. 231-268.

—, "The International Fur Trade and Disempowerment of Cherokee Women, 1680-1775," Thomas D. Hall, ed., *A World-Systems Reader*, (Rowman and Littlefield, Boulder, CO, forthcoming).

Durham, Jimmie (1992): "Cowboys and...Notes on Art, Literature, and American Indians in the Modern American Mind," M. Annette Jaimes, ed., *The State of Native America*: Genocide, Colonization, and Resistance, (South End Press, Boston), pp. 423-438.

Dyson, Stephen L. (1985): *The Creation of the Roman Frontier*, (Princeton University Press, Princton).

Erdrich, Louise (1984): *Love Medicine*: A Novel, (Holt, Rinehart and Winston, New York).

— (1984): *Tracks*: A Novel, (Henry Holt, New York).

Faiman-Silva, Sandra L. (1997): *Choctaws at the Crossroads: The Political Economy of Class and Culture in the Oklahoma Timber Region*, (University of Nebraska Press, Lincoln).

Fenelon, James (1997): "From Peripheral Domination to Internal Colonialism: Socio-Political Change of the Lakota on Standing Rock," *Journal of World-Systems Research* 3: pp. 259-320, (electronic journal: http://csf.colorado.edu/wsystems/jwsr.html)

— (1998): *Culturicide, Resistance, and Survival of the Lakota* (Sioux Nation), (Garland Publishing, New York).

Ferguson, R. Brian (1997): "Tribes, Tribal Organization," Thomas Barfield, ed., *Dictionary of Anthropology*, (Blackwell, London), pp. 475-476.

Ferguson, R. Brian, and Neil L. Whitehead, eds. (1992a): *War in the Tribal Zone: Expanding States and Indigenous Warfare*, (School of American Research Press, Santa Fe, NM).

— (1992b): "The Violent Edge of Empire," R. Brian Ferguson and Neil L. Whitehead, eds. *War in the Tribal Zone*, (School of American Research Press, Santa Fe), pp. 1-30.

Frank, Andre Gunder and Barry K. Gills, eds. (1993): *The World System*: Five Hundred Years of Five Thousand? (Routledge, London).

Gedicks, Al. (1993): *The New Resource Wars: Native and Environmental Struggles Against Multinational Corporations*, (South End Press, Boston).

Gills, Barry K. and Andre Gunder Frank (1991): "5000 Years of World System History: The Cumulation of Accumulation," Christopher Chase-Dunn and Thomas D. Hall, eds., *Core/Periphery Relations in Precapitalist Worlds*, Westview Press, Boulder, CO), pp. 67-112.

Griffen, William (1988a): *Apaches at War & Peace: The Janos Presidio*, 1750-1858, (University of New Mexico Press, Albuquerque).

— (1988b): *Utmost Good Faith: Patterns of Apache-Mexican Hostilities in Northern Chihuahua Border Warfare*, 1821-1848, (University of New Mexico Press, Albuquerque).

Gunawardana, R. A. L. H. (1992): "Conquest and Resistance: Pre-state and State Exapansionism in Early Sri Lankan History" R. Brian Ferguson and Neil L. Whitehead, eds. *War in the Tribal Zone*, (School of American Research Press, Santa Fe), pp. 61-82.

Gutiérrez, Ramón A. (1991): *When Jesus Came, the Corn Mothers Went Away: Marriage, Sexuality, and Power in New Mexico, 1500-1846*, (Stanford University Press, Stanford).

Guy, Donna J. and Thomas E. Sheridan, eds. (1998a): *Contested Ground: Comparative Frontiers on the Northern and Southern Edges of the Spanish Empire*, (University of Arizona Press, Tucson).

— (1998b): "On Frontiers: The Northern and Southern Edges of the Spanish Empire in America," Donna J. Guy and Thomas E. Sheridan, eds., *Contested Ground*, (University of Arizona Press, Tucson), pp. 3-15.

Haaland, Gunnar (1969): "Economic Determinants in Ethnic Processes," pp. 53-73 Frederick Barth, ed., *Ethnic Groups and Boundaries*, (Little Brown, Boston).

Hall, Thomas D (1986): "Incorporation in the World-System: Toward A Critique," *American Sociological Review* 51: pp. 390-402.

— (1987): "Native Americans and Incorporation: Patterns and Problems," *American Indian Culture and Research Journal* 11:1-30.

— (1989a): *Social Change in the Southwest*, 1350-1880, (University Press of Kansas, Lawrence, KS.).

— (1989b): "Is Historical Sociology of Peripheral Regions Peripheral?" Michael T. Martin and Terry R. Kandal, eds., *Studies of Development and Change in the Modern World*, (Oxford University Press, Oxford), pp. 349-372.

— (1991a): "Civilizational Change: The Role of Nomads," *Comparative Civilizations Review* 24: pp. 34-57.

— (1991b): "The Role of Nomads in Core/Periphery Relations" Christopher Chase-Dunn and Thomas D. Hall, eds., *Core/Periphery Relations in Precapitalist Worlds*, Westview Press, Boulder, CO), pp. 212-239.

— (1997): "World-Systems and Evolution: An Appraisal," *Journal of World-System Research*, 2:1-109, (electronic journal http://csf.colorado.edu/wsystems/jwsr.html)

— (1996): "The World-System Perspective: A Small Sample from a Large Universe," *Sociological Inquiry* 66: pp. 440-454.

— (1997): "Frontier," Thomas Barfield, ed., *Dictionary of Anthropology*, (Blackwell, London), pp. 208-209.

— (1998a): "La Plata and Las Provincias Internas: A View From World-System Theory" Donna J. Guy and Thomas E. Sheridan, eds. *Contested Ground*, (University of Arizona Press, Tucson), pp. 150-166.

— (1998b): "The Effects of Incorporation into World-Systems on Ethnic Processes: Lessons from the Ancient World for the Modern World," *International Political Science Review* 19, pp. 251-267.

Hall, Thomas D. and Christopher Chase-Dunn (1993): "The World-Systems Perspective and Archaeology: Forward into the Past," *Journal of Archaeological Research* 1: pp. 121-143.

Heizer, Robert, F. ed. (1978): *Handbook of North American Indians*, Volume 8, California, (Smithsonian Institution, Washington, D.C.).

— and A. E. Treganza (1971): "Mines and Quarries of the Indians of California," Robert F. Heizer and Mary A. Whipple, eds., *The California Indians*: A Sourcebook, 2nd ed., (University of California Press, Berkeley), pp. 346-359.

Hoebel, E. A. (1982): *The Plains Indians*, (Indiana University Press, Bloomington).

Hopkins, Terence K., I. Wallerstein, Resat Kasaba, William G. Martin, Peter D. Phillips (1987): *Incorporation into the World-Economy: How the World System Expands* special issue of *Review* 10: 5/6(Summer/Fall): pp. 761-902.

Horvath, Steven (1977): "The Genízaro of Eighteenth-Century New Mexico: A Reexamination," Discovery, School of American Research, pp. 25-40.

— (1979): "The Social and Political Organization of the Genízaros of Plaza De Nuestra Señora De Los Dolores De Belén, New Mexico, 1740-1812," Ph.D. dissertation, Brown University.

Hoxie, Frederick E., A Final Promise (1984): *The Campaign to Assimilate the Indians*, 1880-1920, (University of Nebraska Press, Lincoln).

Hurtado, Albert L. (1988): *Indian Survival on the California Frontier*, (Yale University Press, New Haven).

Jaimes, M. Annette with Halsey, Theresa (1922): "American Indian Women: At the Center of Indigenous North America," M. Annette Jaimes, ed., *The State of Native America*: Genocide, Colonization, and Resistance, (South End Press, Boston), pp. 311-344.

Johnston, Jim (1978): "The Wintu and Yana Territorial Boundary," *Paper presented to the annual meetings of the Society for California Archaeology*, Yosemite National Park, March.

Jones, Kristine L. (1994): "Comparative Ethnohistory and the Southern Cone," *Latin American Research Review* 29: pp. 107-118.

— (1998): "Comparative Raiding Economies: North and South," Donna J. Guy and Thomas E. Sheridan, eds. *Contested Ground*, (University of Arizona Press, Tucson), pp. 97-114.

Kardulias, P. Nick (1990): "Fur Production as a Specialized Activity in a World System: Indians in the North American Fur Trade," *American Indian Culture and Research Journal* 14: pp. 25-60.

Knack, Martha C. (1987): "The Role of Credit in Native Adaptation to the Great Basin Ranching Economy," *American Indian Culture and Research Journal* 11: pp. 43-65.

Lattimore, Owen (1940): *Inner Asian Frontiers*, 2nd ed, (Beacon Press, Boston, 1951 (Originally *American Geographical Society*).

—, "The Frontier in History," Owen Lattimore, ed., *Studies in Frontier History*: Collected Papers, 1928-58, (Oxford University Press, London, 1962c), pp. 469-491.

— (1962a): "Inner Asian Frontiers: Defensive Empires and Conquest Empires," Owen Lattimore, ed., *Studies in Frontier History*: Collected Papers, 1928-58, (Oxford University Press, London), pp. 501-513.

— (1962b): ed., *Studies in Frontier History*: Collected Papers, 1928-58, (Oxford University Press, London).

Lindner, Rudi Pau (1981): "Nomadism, Horses and Huns," *Past & Present* 92: pp. 3-19..

— (1983): *Nomads and Ottomans in Medieval Anatolia*, Vol. 144 Indiana University Uralic and Altaic Series, (Research Institute for Inner Asian Studies, Bloomington).

Lowie, Robert H. (1954): *Indians of the Plains*, (Natural History Press, New York).

Markoff, John (1994): "Frontier Societies," Peter N. Stearns, ed., *Encyclopedia of Social History*, (Garland, New York), pp. 289-291.

Mathien, Frances Joan and Randall McGuire, eds. (1986): *Ripples in the Chichimec Sea: Consideration of Southwestern-Mesoamerican Interactions*, (Southern Illinois University Press, Carbondale, IL).

McNeill, William H. (1964): *Europe's Steppe Frontier*, 1500-1800. (University of Chicago Press, Chicago).

Melody, Michael E. (1977): *The Apaches*, (Indiana University Press, Bloomington).

Meyer, Melissa L. (1994): *The White Earth Tragedy: Ethnicity and Dispossession at a Minnesota Anishinaabe Reservation, 1889-1920*, (University of Nebraska, Lincoln).

Mies, Maria (1993): *Patriarchy and Accumulation on a World-Scale*, (Zed Books, London).

— and Vandana Shiva, *Ecofeminism*, (Zed Books, London).

Mikesell, Marvin W. (1960): "Comparative Studies in Frontier History," *Annals of American Association of Geographers* 50: pp. 62-74 (1960) [reprinted in Richard Hofstadter and Seymour Martin Lipset, eds., Turner and the Sociology of the Frontier, (Basic Books, Boston, 1968), pp. 152-171.

Miller, David Harry (1993): "Ethnogenesis and Religious Revitalization beyond the Roman Frontier: The Case of Frankish Origins," *Journal of World History* 4: pp. 277-285.

Mishkin, Bernard (1940): *Rank and Warfare among the Plains Indians*, Monograph no. 3 of the American Ethnological Society, (University of Washington Press, Seattle), reprinted by University of Nebraska Press, Lincoln, 1992.

Moseley, Katherine P. (1992): "Caravel and Caravan: West Africa and the World-Economies ca. 900-1900 AD," *Review* 15: pp. 523-555.

Mulroy, Kevin (1993): "Ethnogenesis and Ethnohistory of the Seminole Maroons," *Journal of World History* 4: pp. 287-305.

Nagel, Joane (1996): *American Indian Ethnic Renewal: Red Power and the Resurgence of Identity and Culture*, (Oxford University Press, Oxford).

Ortiz, Alfonso (1979): *Handbook of North American Indians*, Volume 9: Southwest. (Smithsonian, Washington, D.C.).

— (1983): *Handbook of North American Indians*, Volume 10: Southwest, (Smithsonian, Washington, D.C.).

Peregrine, Peter N. (1996): "Archaeology and World-Systems Theory," *Sociololgical Inquiry* 64: pp. 486-495.

— and Gary M. Feinman, eds. (1996): Pre-Columbian World-Systems, *Monographs in World Archaeology* No. 26, (Prehistory Press, Madison, WI).

Power, Susan (1994): *The Grass Dancer*, (G. P. Putnam, New York).

Rafert, Stewart (1994): *The Miami Indians of Indiana: A Persistent People, 1654-1994*, (Indiana Historical Society, Indianapolis).

Reff, Daniel T. (1991): *Diseases, Depopulation, and Culture Change in Northwestern New Spain*, 1518-1764, (University of Utah Press, Salt Lake City).

Robertson, Roland (1995): "Glocalization: Time-Spance and Homogeneity-Heterogeneity" Mike Featherstone, Scott Lash and Roland Robertson, eds., *Global Modernites*, (Sage, Newbury Park), pp. 25-24.

Rose, Wendy (1992): "The Great Pretenders: Further Reflections on Whiteshamism," M. Annette Jaimes, ed., *The State of Native America*: Genocide, Colonization, and Resistance, (South End Press, Boston), pp. 403-421.

Sahlins, Peter (1989): *Boundaries: The Making of France and Spain in the Pyrenees*, (University of California Press, Berkeley).

Seals, David (1979): *The Powwow Highway*: A Novel, (Plume, New York).

— (1992): *Sweet Medicine*, (Orion Books, New York).

Secoy, Frank R. (1953): *Changing Military Patterns of the Great Plains Indians* (17th Century Through Early 19th Century), Monographs of the American Ethnological Society 21, (J.J. Augustin, Locust Valley, N.Y.), reprinted by University of Nebraska Press, Lincoln, 1992).

Shannon, Thomas R. (1996): *An Introduction to the World-System Perspective*, 2nd ed, (Westview Press, Boulder, CO).

Sheridan, Thomas E. (1992): "The Limits of Power: The Political Ecology of the Spanish Empire in the Greater Southwest," *Antiquity* 66: pp. 153-171.

Sherratt, Andrew G. (1993a): "What Would a Bronze-Age World System Look Like? Relations Between Temperate Europe and the Mediterranean in Later Prehistory" *Journal of European Archaeology* 1: 1-57.

—, C. Scarre and F. Healy, eds. (1993b): *Trade and Exchange in Prehistoric Europe*, Prehistoric Society Monograph, (Oxbow Books, Oxford), pp. 245-255.

— (1993c): "The Growth of the Mediterranean Economy in the Early First Millennium B.C," *World Archaeology* 24: pp,. 361-378.

— (1994): "Core, Periphery and Margin: Perspectives on the Bronze Age," Clay Mathers and Simon Stoddart, eds., *Development and Decline in the Mediterranean Bronze Age*, (Sheffield Academic Press, Sheffield), pp. 335-345.

— (1995): "Reviving the Grand Narrative: Archaeology and Long-Term Change" The Second David L. Clarke Memorial Lecture, *Journal of European Archaeology* 3:1-32.

Silko, Leslie Marmon (1977): *Ceremony*, (Viking, New York).

— (1991): *Almanac of the Dead: A Novel*, (Simon and Schuster, New York).

Slatta, Richard W. (1983): *Gauchos and the Vanishing Frontier*, (University of Nebraska Press, Lincoln).

— (1990): *Cowboys of the Americas*, (Yale University Press, New Haven).

— (1997): *Comparing Cowboys and Frontiers*, (University of Oklahoma Press, Norman).

— (1998): "Defending Far Frontiers: Spanish Colonial Military Strategy and Ideology," Donna J. Guy and Thomas E. Sheridan, eds. *Contested Ground*, (University of Arizona Press, Tucson), pp. 83-96.

Smith, Anthony D. (1986): *The Ethnic Origins of Nations*, (Blackwell, Oxford).

— (1991): *National Identity*, (University of Nevada Press, Reno).

Smith, Joan, Collins, Jane Hopkins, Terence K., and Muhammed, Akhbar, eds. (1988): *Racism, Sexism and the World-System*, (Greenwood, New York).

Snipp, C. Matthew (1988): "Public Policy Impacts and American Indian Economic Development," C. Matthew Snipp, ed., *Public Policy Impacts on American Indian Economic Development*, (Native American Studies, Development Series No 4, Albuquerque), pp. 1-22.

So, Alvin Y. (1990): "The Process of Incorporation into the Capitalist World-System: The Case of China in the Nineteenth Century," *Review* 8: pp. 91-116 .

— (1990): *Social Change and Development: Modernization, Dependency, and World-system Theory*, (Sage, Newbury Park, CA).

Socolow, Susan Migden (1992): "Spanish Captives in Indian Societies: Cultural Contact Along the Argentine Frontier, 1600-1835," *Hispanic American Historical Review* 72: pp. 73-99.

Thornton, Russell (1987): *American Indian Holocaust and Survival*, (University of Oklahoma Press, Norman).

—, Tim Miller, and Jonathan Warren (1991): "American Indian Population Recovery following Smallpox Epidemics," *American Anthropologist* 93: pp. 28-45.

Upham, Steadman (1992): "Interaction and Isolation: The Empty Spaces in Panregional Political and Economic Systems," Ed Schortman and Patricia Urban, eds., *Resources, Power, and Interregional Interaction*, (Plenum Press, New York), pp. 139-152.

Wallerstein, Immanuel (1974a): "The Rise and Future Demise of the World Capitalist System: Concepts for Comparative Analysis," *Comparative Studies in Society and History* 16: pp. 387-415 (reprinted in I. Wallerstein, ed. (1979): *The Capitalist World-Economy*, (Cambridge University Press, Cambridge), pp. 1-36.

— (1974b): *The Modern World-System: Capitalist Agriculture and the Origins of European World-Economy in the Sixteenth Century*, (Academic Press, New York).

— (1979): *The Capitalist World-Economy*, (Cambridge University Press, Cambridge).

— (1980): *The Modern World-System II: Mercantilism and the Consolidation of the European World-Economy, 1600-1750*, (Academic Press, New York).

— (1983): "An Agenda for World-Systems Analysis" William R. Thompson, ed., *Contending Approaches to World System Analysis*, (Sage, Beverly Hills), pp. 299-308.

— (1984): *The Politics of the World-Economy: The States, the Movements, and the Civilizations*, (Cambridge University Press, Cambridge).

— (1989): *The Modern World-System III: The Second Era of Great Expansion of the Capitalist World-Economy, 1730-1840s*, (Academic Press, New York).

— (1991): *Geopolitics and Geoculture: Essays on the Changing World-System*, (Cambridge University Press, Cambridge).

— (1993): "World System vs. World-Systems," Andre Gunder Frank and Barry K. Gills, eds., *The World System*: Five Hundred Years of Five Thousand? (Routledge, London), pp. 291-296.

— (1995): "Hold the Tiller Firm: On Method and the Unit of Analysis," Stephen K. Sanderson, ed., *Civilizations and World-Systems*: Two Approaches to the Study of World-Historical Change, (Altamira Press, Walnut Creek, CA), pp. 225-233.

Ward, Carol (1997): "American Indian Women and Resistance to Incorporation: The Northern Cheyenne Case," Paper presented at the International Society for the Comparative Study of Civilization meeting, Provo, UT, May.

Ward, Carol, Elon Stander, and Yodit Solom (1999): "Resistance through Healing among American Indian Women," Thomas D. Hall, ed., *A World-Systems Reader*, (Rowman and Littlefield, Boulder, CO), forthcoming.

Ward, Kathryn B. (1984): *Women in the World System*, (Praeger, New York).

— ed. (1990): *Women Workers and Global Restructuring*, (ILR Press, Ithaca, NY).

— (1993): "Reconceptualizing World-system Theory to Include Women," Paula England, ed., *Theory on Gender/Feminism on Theory*, (Aldine, New York), pp. 43-68.

Ward, Kathryn B. and Jean Larson Pyle (1995): "Gender, Industrializtion, Transnational Corporations, and Development: An Overview of Trends and Patterns," Christine E. Bose and Edna Acosta-Belen, eds., *Women in the Latin American Development Process*, (Temple University Press, Philadelphia), pp. 37-63.

Weber, David J. and Jane M. Rausch (1994): *Where Cultures Meet: Frontiers in Latin American History*, (Scholarly Resources Inc., Wilmington, DE).

Willard, Alice (1993): "Gold, Islam and Camels: The Transformative Effects of Trade and Ideology," *Comparative Civilizations Review* 28, pp. 80-105.

Wilmer, Franke (1993): *The Indigenous Voice in World Politics: Since Time Immemorial*, (Sage, Newbrury Park).

— (1995): "From the Age of Conquest to the Age of Self-Determination: Indigenous Peoples and the Changing Face of International Sovereignty," Paper presented at the International Studies Association meeting, Chicago, February.

Wilson, David R. (1997): "From Isolation to the Iron Age: the Northern Cheyenne and Energy Development," Paper presented at the International Society for the Comparative Study of Civilization meeting, Provo, May.

Wolf, Eric R. (1982): *Europe and the People Without History*, (University of California Press, Berkeley).

RICHARD E. LEE

# AFTER HISTORY?

## The Last Frontier of Historical Capitalism

Old Boundaries. New Boundaries. Crossing Boundaries. Blurred boundaries. We live in a time of what seems to be a heightened sensitivity to the ways material and conceptual boundaries create limits and opportunities in the real world. To say that, however, is not to assert that hitherto social scientists have been unaware of the consequences of privileging one or another set of boundary-making criteria defining the what or whom they study. Indeed, what has come to be known as World-Systems Analysis arose amid, and took form through, critical reflection on the analytic object of inquiries into long-term, large-scale, social change.

The intense interest in large-scale comparative social science of the nineteenth century waned during the first half of the twentieth century. Although the earlier studies had been primarily historical in orientation, they were really comparative in name only, as Roy C. Macridis noted in the mid-1950's; they were descriptive, parochial, static and monographic in approach.[1] With the end of the war in 1945 and U.S. social science's ascendance to dominance on a world scale came a resurgence of large-scale comparisons. There were, however, significant departures from earlier modes of inquiry and two developments could be immediately recognized. One of these was the "emphasis on field studies of 'emerging,' 'new,' 'non-Western' nations" and the other was a "concern for theoretical explication and methodological rigor".[2]

In the post-war period these two changes were embodied in studies of comparative modernization. "Modernization" theory expressed the realization by Western, especially American, social scientists of the increasing importance of the non-West and the non-rich in the context of the geopolitical conflict of the cold war, but sought to understand these crucial areas and peoples by simply extending, or universalizing, the experiences and analytic viewpoints of the West.[3] Only the independent nation-states forming as a result of decolonization were uncommitted, or might possibly be swayed, in the East-West struggle. As Jacob Viner asserted in 1951: "We are seeking willing and strong allies". This attitude was accompanied, nonetheless, with a real concern for well-being. Viner continued: "We have, I insist, interests in the welfare of foreign peoples going beyond our own national security and commercial prosperity".[4] "Thus



*G. Preyer, M. Bös (eds.), Borderlines in a Globalized World, 67-82.*

the attention to explaining inequality – economic development and "the derived concept 'underdeveloped country'" – joined social scientists to policy planners with an anti-communist agenda.[5]

The ideological aspect of the modernization project resulted from observations of the Japanese, German, Italian and Soviet experiences suggesting that "free market" economics and representative democracy might not be the inevitable end point of all societal development. "If the Soviet experience teaches anything," wrote Alexander Gerschenkron,

> it is that it demonstrates *ad oculos* the formidable dangers inherent in our time in the existence of economic backwardness. ... In conditions of a 'bi-polar world' this [may lead to] imitation of Soviet policies by other backward countries and [to] the latter's voluntary or involuntary incorporation in the Soviet orbit.[6]

The result was a preoccupation with political change and the social forces determining its direction. According to Morris Watnick, "technical aid and economic reform" had to be accompanied by the "development of an ethos and system of values which can compete successfully with the attraction exercised by communism".[7]

The second change readily identified by practitioners of post-war social science had to do with the attainment of professional respectability due in large to "refinements in theory and measurement used in the study of cross-sectional relations".[8] In their bid for legitimacy, associated with the "positivist claim that only natural science provided certain knowledge and conferred the power of prediction and control," the social sciences in the U.S. took a turn away from the historical methods of the work alluded to by Macridis to embrace empirical and quantitative analysis with the emphasis on hypothesis testing as a matter of routine practice.[9] The comparative method in the social sciences represented the analogue of the experimental method in the natural sciences, and the "systems" model of interdependent, interacting structures maintaining system equilibrium became increasingly common in social research.[10] As one prominent exponent of the modernization perspective, Gabriel A. Almond, put it, "our capacity for explanation and prediction in the social sciences is enhanced when we think of social structures and institutions as performing *functions* in *systems*"[11] and F. X. Sutton defined a "society" as "a particular kind of social system, viz., one comprehensive and differentiated enough to be self-sufficient".[12]

Structural-functional analysis involving some form of Talcott Parsons's translation of Weberian "rationality" into sets of pattern variables, implemented the comparative method in much of the work relating to modernization. In a dualism with a long heritage in classical sociology,[13] "modern" societies, it was argued, displayed universalistic, specific, and achievement based norms and practices while "traditional" configurations were particularistic, diffuse, and ascriptive. The virtue of these pattern variables was that they provided a "standard means of describing the role-expectations and value-standards in *any* social systems ... important in comparative analysis".[14] Here, however, was a static theory, with modernization no more than a datum. Since it did not explain how or why modernization took place, it could only distinguish those societies which had modernized from those which had not.[15]

Nonetheless, theorists posited contemporary Western social organization, capitalism and democracy as the end point towards which the Third World was "developing". This move was often made explicit,[16] but could also be left implicit in deference to "value neutrality". Not surprisingly, a Soviet version paralleled its Western counterpart; the motor was the same, state-by-state industrialization, but the end result was socialism. What was needed, then, especially for the policy maker, was a model which assumed change. In 1956, W. W. Rostow offered one such schema in the form of a three-stage theory of transformation of "economies," specifically identified as national economies. The middle stage, "take-off" to self-sustaining growth, was defined as an "industrial revolution, tied directly to radical changes in methods of production, having their decisive consequence over a relatively short period of time"; successful "take-off" depended on an increase in the rate of productive investment and a leadership or entrepreneurial sector ready and willing to exploit the expansion.[17] By the time his model appeared in book form in 1960, the number of stages had grown to five, but lack of an account for the temporal process of change persisted. Rostovian theory simply failed "to specify any mechanism of evolution which links the different stages".[18]

On the empirical side, criticism of the descriptive suppositions of the modernization perspective accompanied demonstrations of its short-comings as theory. Reservations were advanced early in the 1950's by Raul Prebisch and the E.C.L.A. group (U.N. Economic Commission for Latin America). They observed anti-Ricardian, deteriorating terms of trade between "core" and "periphery" suggesting that increased contact with the core, metropole or center impeded development in the periphery or satellite.[19] The logic of modernization was thus inverted, but the solution, the "import substitution" model which became the mainstay of developmentalism, did not challenge the dualistic view of Third World social structures, or their representation in terms of stages in an evolutionary pattern, or the corollary that Western social structures and levels of development could be generalized as "advanced industrial societies" over the entire globe.

Whatever "system" these analysts studied, they were primarily concerned with outcomes at the level of the state. This held not only for those working from the modernization perspective and their developmentalist critics as well, but, given the "socialism in one country" doctrine, for those grounded in communist orthodoxy too. The cold warriors were concerned with protecting U.S. supremacy, or attacking it, by building coalitions of states. Those analysts working to improve material conditions in the Third

World saw the state as a primary agent in reproducing the industrial revolutions which, it was theorized, accounted for First-World development.

If nation-state "societies" comprised the most common unit of study (practical for data collection and supposedly fulfilling the requirement of independence for comparative analysis), there were, of course, two other conceptual possibilities in the choice of analytic unit. On the one hand, it was certainly possible to conceive of smaller elements of who or what was changing or needed changing, "traditional" societies or "cultures," and operationlize them in the form of "tribes" as anthropologists did. There were some, especially colonial administrators acting in their own interests, who, like Malinowski, argued that in the colonial situation these were the relevant units. Building on the critiques of this view by M. Gluckman and G. Balandier, Immanuel Wallerstein argued in 1966 that, in fact, the colony was the proper unit for the study of the process of change "within a world context of modernization". It was within this framework that the question of the legitimacy of the colonial governing authority nourished nationalist movements; "what emerged as a consequence of the social change wrought by the administration was a nationalist movement which eventually led a revolution and obtained independence".[20]

This is a decisive argument. It is based on the proposition that colonial boundaries, and by extension those of the (emerging) states, are not pre-given; indeed, they may arbitrarily embrace multiple "cultures" or divide territories previously identified with one single "culture". Rather than a fact of nature, they are imposed, not without local resistance, and even fluctuate, as a product of contentious agreement among sovereign powers. The political entities thus geographically demarcated inevitably encompass a stratified population over which the monopoly on the (legitimate) use of force resides with the central authority. To take a single "culture" as the unit of study restricts the analyst in describing the structures of power where the struggles for change are actually played out, and this restriction effects the range of desirable strategic outcomes and the modes of effective tactical engagement which can be envisioned by change-agents. There is, thus, a political component to the choice of the more, or less, inclusive unit.

On the other hand, designating a larger system of relations than the colony/state as the unit of study presented a second methodological alternative. Neither modernization theorists nor developmentalists considered underdevelopment to be a necessary consequence of capitalism as such, although they might argue that there simply was not enough of it in the Third World. Others, however, did conceptualize the problem in terms of a direct relationship between capitalism and inequality. Reviewing Rostow's *The Stages of Economic Growth: A Non-Communist Manifesto* (1960), Paul Baran and Eric Hobsbawm maintained that "all economic development between the 'traditional' society and the appearance of the USSR was actually *capitalist* development ... which calls therefore for an analysis of the specific characteristics of *capitalism*".[21]

In his analysis of underdevelopment in Latin America, André Gunder Frank built on Baran's contention in the *Political Economy of Growth* (1957) that exploitation of the Third World to the profit of metropolitan capitalism continued, in fact became more efficient, after the end of the colonial period. Marxist orthodoxy predicted the spread of uniform capitalist class relations over the entire capitalist world; in a series of articles written in the mid-1960's Frank contended that empirically this was not, nor had ever been the case. The reality, he claimed, was one of a polarization which took place through incorporation into a structured relationship of metropolis and satellite.

> Economic development and underdevelopment are not just relative and quantitative ... economic development and underdevelopment are relational and qualitative, in that each is structurally different from, yet caused by its relation with, the other. ... One and the same historical process of the expansion and development of capitalism throughout the world has simultaneously generated – and continues to generate – both economic development and structural underdevelopment.[22]

Frank firmly rejected the dualist model of simultaneously occurring traditional and modern sectors in "peripheral satellite countries". It was the same metropolis-satellite structure which characterized the capitalist system at all levels, and this "structural underdevelopment at the national and local level ... was created and is still aggravated by the structure and development of the world capitalist economy".[23] Contending that "in chainlike fashion the contradictions of expropriation/appropriation and metropolis/satellite polarization totally penetrate the underdeveloped world creating an 'internal' structure of underdevelopment" within a "virtually world-embracing system,"[24] Frank called attention to the centrality of the world market.

Ernesto Laclau responded that Frank had confused "participation in a world capitalist economic system" with a "capitalist mode of production" whose "fundamental economic relationship ... is constituted by the free labourer's sale of his labour-power," the necessary condition for which "is the loss by the direct producer of ownership of the means of production".[25] Thus Frank's affirmation that Latin America had been capitalist since the conquest was patently not true. But such a definitional argument gave little weight to the fact that the primary goal of the capitalist is profits, which, although extracted in the production process in the form of surplus value, have still to be realized in exchange.

The dualist model that Frank rejected had been central to the debates of the early 1950's about the original "transition from feudalism to capitalism" in Europe that were ignited by the publication of Maurice Dobb's *Studies in the Development of Capitalism* in 1946. During the course of the exchanges, Paul Sweezy hit on the *gestalt* of specifying the unit of analysis:

> Historical forces which are external with respect to one set of social relations are internal with respect to a more comprehensive set of social relations. And so it was in the case of Western European feudalism. The expansion of trade, with the concomitant growth of towns and markets, was external to the feudal mode of production, but it was internal as far as the whole European-Mediterranean economy was concerned.[26]

It is in this context that, from the early 1970's, Immanuel Wallerstein began to argue for a single, singular and overarching unit of analysis for the study of social change in the modern world. Wallerstein stated the question thus:

> Western Europe, at least England from the late seventeenth century on, had primarily landless, wage-earning laborers. In Latin America, then and to some extent still now, laborers were not proletarians, but slaves or 'serfs'. If proletariat, then capitalism. Of course. To be sure. But is England, or Mexico, or the West Indies a unit of analysis? Does each have a separate 'mode of production'? Or is the unit (for the sixteenth-eighteenth centuries) the European world-economy, including England *and* Mexico, in which case what was the 'mode of production' of this world-economy.[27]

His answer was that Frank and Sweezy, like Mao Tse-Tung who argued for the view of "socialist society" as a process rather than a structure, were implicitly taking the "world-system rather than the nation-state as the unit of analysis".[28]

Wallerstein directly linked his term "world-system" to Fernand Braudel's concept "*économie-monde*" and the English-language term he derived as its equivalent, "world-economy". "World economy," as used by economists, alluded to "the structure of trade and financial flows between sovereign states" and "world" referred "to the fact that what economists were analysing were flows over the entire globe". *Économie-monde*, in contrast, referred, first, "not to *the* world, but to *a* world" and second, not to the "economic relations *among* constituted political units inside that world, but to the economic processes *within* that world in its entirety".[29] As a logical consequence there followed a coherent set of exhaustive and mutually exclusive typologies of historical social systems: small "autonomous subsistence economies" or minisystems, and two varieties of large "worlds," "defined by the fact that their self-containment as an economic-material entity is based on extensive division of labor and that they contain within them a multiplicity of cultures". These two varieties of world-systems are "world-empires," "in which there is a single political system over most of the area" and "world-economies," "in which such a political system does not exist over all, or virtually all of the space".[30]

Axiomatically, at any point in time, the outside boundaries of the modern world-system, or capitalist world-economy, have been coextensive with the geographic scope of its axial division of labor and integrated production processes (observable, for instance, in terms of trade in bulk goods or necessities). Furthermore, the modern world-system is unique among social systems in that, beginning in the sixteenth century, it expanded its boundaries from its European center to incorporate the Western hemisphere and then, from the end of the nineteenth century, took in the entire rest of the globe. Operationalizing this larger (relational) unit, therefore, presented a problem of conceptualization in that its boundaries in space and time, that is, its geographic extent and its historical development, were interdependent. It would have to be understood as a spatio-temporal totality.

The modern world-system is, then, a historical system – systemic (possessing continuities in its relational patterns), in that its structures have remained qualitatively recognizable over the long term, and historical (exhibiting irreversible change over the long term), in that it came into existence at a specific time and place, underwent a spatio-temporal development which rendered it at all times and places different, and ostensibly will eventually cease to exist. The categories we use in its analysis are products of its development so consequently must "*all* ... be analyzed as processes, rather than as categories".[31] Synchronically, inequality, for instance, appears as a measure of an attribute of an entity relative to a measure of the same attribute of a similar entity. Diachronically, however, the entities themselves emerge as products of the processes reproducing the structures of the system through time: instead of inequality among states, polarization of the system.

The great question for both analysts and activists has always been why the exploited majority has not simply risen up and changed the rules. Historically, world-economies have been unstable and have generally transformed into empires or disintegrated. The modern world-system, in contrast, has not (yet) met either fate.

> [T]he secret of its strength ... is the political side of the form of economic organization called capitalism ... [which] as an economic mode is based on the fact that the economic factors operate within an arena larger than that which any political entity can totally control. This gives capitalists a freedom of maneuver that is structurally based.[32]

This political organization which consists of the monopoly over the (legitimate) use of force being distributed among a multiplicity of entities we call states is the second way the modern world-system is unique among social systems. What matters for the system as a whole is not where state borders are drawn (they have, in fact, changed greatly over time), but rather that there exists a fragmenting mechanism per se (the process of state formation) defining a hierarchical ordering of multiple centers of power which can impose resolutions to struggles among competing interests, with maximum legitimacy, only within their exclusive geographic perimeters. States (and the security of their "sovereignty") exist solely as members of an interstate system, each by the leave of the others, and this interstate system takes its place beside the axial division of labor as the second primordial structure of the modern world-system.

Classes, as economic phenomena, are formed at the level of the division of labor, at the level of the world-economy; the answer to the political question why the exploited majority simply does not rise up, is of course that it does, periodically. Actual class struggle, however, always remains fragmented since political movements organize to effect change where the primary organs of power and decision-making are located, in the states. Now given the structure of the world-economy, capital has always held the advantage over labor in the long term. Nonetheless, individual, competing capitalists figure their bottom lines in the short term and workers have to satisfy their needs every day. Considering the cost of active struggle to profits and wages, any deployment of force over a significant period of time is decidedly unattractive. In the medium term, the least costly outcome is the reestablishment of consensus, even though it entails the expense to local capitalists of granting some material gains to workers. These gains are kept to a minimum, for workers too absorb an expense in accepting less than they would like, by the addition of a codicil promising further progress at some unspecified time in the future.

Expanding on the first point, the distribution of aggregate surplus at any point in time is a zero-sum game. Acceding to some, even minimal, demands of labor in one locale has to be made up in another if ceaseless accumulation is to continue, or, since that could lead to a vicious circle wiping out accumulation altogether, new sources of surplus have to be found. Indeed, this is what has happened historically as the world-economy has expanded to incorporate fresh pools of cheap labor at the bottom of the wage scale to make up at the system level what was conceded locally.

The "globalization" model acknowledges implicitly that the economic processes of historical capitalism have not changed over the past five centuries, but this is not the way the model has generally been understood. In the contemporary world, the perceived openness of the international economy and the ease with which it slips the bonds of state regulation which globalization decries, express the recognition that the cycles of endless accumulation – expansion, incorporation, exploitation, and appropriation over long distances for reinvestment – take precedence over regulative policies any state or states might try to impose. This is exactly what "world-economy" means; a world-economy functions within and over the entirety of the "world" defined by the spatio-temporal extent of its processes. Nonetheless, globalization has both correctly identified and recognized as important a fundamental change relating to the politics of the modern world-system: the "external" geographic boundaries of the world-economy have disappeared. The reason this is important, however, has not to do with the cyclical downturn in the perceived capacity of the states to regulate "international" capital. The significance lies rather with the political consequences of the fact that there is no longer an "outside" available for incorporation to replenish the lowest strata of the world division of labor and produce the surplus necessary to stave off class struggle while maintaining the endless accumulation of capital.

This brings us to the second point concerning the periodic settlements between capital and labor, the promise of progress. As world-scale class conflict played out in localized struggles over the eighteenth and nineteenth centuries, the contradictory demands of radicals for freedom and democracy (echoing the voices of working class victims of variously coercive modes of labor exploitation), of conservatives for order over anarchy, and of capital for assured pools of cheap labor were answered with a politics of "consensus" which inscribed some groups into subordinate positions on socially constructed but politically functional status hierarchies of race and gender. These hierarchies were translated and naturalized into "nations" of cultural/historical peoples and the dominant, politically responsible social subjects, the "citizens" of which they were made up, and the excluded "others" relegated to a secondary station legitimating their exploitation. The process resulted in the collapse of clear ideological alternatives on the left and the right and the emergence of the "new liberalism" at the end of the nineteenth century.[33]

During the first half of the twentieth century and following the incorporation of the last external arenas, the new-liberal consensus was extrapolated worldwide in the form of Wilsonian "self-determination of nations" and Rooseveltian "economic development," the structural equivalents "of universal suffrage and the welfare state at the national level within the core zone".[34] This world-liberal compact relied on strengthened state structures and piecemeal reform to insure order, that is, keep democratic tendencies in check. Its unstable equilibrium pledging progress prevailed for upwards of a century, but the promise wore thin, especially for women, ethnic and racial "minorities" and the young in the core and (ex-)colonial peoples in the periphery on whose marginalization it had depended.

Herein lies the import of the extension of the external boundaries of the modern world-system to the maximum and the consequent disappearance of any external arena. By the 1960's the note had come due but there was no one left ("outside" the system) to whom the promise of progress had not been made to bring on-line to pay for its (partial) fulfillment for those to whom it had been made. Even the modernizers could see that the sequential model did not describe development in the real world and all of the social, national and Old Left movements which had bought into the promise by targeting state power found themselves targets, along with the powerful institutions guaranteeing the processes of endless accumulation, in the world revolution of 1968.

So, is historical capitalism living on borrowed time? The squeeze on the middle strata and the intensified, indeed intensifying, exploitation of the lower strata suggest that it may be.[35] Given the stipulation of its initial spatio-temporal confine[36] and the disappearance of its geographic perimeter, the real question concerns its ultimate bound. In addressing this issue, I want to recall the fact that world-systems analysis is a perspective that has developed as heuristic and polemic, rather than theory. It is in this spirit that I will assert that there has been a third structure to be placed beside the axial division of labor and the interstate system as constituted by and constitutive of historical capitalism. I shall call this the structure of knowledge.[37] It consists of a set of intellectual antinomies such as objective/subjective, order/chaos, universal/particular and truth/value. Coextensive over time and space with the modern world-system, it has become the dominant organizational model "disciplining" human cognition and has been produced and reproduced in and through the institutional structures of the disciplines of knowledge production and naturalized as "common sense". The process through which it has developed historically I shall call, without need of great imagination, "rationalization" – the cultural process of the modern world-system.

Beginning in the sixteenth century,[38] the study of natural things was progressively separated from and privileged over what came to be characterized as the arts or humanities; the two domains were grounded in the dualism of nature and humans, of body and mind, of physical or secular and social or spiritual. In 1637, René Descartes established a set of rules of right reason and a reductive and deductive method that would lead to useful knowledge in the form of laws to "make ourselves, as it were, masters and possessors of nature".[39] Arguing against the Scholastics, it was the search for Truth, not a consideration for values, that drove Descartes's thought. Half a century later, Isaac Newton synthesized Francis Bacon's new "Organon," an experimental, empirical approach, with Descartes's highly individualistic project. Built on the model of celestial mechanics, classical science posited that observable effects were physically determined and the discovery of universal laws governing such determination would lead to accurate prediction, both future and past. Concomitantly, the espousal of values intrinsic to classical rhetoric underpinned the other face of the revolt against scholasticism and the humanities monopolized social criticism until the rise of the social sciences from the middle of the nineteenth century. This (always contested) divorce of systematic knowledge from human values, deepened with the encroachment of positivism on the domain of social inquiry. The intellectual hierarchy was sealed with John Stuart Mill's arguments for the application of the principles of the exact sciences to the moral sciences and Auguste Comte's move to establish positivism as the foundation for the production of social knowledge.

From the 1880's through the 1920's, this secular trend underwent a major restructuring closely related to the decline in the theological grounding for "universal" history reflecting the long-term secularization of knowledge and the rise of nationalist agendas hierarchizing difference in constructions of "peoples". The *Methodenstreit*, or controversy over the purposes, characteristics, methods and domain of sociocultural knowledge in reaction to positivism revolved around the relationship between meaning or values and systematic knowledge. In philosophy, efforts to secure rigorous certitude without sacrificing human finitude were undermined by the project itself, partaking as it did of the same fundamental Cartesian commitment to truth grounded in the "scientific objectivity" of the "self-knowing subject".[40] The outcome of the marginalist revolution established economics as a value-free discipline displacing political economy, and the historicists' project in general was finally put to rest by Max Weber. Weber argued against both the positivists and their opponents. He held fast to the axiological dimension identifying interpretation or understanding as the goal of human studies and at the same time emphasized the verifiability of knowledge in the sense of "*sufficient* ground".[41] Operationally, however, he lifted his "ideal type" out of time and context and, as Ernst Breisach observes,

> historians [were] separated completely from the world of values they investigated. They [became] totally detached observers who objectively created islands of explained actions in a landscape of total obscurity.[42]

In England the controversy was more pragmatic than philosophical. The essentially political agenda envisioned the replacement of the binary opposition of the Authority of Tradition to the Chaos of Radicalism with the benign synthesis of Ordered Change through Scientific Control. In place of appeals to values, which had underpinned the politics of both the right and the left, the empirical, managerial social sciences increasingly ordered collective decision-making implementing Mill's suggestion that from the "science of society" come "guidance".[43]

Overall, the *Methodenstreit* determined the intellectual and institutional arrangements which would implement the construction of knowledge in the social sphere and furnish the indispensable instruments of the reformism of the new-liberal consensus and its promise of progress replacing the real, but defeated, political alternatives of the left and the right. Although it did not go unchallenged, the resulting organization of the disciplines was firmly in place and largely taken for granted during the 1945-68 period. It opposed universal science, the empirical and positivistic sphere of truth, expressing the Enlightenment ideal of endless progress implemented in an ultimately law-like, and therefore predictable, world, to the particularistic humanities, the impressionistic and chaotic realm of values. The social sciences to a certain extent vacillated between nomothetic scientism and idiographic humanism. Some, the more nomothetic – economics, political science, and sociology – began with the description of empirical reality to arrive by induction at abstract laws independent of time and space. Others, the more idiographic – history, anthropology, and Orientalism – also began with empirical description but treated all particulars as equal. The one ignored difference, the other denied structure. Politically, the separation of the social science disciplines in the name of these two universalisms and the sectorializing effect that separated market, state and civil society into putatively independent domains made it far more difficult to perceive the underlying organizational patterns or the feedback mechanisms of large-scale social relations, and thus more difficult for activists to organize to change them.[44]

Over the past three decades, this organizational pattern has reached the limit of its development. The process of rationalization has entered into crisis. The attendant transformation is already changing the way we view the world and it will eventually alter the possibilities for human action which we are able to imagine.

The structuralisms spelled the demise of European humanism and positivism alike, and from the late 1960's, developments at the level of theory were mirrored on the ground of practice. Those groups which had theretofore lacked a "voice" gained admittance to the academy and began to transform it from the inside by applying their differently situated knowledge of the workings of the social world. Since then, multiple, not always harmonious, varieties of feminism have contested received premises of knowledge formation through a conception of values expressed in hierarchies of difference and power and have directly undermined the (male) universalism and objectivity by which science laid claim to a distinctive arena of knowledge production. Their work disputed "essentialist" categories of man and woman and indicated the female body as a pivotal site of positioning women in society through scientific discourse. In a similar fashion, scholars and activists working in the area of race and ethnicity have, as they produced their own empirical studies, built up theories of difference that challenged (Western) universalism and objectivity. Their work likewise unveiled how the essentialism of received categories of difference functioned to inscribe whole groups into subordinate positions.

Over the same period, the very premises of science have been undermined from the inside.[45] It took the better part of four centuries for what we now think of as the scientific model to dominate our common sense view. That model included the discrimination between true and false, in a world of independent, "objective" elements. It included the idea that explanations should be brief and simple and at their best couched in laws admitting predictability. These are exactly the notions which have lost their intellectual legitimacy. They continue, however, to regulate our everyday thinking. They are not genetically encoded, the product of a universal human mind; they were constructed and may be changed. By the same token, they are not purely a matter of independent, personal choice, or cognitive individualism. They constitute what Eviatar Zerubavel has called a "social mindscape"[46] and are shared by a thought community far beyond those who call themselves scientists.

Contingency, context-dependency, the collapse of essentialisms, and multiple, overlapping temporal and spatial frameworks are moving the humanities in the direction of the historical social sciences; that chance and necessity are indivisible and give rise to irreversibility and creativity in natural systems are moving the sciences in the same direction. Coinciding with these developments, the intellectual sanctions and practical justifications for independent disciplines in the social sciences is disintegrating.

So, what conclusions are we to draw from the simultaneous exhaustion of the economic processes insuring endless accumulation while containing class struggle and the collapse of their intellectual foundations? Are we on the brink of what Francis

Fukuyama called a "post-historical period [when] there will be neither art nor philosophy, just the perpetual caretaking of the museum of human history?" Is this

> not just the end of the Cold War, or the passing of a particular period of postwar history, but the end of history as such: that is, the end point of mankind's ideological evolution and the universalization of Western liberal democracy as the final form of human government?[47]

Decidedly not. The upper bound of the trajectory of historical capitalism is not a point of arrival. It is a frontier of transition implying an ethical imperative to make profoundly political choices. The real story of the post cold-war world is not the "victory of the West" but the disintegration of the liberal compact which began in 1968 and was completed in 1989.[48] This incarnation of liberalism was a politics of medium-term increments of reformist change adding up to endless (long-term), linear, progress. It depicted a golden, extrapolatable, "now" with no allusion to either a future transformation (socialism) or an idyllic past (conservatism). The parallel to Newtonian dynamics is clear. Science itself offered the linear development model, based empirically and epistemologically on independent units. But in the post cold-war world, liberalism has proved unable to deliver on its universalist message of progress and science now provides us with alternative models of physical reality, relationally constituted self-organizing systems and fractal geometry, and of change and transition, complexity theory and chaos theory – all in defiance of the law of the excluded middle underpinning classical science, classical logic, and current common sense. The recognition of the indeterminacy of meaning in the humanities and the "alternative knowledges" brought to bear in the social sciences by the expansion of faculty and student body after 1968 to include those speaking from marginalized subject positions have highlighted the political dimension of knowledge formation and undermined the idea of scholarship as a perfectly disinterested activity amenable to objective evaluation.

Although the "postmodern" problematizes any nineteenth-century idea of the "social," we have not reached the end of responsibility and social agendas. We are hardly at the "end of history". To the contrary; we are on the frontier "after history" when time and space can no longer be treated as neutral parameters but must be viewed as socially constructed and interdependent processual categories. Indeed, the epistemological status of "history," argues Elizabeth Deeds Ermarth, may be taken as "an inflection of culture since around 1400".

> "History" as a category, like "time" and "space," as we have come to conceive of it over many centuries, is an instance of representation that we have almost completely naturalized. ... Whereas historical time is like "a road" and its life "a kind of journey" ... postmodern time belongs to a figure, an arrangement in which "the other world surrounds us always and is not at all *the end of some pilgrimage*".[49]

The present transition is the last frontier of historical capitalism. It is a *time* for optimism, not resignation, for change there will be. The future abounds with possibilities, but not all equally desirable. It is too, then, a *space* for committed, purposeful action, as no final outcomes are predictable. Lasting for the next 30-50 years perhaps, the transition will be rich in fluctuations, that is, social instability – a lack of order already comprises the "new world order". Unstable systems, in fact, impose fewer constraints, fewer limits. The exercise of free will – for instance, in the form of interpretative scholarly work meaningful for these times – is thus less restricted and, capable of massive amplification, could constitute an irreversible and determining moral choice for a qualitatively different social world "after history".

## NOTES

1 Roy C. Macridis (1963 (1955)): "A Survey of the Field of Comparative Government," reprinted in Harry Eckstein and David E. Apter, eds., *Comparative Politics: A Reader* (Glencoe, Free Press), pp. 43-52.

2 Gabriel A. Almond (1966 (1965)): "A Developmental Approach to Political Systems," reprinted Jason L. Finkle and Richard W. Gable, eds., *Political Development and Social Change* (New York, John Wiley & Sons), pp. 96-118, at p. 96.

3 The movement began with the creation of the Committee on Economic Growth of the Social Science Research council in 1950 by Simon Kuznets and a conference at the University of Chicago in 1951. It was institutionalized in the journal *Economic Development and Cultural Change* founded in 1952. For papers from the 1951 University of Chicago conference, see Bert F. Hoselitz, ed. (1952): *The Progress of Underdeveloped Areas* (Chicago, University of Chicago Press). For examples of representative work, see Bert F. Hoselitz and Wilbert E. Moore, eds. (1963): *Industrialization and Society* (The Hague, UNESCO-Mouton) and Jason L. Finkle and Richard W. Gable, eds. (1966): *Political Development and Social Change* (New York, John Wiley & Sons).

4 Jacob Viner (1952), "America's Aims and the Progress of Underdeveloped Countries," Bert F. Hoselitz, ed.,: *The Progress of Underdeveloped Areas* (Chicago, University of Chicago Press), pp. 175-202, at pp. 175, 176.

5 Hoselitz ( 1952): p. v.

6 Alexander Gerschenkron (1952): "Economic Backwardness in Historical Perspective," Bert F. Hoselitz, ed., *The Progress of Underdeveloped Areas* (Chicago, University of Chicago Press), pp. 3-29, at p. 29.

7 Morris Watnick (1952): "The Appeal of Communism to the Underdeveloped Peoples," Bert F. Hoselitz, ed., *The Progress of Underdeveloped Areas* (Chicago, University of Chicago Press), pp. 152-72, at p. 172.

8 Wilbert E. Moore (1963): "Introduction: Social Change and Comparative Studies," *International Social Science Journal* XV: pp. 519-527, at pp. 519-20.

9 Dorothy Ross (1991): *The Origins of American Social Science* (Cambridge, Cambridge University Press), p. 390. See Richard H. Wells and Steven J. Picou (1981): *American Sociology: Theoretical and Methodological Structures* (Washington, D.C., University Press of America), p. 115, for a quantification of the decline in interpretative studies and the rise in survey-based analyses: the latter reached 70% during the 1950-1964 period and 80% during the 1965-1978 period for the data set used.

10 American social science embraced the Durkheimian view that "assumes an indissoluble connection between theory and comparative method ... 'Comparative sociology is not a particular branch of sociology; it is sociology itself'. ... In its broadest interpretation this canon of method emphasizes that a proper science deals with the general rather than the unique; a multiplicity of empirical cases must be brought together under the abstract categories of a theory," wrote F. X. Sutton "Social Theory and Comparative Politics," reprinted Harry Eckstein and David E. Apter, eds. (1963 (1955)): *Comparative Politics: A Reader* (Glencoe, Free Press), pp. 67-81, at p. 67.

11 Almond (1966 (1965)): p. 97.

[12] Sutton (1963 (1955)): p. 68.

[13] E.g., Tönnies (*Gemeinschaft-Gesellschaft*), Maine (status-contract), Durkheim (mechanical-organic).

[14] Sutton (1963 (1955)): p. 69.

[15] Figuring prominently in the development of the structural-functionalist perspective were Bronislaw Malinowski, Alfred Radcliffe-Brown, Talcott Parsons, and Robert K. Merton. The Vienna Circle had rejected the view that distinguished between the natural and the social sciences and associated being itself with exhibiting a value on a variable. Paul Lazarsfeld, in collaboration with Robert K. Merton, institutionalized these principles at the Bureau of Applied Social Research at Columbia University. The form of social science they developed, based on survey research and statistical methods combined with structural-functionalist theory, became a model for the world.

[16] E.g., S. N. Eisenstadt (1966): *Modernization: Protest and Change* (Englewood Cliffs, N.J., Prentice-Hall), p. 1.

[17] W. W. Rostow (1964 (1956)): "Takeoff into Self-Sustained Growth," Amitai Etzioni and Eva Etzioni, eds., *Social Change: Sources, Patterns, and Consequences* (New York, Basic Books), pp. 275-90, at p. 289.

[18] Paul A. Baran and E. J. Hobsbawm (1961): "The Stages of Economic Growth," *Kyklos* 14: pp. 234-42 , at p. 236.

[19] See W. Baer (1962): "The Economics of Prebisch and ECLA," *Economic Development and Cultural Change* X: pp. 169-82.

[20] Immanuel Wallerstein, ed. (1966): *Social Change: The Colonial Situation* (New York, John Wiley & Sons), pp. 1, 7.

[21] Baran and Hobsbawm (1961): p. 237.

[22] André Gunder Frank (1969 (1967)): *Capitalism and Underdevelopment in Latin America: Historical Studies of Chile and Brazil*, Revised Edition (New York, Monthly Review Press), p. 9. The construction of this relation over the long term, "the development of underdevelopment," became the theme of dependency theorists.

[23] Frank (1969 (1967)): pp. 10, xxi.

[24] Frank (1969 (1967)): pp. xxi, 36.

[25] Ernesto Laclau (1971): "Feudalism and Capitalism in Latin America," *New Left Review* 67: pp. 19-38, at pp. 38, 25.

[26] Paul Sweezy (1978(1953)): "A Rejoinder," Paul Sweezy, et al., *The Transition from Feudalism to Capitalism* (London, Verso), pp. 102-8, at p. 105.

[27] Immanuel Wallerstein (1979 (1974)): "The Rise and Future Demise of the World Capitalist System: Concepts for Comparative Analysis," *The Capitalist World-Economy* (Cambridge, Cambridge University Press), pp. 1-36, at p. 10.

[28] Wallerstein (1979 (1974)): p. 13.

[29] Immanuel Wallerstein (1993): "World-System," William Outhwaite and Tom Bottomore, eds., *The Blackwell Dictionary of Twentieth-Century Social Thought* (Cambridge, MA, Blackwell), pp. 720-21, at p. 720.

[30] Immanuel Wallerstein (1974): *The Modern World-System I: Capitalist Agriculture and the Origins of the European World-Economy in the Sixteenth Century* (New York, Academic Press), p. 348. Beginning with *The Modern World-System I* and "The Rise and Future Demise of the World Capitalist System: Concepts for Comparative Analysis," both published in 1974, Wallerstein has elaborated the consequences of the analytic model in a flood of books and articles, often in close collaboration with Terence K. Hopkins, or with students and scholars at the Fernand Braudel Center for the Study of Economies, Historical Systems, and Civilizations founded in 1976 at the State University of New York at Binghamton, or with other colleagues world-wide.

[31] Immanuel Wallerstein (1979): "Theoretical Implications: A Roundtable Discussion Between Giovanni Arrighi, John Higginson, Bernard Magubane, John Saul, and Immanuel Wallerstein," *Review* III: pp. 355-360, at p. 357.

[32] Wallerstein (1974): p. 348.

[33] I have explored this thesis, particularly the way rhetorical mechanisms were deployed in response to the Irish and Jamaican rebellions and the reform movement in England in the 1860's and thereafter, in my "The Politics of Accumulation: Race, Gender, and the World Class Struggle in Victorian England," under review.

[34] The zones of "real existing socialism" were not excluded: the Leninist program, "not world revolution but anti-imperialism plus socialist construction ... on inspection turned out to be mere rhetorical variants on the Wilsonian/Rooseveltian concepts," argues Immanuel Wallerstein (1995): in *After Liberalism* (New York, New Press, 1995), pp. 137-38.

[35] The answer contained in Terence K. Hopkins, Immanuel Wallerstein, et. al. (1996): *The Age of Transition: Trajectory of the World-System, 1945-2025* (London, Zed) is a definitive yes.

[36] Such a stipulation is far from universally accepted. See, for instance, the essays, including Wallerstein's response, in André Gunder Frank and Barry K. Gills, eds. (1993): *The World System: Five Hundred Years or Five Thousand?* (New York, Routledge).

[37] The interrogation of the articulation among the now three structures of historical capitalism has only just begun. See Immanuel Wallerstein (1991): *Unthinking Social Science: The Limits of Nineteenth-Century Paradigms* (Cambridge, Polity Press); Gulbenkian Commission for the Restructuring of the Social Sciences (1996): *Open the Social Sciences: Report of the Gulbenkian Commission on the Restructuring of the Social Sciences* (Stanford, Stanford University Press); and my *TimeSpace of Cultural Studies: English Cultural Studies in the Post-1945 World-System*, under review.

[38] I have set out the following argument in more detail in Richard Lee (1998): *Complexity Studies and the Human Sciences: Pressures, Initiatives and Consequences of Overcoming the Two Cultures* (Mexico City, CIIECH).

[39] René Descartes (1980 (1637)): *Discourse on Method and Meditations on First Philosophy*, translated by Donald A. Cress (Indianapolis, Hackett), p. 33.

[40] Charles R. Bambach (1995): *Heidegger, Dilthey, and the Crisis of Historicism* (Ithaca, Cornell University Press), pp. 181-2.

[41] Max Weber (1975): *Roscher and Knies: The Logical Problems of Historical Economics*, translated and with an Introduction by Guy Oakes (New York, Free Press), p. 194.

[42] Ernst Breisach (1983): *Historiography: Ancient, Medieval, and Modern* (Chicago, University of Chicago Press), p. 284.

[43] John Stuart Mill (1988 (1843)): *The Logic of the Moral Sciences* (La Salle, IL, Open Court), at p. 64.

[44] See Wallerstein (1991): pp. 191-92.

[45] For a comprehensive review of this literature, see Richard Lee (1992): "Readings in the 'New Science': A Selective Annotated Bibliography," *Review* XV: pp. 113-71.

[46] Eviatar Zerubavel (1997): *Social Mindscapes: An Invitation to Cognitive Sociology* (Cambridge, MA, Harvard University Press).

[47] Francis Fukuyama (1989): "The End of History?" *The National Interest* 16: pp. 3-18, at pp. 18, 4.

[48] See Wallerstein (1995).

[49] Elizabeth Deeds Ermarth (1992): *Sequel to History: Postmodernism and the Crisis of Representational Time* (Princeton: Princeton University Press), at pp. 4, 54, 16 (emphasis added).

# II Defining Borderlines in the World-System: The Emergence of New Memberships

GERHARD PREYER

# GLOBALIZATION AND THE EVOLUTION OF MEMBERSHIP

*Damit, daß wir immer und überall*
*Grenzen haben, sind wir auch Grenze.*
*Georg Simmel*

## 1 FUNCTIONS OF MEMBERSHIP AND BORDERLINES OF SOCIAL SYSTEMS

Nation states, families, ethnic groups, villages, and economic organizations – every collectivity – need to draw a line between what or whom is, or is not, permitted within it. Lacking the determination of such lines of discrimination, namely the production, reproduction and stabilization thereof, the collectivity disappears. Today, we find ourselves in a global world-system which has begun to show its own dynamic. It is a system without any center. It is not controlled by goals, norms or political directives, and its own dynamic is not focused within geopolitical borderlines or by the locality in general. In the following I sketch the deconstruction and reconstruction of borderlines and the emergence of new membership conditions within global settings in the context of the evolution of codes of membership. Also, one needs to mention an essential change in contemporary social sciences as a theoretical consequence of the analysis of the process of globalization. The subject of theorizing social process is not society as a regional or territorial marked unit, not the *societas civilis*, or like Parsons (1966, 9) has argued: "A society is a type of social system, in any universe of social systems, which attains the highest level of self-sufficiency as a system in relation to its environment." The realm of the social are the inter-societal communication networks, that is world-systems as Chase-Dunn and Hall (1998) referred to it in the plural, which have restructured all local social structure (on the concept of world-systems, see Wallerstein 1998, Chase-Dunn and Hall 1998, Chase-Dunn 1999).

All borderlines are fixed by membership in social systems and its types of operations. Without any such condition, there is no social field and no communication. The communicative ascription of actions, or of omissions, also establishes the prohibitive or exclusive structure, is only possible, if a social system is able to program its code of



*G. Preyer, M. Bös (eds.), Borderlines in a Globalized World, 85-98.*

membership. In this respect social systems are closed systems, that is elements and structures can only exist in such systems if there is a continuation of pattern maintenance of its code of membership. The process of closing of these systems is given at the level of decision regarding membership (see Preyer 1998a and b). Yet borderlines are not to be conceived as breaking down when contacting an environment. On the contrary, they can only be seen in a relationship to a particular environment.

From this assumption we can conclude that there are three universal functional requirements of continuation of social systems in general:

1. *external* borderline maintenance, that is the stabilization of the external boundaries
2. maintenance of *internal* organization, that is the stabilization within the established boundaries
3. *crossing* and *changing* of borderlines in confronting the functional requirement of the restructuring of these processes.

It is the dual closing of social systems on the basis of programming its code of membership which opposes social systems to their environment. The evolutionary variation of inclusion and exclusion are determined by the differentiation of conditions of membership on the basis of codes and systems of orientation – so-called *Leitorientierungen* – of factual social action systems. Comparative evolutionary studies deliver significant evidence for this assumption. We also have evidence for the problem that codes of membership are confronted by inflationary and deflationary processes. The expansion of membership to different groups of people in the economic system does not induce an inflation, but in the case of the increase of members in the university, political, and societal systems there is evidence for inflationary processes. In the system of modern society the differentiation of conditions of membership takes effect of the following set of inclusions of people in the societal system (on inclusion-exclusion see Luhmann 1997, 618–634):

1. *political* inclusion: increasing equality of opportunity in the case of political decisions
2. *economic* inclusion: increasing equality of opportunity in the case of the participation of economic exchange
3. *social* inclusion: formal rights and citizenship, pluralism, associations
4. *cultural* inclusion: increasing equality of opportunity in the case of the participation in the educational system and the higher education (see also Münch 1984, 261–301).

These inclusions have developed some of the social problems of contemporary Western societies, for which there are no simple solutions to handle the consequences of the so-called "logic of inclusion". In the global world-system emerges big regions of exclusion. Yet per definition there are no inclusions without accordant exclusions. Inclusions are also limited in the system of modern societies by ascriptive solidarities, for example membership in regions, businesses, kinship, neighborhood, etc. But the decline in exclusionary ascriptive solidarity, for example of kinship system and social stratification, is partially compensated by secondary associations (*Selbsthilfegruppen*) which have emerged in connection with the crisis of the welfare state (Hondrich and Koch-Arzberger 1992). In sum, evidence shows that there are conflicts, but also a growth of solidarity, in the developments of Western societies. For an evolutionary characterization of membership one can establish three levels of analysis: the societal action system and its differentiation, systems of organizations, and systems of elementary interactions.

### *1.1 The Societal Action System and its Forms of Differentiation*

The societal system is a point of orientation for all members of social systems. This enables us to begin, continue, and end with interaction. Thus, the societal is maintained. Should someone ask the question why he knows that there is a societal system, in those cases when the episodes of communication are ended, the answer is simple: communication only exists within a societal system. It is a point of orientation for the interaction process and its structuring. In retrospect, it is beneficent for the evolutionary research to distinguish levels of membership in order to characterize forms of differentiations. In a structural characterization of processes of inclusions it can be shown that there is not only a differentiation of the conditions of membership, but also a process to make the membership variable.

In contrast to some sociologists, yet inspired by others such as Max Weber and his concept of *Verband*, I describe the forms of differentiation in a structural manner as differentiation and variations of membership in general. The strategy is helpful particular in the analysis of the structuring of the membership code in a global world-system because it is *one* of its dynamics that globalization and particularization go hand in hand. We have evidence – excepting the center-periphery differentiation – to distinguish four forms of differentiation:

1. The *segmentary* differentiation: there is consensus among most sociologists that one finds the kinship system as the basis of the differentiation of situations and its functional requirements at the lowest level of social evolution. Kinship is the primordial code of membership. Clan eldership as well as chieftainship are generally associated with the social status within the system. Inclusion and exclusion are determined by this status. It is significant for this form of differentiation that all members can only be

in one social unit. It is obvious that the social system of this kind is of low complexity. Segmentary differentiation is characterized as an determination of membership by the kinship system, clan, or tribe.

2. The *stratificatory* differentiation: the membership of this form is defined by the stratification of social units. Also in this case the member can only be in one unit (cast, nobility). As result of this restriction, non-similar social units exist. Membership is determined by the social status within the social system of stratification which limits the extension of reciprocity of its members. Complexity is higher than in the case of segmentary differentiation but is limited by the form of differentiation. In this case, we characterize the condition of membership in respect to the units of stratification ordered according to the religious status, nobility, or the various types of bureaucratic civil and military organizations.

3. The differentiation of *political* and *legal* organization from the ascriptive properties of the kinship system is a process in which the condition of membership has been variable, and whose features are a higher order of inclusion of common people. In connection with this form we find the tendency to develop complex bureaucratic structures. The essential feature of stabilization of this structural component of social organization is the office (*Amt, Stelle*). In particular, this makes possible a higher allocation of resources and is evidenced in the broader scale of tasks such as the military, irrigation, canals of the river valley civilizations. In consequence, the problem of loyalty of the common people, the balance of conflicting interests and the rhetoric of political ideologists was born. In the development of the modern market system in "old" Europe, the national state was of protectional and innovative significance. In Great Britain, in contrast, the state was protectional but not innovative.

4. The *functional* differentiation: the specialization of social action systems with their own codes and orientation, for example the modern economic and political action system (democratic constitutionalism), is a late consequence of social evolution. Functional differentiation means the abstraction of analytical functions from concrete social units. This process is being reinforced in a global world-system. For the system of modern society, a high degree and growth of complexity is typical. This emerged as a result of the differentiation of the societal system, the system of organization, and the system of interaction. The conditions of membership are determined by the functional action system and by formal organizations. The differentiation implies that codes of membership are determinated by the particular social systems. Functional differentiation is not to be misunderstood. It is true that we also find in this social universe forms of segmentary and stratificatory forms of differentiation in what Parsons called "diffuse prestige". Social stratification exists in all differentiated social systems but these forms do not structure the action system in its entirety. At the level of functional differentiation, the development towards a global world-system has begun. In this sense this evolutionary level is a prerequisite for globalization.

### *1.2 Systems of Organizations*

The differentiation of formal organizations regarding membership in a social action system is of a higher order because there is an explicit determination of entry into and withdrawal from the social unit as well as an established hierarchy of positions (*Stelle, Amt*). Formal organizations are a warrant and connection of action and thus they are also a mechanism of selection and stabilization. It is an essential feature of formal organizations to reduce expectations by its formal line of positions (*Stellen*) and to regulate membership. One of the main features of this social unit is: the formal positions are constant but the candidates (the possible members) are contingent. They are part of the environment of the system of organizations.

In a global world-system the operation of organization is structured by the technology of new media. This basis of its operations generates new formal line of positions in general. The new prototype of these organizations is not characterized by fragmentation but by segmentary structures. In the process of this development, new conditions of membership in organizations emerge. Foremost, there is the requirement that all members are trained to work in a team system of the network of organizational structure and acquire "computer literacy". The latter is a new feature of the working system in all occupations. For all organizations the trend is toward the virtual. In the modern system of society, organizations have dominated our social activities, but a global world-system cannot be organized and regulated as a whole: it is a chaotic system.

### *1.3 Systems of Elementary Interactions*

Communications are instrumental (intentional) actions and are born by connecting and differentiation of information, the announcement thereof, and the expression of self (on the concept of communicative action, see Ulkan 1997). All acts of communication have as their focus the decision about the consent and dissent on their continuation, a decision which would not exist without communication. In elementary interactions between persons, the participants are likewise addressee and agent of orientation. The difference between organizations and elementary interactions is that the conditions of membership are, at first, the presence of persons, and second, the participants, ability to decide about who is present or who is not. A person's presence defines the borderline of this social system. Elementary interactions have a short period and the stabilization is only possible by means of the creation of structure; for example, generating "closeness" and "distance," finding themes of communication, selecting the role of participation, showing consideration, etc.

The consequence of new media and electronic communication is that the presence of a person acquires a new definition: the membership within the systems is defined not by a *direct* presence, but by electronic involvement and thus a *virtual* presence. Communication and acknowledgment is not bound by the process of spacio-temporal presence. An e-mail address is now enough to continue with the communicative operations. Presence is now defined via electronic network systems. This leads to a fundamental change in the structure of all social systems. Yet, it is to note that systems of elementary interactions are not the model to grasp the societal system and its complexity (Luhmann 1997 vol. II, 826). It is a common fault of many social scientists to model social systems with patterns of elementary interactions.

## 2 FEATURES OF NATIONAL SOCIETAL COMMUNITIES IN THE SYSTEM OF MODERN SOCIETY AND TRENDS OF DEVELOPMENT

The development of the system of modern society is characterized significantly by the fact that religious and cultural pluralism have led to a differentiation in the religious, political and professional complex in the social structure. One of the processes was the stabilization of the modern market system by the nation states and its competition on a world market of protection (Bornschier 1988, Bornschier and Trezzini 1996, on European nation building see also Bös 1998). The center of this development was in 17th century Great Britain, The Netherlands, France and, peripherally, Germany. The breakdown of this development followed in the 19th century with the appearance of new leadership societies, that is the United States of America and Germany, as a consequence of the industrial and democratic revolutions. One of the results of this breakdown was that the institutional arrangements of the early modern period were remodeled. The extension of the modern culture reduces the significance of the ascriptive status-allocation of monarchy, nobility, state church as well as the economic kinship system. The further development of modern culture was driven by the expansion of standard language, general education, and common traditions within the European nation states. The innovations in the societal community were the emergence of associations, the sovereignty of national states, citizenship, and the democratic constitutionalism. For economic development, the markets of factors of production, professional services, and an economic rationality of administration became significant. In the United States of America, two features were essential for the societal community, namely, associations and professions, which are, in addition, based on employment rather than on possession.

Inter-cultural and inter-societal comparisons provide us with evidence of different codes of membership and features of national societal communities in the system of Western modern society. The function of programming these codes is to close the societal community.

• Characteristic of the societal system of *Great Britain* is a ranked and differentiated community which leads to a connection between tradition and modernity. The main features of the societal community are the fair distribution and balance of interests, and also the acceptance of social authorities and differentiation. This background consent was destroyed during the Thatcher era and the re-structuring of British society was initiated.

• The societal community of the *United States of America* is characterized by a particularization (WASP or other ascriptive properties on ethnicity, religion, and gender), but one typically also finds the freedom of association, the rights of citizens, and the local autonomy from the state, that is the freedom from the despotism of the state. This is a matter of entering into free contracts, a free development of public opinion, and a coordination of grades of freedom. The societal community is therefore to characterize by the equality of chances, the system of checks and balances, but also particularization.

• In contrast, the development of modernization in *France* is characterized by a stratified societal community in the sense of a hierarchy of nobility, classes, and professional groups. Thereby the inequality of the members of the societal community and a leveling out of administration are typical. This structure is one of the problems of modernization in France under the conditions of globalization.

• What was significant in *Germany* was a closed and differentiated (hierarchical) societal community consisting of a working class, the farming community, business persons, members of the educated class (academes) – until the developments following the First and Second World Wars. The dominated features of the societal community was the cultural universality and an equal administrative treatment. In Germany's "welfare state" after the Second World War a leveling – more or less – of membership and also a inclusion of alien people has been typical. The inclusion of foreigners leads – like in the European countries in general – to one of the main conflicts in Germany's societal community after the *Wiedervereinigung*.

In France, Germany, also Italy, in contrast to other Western societies, conflicts between religious traditionalism and secular modernity were typical.

• The case of *Japan* is informative because we discover a porous particularized and hierarchical societal community which is ordered by isolation. Yet, the community is not structured by castes. It is typical that in this unique case of a societal community the kinship system is not significant for social integration, and there is no functional universalistic cultural orientation. A significant feature of Japanese culture is to bring into line the "ideal" with reality. Thereby universalistic terms have no functional place in this type of social system. The Japanese society is a set of competing groups. The code of membership is defined by primordial, ascriptive, sacral, and hierarchical settings. The hierarchy is structured by a system of social positions on the basis of seniority, which itself is not competitive. In Japan's society the foundation of all communication is an intuitive understanding unlike social intercourse of Western culture. For Western social scientists this concept of communication is difficult to grasp. A Japanese colleague has answered my question "What is the mystery of Japanese power?" with: "Japanese make a blend". (On Japan, and the United States of America, see Preyer and Schissler 1996; on a sketch on Japanese social structure and cultural orientations, see Eisenstadt 1998, 43–46; on Germany, Great Britain, Italy, and France, see Preyer 1998b, see also Münch 1986; on further empirical research on European societies, Hradil and Immerfall 1997).

The trends of development – this is consensus among many social scientists – are going towards individualism, decentralization, association, and globalization. Yet also fundamentalistic reactions of all sorts are typical. Since the 19th century, a new pattern of stratification which has institutionalized individual responsibility and a partial equality of opportunity has emerged. In retrospect, this proved to be functionally adequate for the changed situation in economic, social, and political life. But at the same time, the religious, ethnic, kinship, and national collective identities did not vanish. One of the essential features of communication under the condition of modernity is the differentiation between person and a system of roles. If someone has to identify me in the performance of my role, he or she does not identify me with it, I hope. Yet, what is there to rely on if there remains behind the identification of "my role" a black box and "I myself" remain in all communicative descriptions non-transparent? This is the reason for the "cult of the individual" (Durkheim) and today "of authenticity" – both are secular religions – because it seems that the recursion of communication is only possible by such cults. In addition modern individualism is a societal self-description, and also a pattern for ascriptions of actions and experiences that is make happen something (*Erlebnisse*) in communication.

The 19th century was the ideological century. In its descriptions of the particular social systems such as in economic theory and the theory of the state it has dominated self-description of the society and political programs of the 20th century (on the function of self-description of society, see Luhmann 1997, ch. 5.) Yet, to confront with the growth of complexity and contingency of functional differentiation and of a globalized world-system the realization of inclusions such as in a global "community," claims of global "solidarity," "participation" and "democracy" falls through. All this is not to program in a global world-system, and there is no chance to institutionalize the so-called *Weltbürgerrechte* in such "system". The execution of these rights would be a civil war in continuation. We have to minimize our claims of controlling social systems because all solutions of functional imperatives of such systems can only be "*ein Kleinarbeiten von Systemproblemen*".

## 3 THE GLOBALIZED SOCIETY

Since the beginning of the nineties social scientists have recognized a new sequence in the development of the modern system of society. This was not present in the time of the Cold War, but has its roots there. We perceive today the absolute end of the ideologies of the 19th century which have been dominating us. The application of modern technologies of communication leads to new forms of economic cooperation and organization, political regulations, and structures of communication. The result is a trend to delocalization (Virilio 1996) of all social systems. This means that all ideas of the perfection of the social are coming to an end. The mobilization of society is evidence for the non-perfectibility and non-ideality of the social. In this sense, the ideology of modern culture has no future.

At first it is helpful to clarify the meaning and dimensions of globalization which are elaborated in the sociological research. For it, the overview of Chase-Dunn (1999) is helpful for our orientation. It shows: globalization is a multidimensional process and happens like all social processes simultaneously. Yet, I refer to it with some modified directions of proliferation (a summary and evaluation of the results of research in the 80s and beginning 90s is presented in Featherstone et. al. (eds.) 1995):

1. *Common ecological constraints* means that ecological problems like for example shortage of natural resources operate globally, and generate more and more systemic constraints. The consequence is the imperative of more investment in natural scientific research for the successful solution of common ecological problems.

2. *Cultural globalization means* that there is an expansion of Western values (incorporated in social constitutions), and an adaption of Western institutional practices as well. Yet also for example Japanese strategies of management and forms of organization of corporation have been taking effect in the Western economic system; Asian religions like Buddhism influence intellectual orientations etc. It is evident that for example the lean production and management are accepted in the Western economic systems. Perhaps, the consequence is a new cultural syncretism which leads to "globalization as hybridization" and "structural hybridization," as Pieterse (1995) has called it. In this sense – in difference to Robertson (1995) – globalization involve not "universalization" nor even "multiculturalism" but "interculturalism". Hybridization means 'the way in which forms become separated from existing practices and recombine with new forms in new practices'. (Rowe and Schelling 1991, 231).

3. *Economic globalization* means that we at present live in a time of the development of a new economic global system and relationship, namely a network of production, financial market, services, and marketing of transnational corporations. There is today a free financial market and all global players decide on investments following a new economy of scale.

4. *Political globalization* means the evolutionary emergence of an international political structure and constraints of its institutionalization. In the Eurocentric world-system an interstate system emerges since the 17th century which is characterized by a balance of power. One of the main features of this "system" is that the mechanism of stabilization is structured by competition of states more and more in the global marked of protection.

5. *Globalization of communication* means to participate in the system of communication of cooperating electronic media (*Medienverbund*). In consequences a delocalization of the social emerges. These technologies make possible an exchange of information around the globe without any control by organizations and nation states. It is to be expected that electronic virtualization will change our understanding of the social, history, and also of consciousness (Preyer 1998b, 31–44).

In the following, I shall speak of glo*b*alization in the sense of an expansion and of "glo*c*alization," a concept introduced by Robertson (1995), as re-organization of social systems as a mechanism of building networks of such systems to make a blend.

### *3.1 The New Societal Model*

A globalized society refers to a new model of the societal which takes the place of the post-Second World War Keynesian model. A part of it is a post-hegemonial culture and a new code of membership: the network code of membership. The global world-system is characterized by the fact that societal action system, organization, and interaction are structured by an electronic complex. In this system, all conditions of participation are controlled and determinated by the operations of electronic networks. Therefore a new code of membership and new mechanisms of inclusion and exclusion emerge. This "code" and these "mechanisms" close the systems of communication by specific conditions of participation. Yet, globalization and particularization are not exclusive in nature. Both happen simultaneously in a global world-system. The dynamics of development lead to a globalization of the economy and science in contrast to a particularization of law, communities, political regulations and culture. The unification of for example EU law and regulations show in particular the typical tensions between generalizations and specification of such developments in the context of globalization, for example there are particular historical, and cultural communities of law in Europe, and EU unification leads to an inflation of the code of the legal system in its own domain. It is further not to expect that the traditional and common law disappears in a global system.

Many social scientists and economists expect that the global market system is not limited in a protectionistic way and that economic exchange will expand around the globe. Corporations establish global chains of production of economic value and have thus a better economy of scale. A global economic system also establishes a global financial market and leads to an autonomous financial policy. A global economy is a knowledge-based system with the knowledge centers carrying a new significance, playing a new role as a result of the innovations in the key and pace-making technologies. They have to transform in an early stage of its development into product construction of occupations in the market system. The particularization of the legal, communal, and political systems is a result of the fact that the optimization of effectivity and legitimization can be achieved not at the global level, but only in a differentiation of levels in the solution of political problems: community and regional administrations gain greater competencies in solving their own problems through the principle of subsidiarity. Yet this means that in a global world-system a dismantling of universal competencies in politics and a fall of open communities of citizenship is taking place. This process has as a further consequence that more state-owned enterprises are being privatized. A political control of this system is no longer possible. It is the end of a power-based intra-structure of the modern organization of states (Willke 1997). The structurations between the global and the local are surely one of the foci of research and theorizing in future social science.

### *3.2 Post-hegemonial Culture*

Economy, law, science, and politics are social systems with specific functions and of individual and collective actors. In these systems we find a development of different codes of membership, for example among colleagues, interest groups, relations of friendship etc. The significant orientations and rules are a result of the historical development of the system of modern society. These "codes" are programmed more or less inclusively or exclusively. Both are two sides of a form of social integration. But these orientations and rules are always subject to conflict and are a result of the management of risk. A characteristic development in a global world-system is the expansion of differentiated social systems, negotiation, building of networks between systems, and the effort to find compromises. Yet this does not mean that negotiation is a central mechanism of inter-coordination and regulation of conflict between social systems. There is a gap between the sequences of interaction in which we participate and the uncontrollable complexity of societal system as well as the uncoordinated and differentiated horizon of time of social systems. Negotiation is an indication of problems, but not its solution, because all solutions have consequences which cannot be controlled, for example decisions of investigations, jurisdictions etc. There is also the requirement to implement the decisions made in terms of problem solutions, which are dependent on the allocation of resources.

Globalization and glocalization lead to a drop of universal cultural claims and competencies. There is an internal connection between a global economic system and the contemporary postmodernism, that is the plurality of cultural orientations. In a global world-system there is no single concept of culture which dominates all others (Bergesen 1998). In this sense, the culture is of a post-hegemonial nature. Postmodernism is a cultural orientation that breaks with the system of orientation of modern culture. It is caused by the end of the literal culture and the return of pictures in the epoch of multimedia. The media machines remove all temporal and spatial distances by means of synchronization and virtualization. World-time becomes media-time and it is an interface of different times. We are at the beginning of this development and it is to be expected that our parameters of rationality are in a process of change. All these processes are reinforced by the fact that, in a global world-system, all operations are simultaneous.

### *3.3 Membership of Networks*

If we apply the theory of membership to a global societal world-system, it is revealed that there is no programming of membership in this system: the complexity of a global world-system cannot be programmed in the inter-coordination of the subsystems. This "system" shows a change of membership and of participation because both are structured at the level of networks. One of the features of this communication is that the participants of networks make, and break, contact quickly. With the electronic media, not only virtual firms but also the system of universities, the public administration and the private household are operating on this basis, for example on-line offers of courses, video-lectures or electronic banking. Electronic networks replace significant parts of the traditional infra-structure. The network is the medium for reciprocal awareness and for gaining information. The process of inclusion and exclusion in these social networks leads to a dramatic sharpening of the differences between societal system, organization and interaction. These processes end not in a spatial integration of the social but in a "heterarchical order" of all social systems (Luhmann 1997, 312 ff.), that is the discrimination of communication in networks. Thus, another socio-structural semantics emerges.

Glocalization means an incorporation of global processes into the local and a networking of the local with the global. The system of communication of the global world-system is to be analyzed as a social network where new mechanisms of inclusion and exclusion emerge. We live in what Münch (1991) has called a "mobilized society" and social scientists have stated that the social systems change in their structure. Culture, social communities, politics and the development of the economy operate in new constellations. This situation programs new conflicts of interests of the participants. At present we do not know the models of political regulation in this field. The assumption is that the future models are not global regimes, and we do not expect that the UN is able to manage coming conflicts in the world-system. The Kosovo conflict and the military operations of the Nato is an evidence for this trend. Yet, in a global world-system, this is a requirement that the world market of protection has to satisfy. If not, we are headed towards a global civil war, not of political ideologies but of fundamentalists of all sorts. All social systems have to reorganize their codes of membership in a global world-system and must qualify their conditions of participation. This is the imperative for the survival of social systems in a global world-system. There is nothing that we can do about that, but we have to adapt ourself to these uncontrollable operations. The lamentation and uneasy feeling in particular of "intellectuals" today is understandable in view of this new situation.

Rep.from *Association. Journal for Legal and Social Theory*. Vol. 4 2000 Number 1

## References

Bergesen, A. (1998): "Postmodernism: A World-System Explanation," in G. Preyer (ed.), *Strukturelle Evolution und das Weltsystem. Theorien, Sozialstruktur und evolutionäre Entwicklungen*, (Frankfurt am Main, Suhrkamp), pp. 338–347.

Bös, M. (1998): Zur Evolution nationalstaatlicher Gesellschaften, in G. Preyer (ed.), *Strukturelle Evolution und das Weltsystem. Theorien, Sozialstruktur und evolutionäre Entwicklungen*, (Frankfurt am Main, Suhrkamp), pp. 239-260.

Bornschier, V. (1988). *Westliche Gesellchaft im Wandel*. Frankfurt am Main, Campus.

— and B. Trezzini (1996). "Jenseits von Dependencia- versus Modernisierungstheorie: Differenzierungsprozess in der Weltgesellschaft und ihre Erklärung, in H.P. Müller (ed.), *Weltsystem und kulturelles Erbe*. (Berlin, Reimer),pp. 283–302.

Chase-Dunn, C. "Globalization: A World-Systems Perspective," in this Vol.

— and T.D. Hall (1998): The Historical Evolution of World-Systems, pp. 316–337 in G. Preyer (ed.), *Strukturelle Evolution und das Weltsystem. Theorien, Sozialstruktur und evolutionäre Entwicklungen*. Frankfurt am Main, Suhrkamp.

Eisenstadt, S.N. (1998): "Social Division of Labor, Construction of Centers and Institutional Dynamics. A Reassessment of the Structural-Evolutionary Perspective," in G. Preyer (ed.), *Strukturelle Evolution und das Weltsystem. Theorien, Sozialstruktur und evolutionäre Entwicklungen*, (Frankfurt am Main, Suhrkamp), pp. 29-46.

Featherstone, M., S. Lash and R. Robertson (eds.; 1995): *Global Modernities*, (London, Sage).

Hondrich, K.O. and C. Koch-Arzberger (1992): *Solidarität in modernen Gesellschaft*, (Frankfurt am Main, Fischer).

Hradil, S. and S. Immerfall (1997). *Die westeuropäischen Gesellschaften im Vergleich*. Opladen, Leske und Budrich.

Luhmann, N. (1997): *Die Gesellschaft der Gesellschaft*, vols. 1 and 2., (Frankfurt am Main, Suhrkamp).

Münch, R. (1984): *Die Struktur der Moderne. Grundmuster und differentielle Gestaltung des institutionellen Aufbaus der modernen Gesellschaft*, (Frankfurt am Main, Suhrkamp).

— (1986): *Die Kultur der Moderne*, Bd. 1: *Ihre Grundlagen und ihre Entwicklung in England und Amerika*, Bd. 2: *Ihre Entwicklung in Frankreich und Deutschland*, (Frankfurt am Main, Suhrkamp).

— (1991): *Dialektik der Kommunikationsgesellschaft*, (Frankfurt am Main, Suhrkamp).

Parsons, T. (1966): *Societies. Evolutionary and Comparative Perspectives*, (Englewood Cliffs, Prentice-Hall).

Pieterse, J.N. (1995): "Globalization as Hybridization," in M. Featherstone, S. Lash and R. Robertson (eds.), *Global Modernities*, (London, Sage), pp. 45-68.

Preyer, G. (1998a): "Mitgliedschaftsbedingungen. Zur soziologischen Kerntheorie einer Protosociology," in G. Preyer (ed.), *Strukturelle Evolution und das Weltsystem. Theorien, Sozialstruktur und evolutionäre Entwicklungen*, (Frankfurt am Main, Suhrkamp), pp. 71-123.

— (1998b): *Die globale Herausforderung. Wie Deutschland an die Weltspitze zurückkehren kann*, (Frankfurt am Main, Frankfurter Allgemeine Zeitung).

— and J. Schissler (1996): *Integriertes Management. Was kommt nach der Lean-Production*. (Frankfurt am Main, Frankfurter Allgemeine Zeitung).

Robertson, R. (1995): "Globalization: Time-Space and Homogeneity-Heterogeneity," in M. Featherstone, S. Lash and R. Robertson (eds.), *Global Modernities*, (London, Sage), pp. 25-44.

Rowe, W. and V. Schelling (1991): *Memory and Modernity: Popular Culture in Latin America*, (London, Verso).

Simmel, G. (1999): Die Transzendenz des Lebens, in *Gesamtausgabe*, vol. 16 (ed. by O. Rammstedt and G. Fitzi), (Frankfurt am Main, Suhrkamp).

Ulkan, M. (1997): "Kommunikative und illokutionäre Akte," in G. Preyer, M. Ulkan and A. Ulfig (eds.), *Intention, Bedeutung, Kommunikation. Kognitive und handlungstheoretische Grundlagen der Sprachtheorie*, (Opladen, Westdeutscher Verlag), pp. 22-42.

Virilio, P. (1996): *Fluchtgeschwindigkeit*, (München, Hanser).

Wallerstein, I. (1998): "Evolution of the Modern World-System," in G. Preyer (ed.), *Strukturelle Evolution und das Weltsystem. Theorien, Sozialstruktur und evolutionäre Entwicklungen*, (Frankfurt am Main, Suhrkamp), pp. 305-315.

Willke, H. (1997): *Supervision des Staates*, (Frankfurt am Main, Suhrkamp).

BARRIE AXFORD

# ENACTING GLOBALIZATION

## Transnational Networks and the Deterritorialization of Social Relationships in the Global System

### 1 INTRODUCTION

Bordernization, de-bordernization and re-bordernization are all features of the contradictory processes of globalization. The boundaries between societies and cultures, never as firm as much social science supposed, are becoming inchoate under the impact of new economic flows, mass and specific population movements, changes in transportation and communications and, most germane to this essay, the ubiquity of transnational networks of actors, which are fast becoming the "new social morphology" of the globalized world (Castells 1996, 469). The idea of a borderless world constituted of spaces rather than territories, of "global webs" (Reich, 1991) and "actor-networks" (Latour, 1993) is a concept that has been appropriated for different purposes depending on the predilection of the theorist. Recently fashionable accounts of the boundary – dissolving power of economic transactions (Ohmae, 1990, 1993) rely on the network analogy to demonstrate the functional rationality carried through regional and global economic flows which, it is argued, are making territorial jurisdictions and national economies redundant. There is an implicit neo-functionalist logic on offer in work of this sort, to the effect that exogenous economic forces will eventually trigger changes in consciousness and spawn, among other things, global consumers, global managers and global companies. But in such imaginings actors more often than not are globalized simply by being there, caught up in the power of global flows, and the social morphology that results is one of thin and instrumental networks, or else, as in micro-realist reworkings of the character of world society, denser networks of transactions and interdependence and relationships dominated by power and interests (Meyer et al, 1997). When all is said and done, diversity of outlook is admissable in a world where new forms of spatial practice are now widely in evidence, and where the deterritorialization of social relationships is in train, but where old scripts and even older fictions – about fixed identities, feelings of ontological security, authenticity and, of course, about territoriality, still abound (Mann, 1996).



*G. Preyer, M. Bös (eds.), Borderlines in a Globalized World, 99-124.*

My interest in transnational networks lies not only in the opportunity they afford to interrogate definitions of political, economic and cultural space, in which task students of "postmodern geographies" are now fully engaged (Agnew and Corbridge, 1995; O'Tuathail, 1998; Luke, 1996, 1998) but in their ontological status as social actors and as contexts for the transformation of identities. As part of a modified structurationist perspective on globalization, which I will elaborate later in the piece, ( see Axford, 1995) I intend to address the ways in which transnational networks are re-shaping and re-constituting world society through the possibilities they offer for re-imagining the scale of social organisation and for re-defining the self-definitions of actors who make up such networks. A structurationist perspective, albeit one influenced by arguments from institutionalist analysis (Meyer et al, 1987; Meyer, 1997; Wendt, 1992, 1994) privileges an understanding of a networked globality in which actors both construct the world they occupy and are embedded in chronic structures of meaning and culture. In other words it reflects the messiness and indeterminateness of the global condition, and of all life. As I will argue, it also has the merit of avoiding the reductionism or the excesses of some other theoretical positions on globalization whose provenance lies either in warmed over realism (Jakobson, 1997) or chiliastic postmodernism (Inglis, 1996).

The concept of "transnational networks" is used here to designate all sorts of connections between individuals, groups, formal organisations, and movements across national borders (Hannerz, 1996, 6). In this paper I am more concerned with networks of actors, rather than networks from which human agency is absent, or only secondary. At its most basic the idea of network implies nodes and the manner of their interconnection, not centres or peripheries, which in itself challenges binary descriptions of world order; while transnational, played deadpan, suggests only different sorts of traffic across borders. Both these definitions beg awkward questions, notably about the "power of flows" between nodes, about criteria for inclusion and exclusion in networks (Castells, 1996, 469) and about the real charge in the concept of transnationality (and certainly in the the more loaded "postnationality") which is that the connections are not between territorial states, but outside their remit, and may either directly or implicitly challenge the identities bracketed by these jurisdictions. I do not mean to suggest that transnational networks have established the global frame of reference as the only meaning frame for actors , because apart from considerations such as the actual spatial reach of networks, it is clear that being "constrained to identify" with the global condition, as Robertson puts it (1992) can take many forms, from whole-hearted embrace to robust opposition. Football hooligans are globally connected, and their connectivity aims to subvert or bypass the possibility of national and international surveillance and regulation, but the loyalty of gang members or "firms" is resolutely local or national. Hannerz (1990 and 1996) following Kroeber (1945) proposes that transnational networks be understood to constitute a global ecumene of interconnectedness, a convenient expression for an "interwoven set of happenings" tying the world together in complex fashion (1945, 9). As will become apparent, I am happy with this designation because it covers both the spatial reach of networks in various domains and the key matter of consciousness. However, a global ecumene need not imply a single world, if by that is meant more than a quantitative change in the scale and density of social relationships and organisation. In other words it leaves the key issue of transformations in meaning structures and identity conveniently moot, or subject to further empirical investigation.

Throughout what follows I will develop an argument on the need to see transnational networks as part of a restructuration of space and as at least a metaphor for new and often incipient kinds of social organisation and identities. This in turn allows for a treatment of globalization as a contested and enacted process. I will begin by looking at interpretations of globalization, and of networks as features of that process. These interpretations will include realist assumptions about the ontology of actors, macro-realist arguments which relegate action to the rim of social explanation, and purely phenomenological or postmodernist accounts of social action. I will then talk about bordernisation and de-bordernisation as key facets of globalization and discuss the utility of the network metaphor as a means of understanding this dialectic. Then I want to explore the network metaphor more directly, through a consideration of transnational networks, which can be described as being either "thick" or "thin," and which vary as to content, spatial extension and consciousness (Mann, 1998). Finally I will look at some areas of transnational network practice, drawing upon work being done on the European Information Society Project as a way of re-imagining European unity; by discussing examples of what I will call radical connectivity in relation to cyberscapes and mediascapes, and reflect on the notion of global mutualities, or a global sub-politics as outlined in Beck's recent work, and seen too in the burgeoning literature on transnational social movements. In conclusion, I will assess the utility of the network metaphor as a way of understanding contemporary globalization, and point to some areas where more work needs to be done.

## 2 THEORY: GLOBALIZATION AND TRANSFORMATION

For the various strands of world-systems analysis, the current frisson of globalization is just one more iteration of a world-historical process that now wraps the entire world within its geography (Wallerstein, 1997). As a cultural script territoriality is important only in the sense that the nation-state is the bounded political actor through which the global division of labour is conveniently expressed, inter-nation competitiveness being a functionally required aspect of world-economic integration. As in other realist accounts, the ontology of state and other actors is treated as unproblematic. In a recent paper, Giovanni Arrighi again argues the case for treating current globalization as part of evolutionary changes in world capitalism (1997). In his account transformations bruited as unique to current globalizing trends – the information and communications revolution, the creation of a borderless world in bonds, currencies and equities, and the sheer ubiquity of "transnational connections" (Hannerz, 1996) for example in cultural software and political activism, is interesting only because of its "scale, scope and complexity" (1997, 2).

Still one-dimensional, but more convinced of the transformative power of current globalizing forces, are positions which traffic some version of a global entropic field where all differences between local structures and boundaries are dissolved, where identities are protean and actors become interchangeable at some abstract global level (Erikson, 1991; Albrow, 1996; Waters, 1995). Both polarities are convinced of the power of exogenous and global constraints while remaining at odds on the sort of global system that results.

Between these poles subsist a variety of approaches whose stock-in- trade is a modification of basic realist arguments about the morphology of inter-national relations (Jakobson, 1997; Keohane, 1986). As I suggested earlier, some of this is micro-realist in character (Meyer et al, 1997), pointing to ever denser networks of transactions and interdependence between still autonomous territorial states. Neo-liberalism too (Keohane, 1986) though more catholic in its treatment of international actors, remains enamoured of the rootedness of collective action in the rational cooperation of territorial (state) actors. Other arguments, part of a paradigm shift in disciplines such as Anthropology, and convinced of the networked nature of social relations, depict a world in which remote connections, dispersed networks and hybridized identities are replacing the older mosaic of separate cultures, societies and localities to create an ecumene of interconnectedness (Friedman, 1997; Hannerz, 1996). At the very least, such visions intimate or look to confirm a radical deterritorialization of social organisation in which processes of globalization are redrawing the economic, political and cultural geographies of the modern world. At most they suggest a world in which "boundaries, structures and regularities" (Appadurai, 1996, 46) are nugatory. Much of the work in the latter categories also bears on the ways in which globalizing forces alter the frame of social agency as they render traditional boundaries (territorial and otherwise) and subjectivities ambiguous and possibly unsustainable, except by dint of retrenchment or through reinvention (Shapiro, 1997, 2). While this is a facet of what I call the restructuration of territorial imaginaries and identities, it is also the subject of a fully fledged and often romantic discourse about the entwinings of the local and the global, about local resistance, and about the authenticity or otherwise of global cultures.

Finally there are those positions that traffic right up to and over the edge of postmodernist deconstructionism. Such work can be found in treatments of an emergent postmodern geopolitics (Lefebvre, 1974; Luke, 1995; Agnew, 1998; O'Tuathail, 1998) in which dominant representations of space, or the Euclidean world of "spatial blocs, territorial presence and fixed identities," (O'Tuathail, 1998, 6) of binary geographies and rationalistic discourse, gives way to what O'Tuathail calls post-spatial binaries (as in Benjamin Barber's Jihad versus McWorld, 1995) or the space of flows outlined in Appadurai's allusive references to global scapes and contingent global subjects (O'Tuathail, 1998; Appadurai, 1990 and 1996). Seductive as these images may be, and I must confess that I am more than willing to flirt, ideas about postmodern geopolitics have to be tempered by the recognition that everywhere a growing number of postmodern characters still perform in resolutely modernist scripts (Rosenau and Bredemeier, 1994). For all that, my argument will be that globalization is contributing to an undoing of the present, where that refers to the cultural scripts and structural forms and identities of modernity. In particular, I will argue that transnational networks increasingly populate a global cultural and political economy where territoriality as the most powerful constitutive rule is in retreat (Axford and Huggins, 1998). Transnational networks are a convenient, perhaps even the paradigm expression of the labile and transformative qualities of the current phase of globalization in which many social relationships are stretched over ever greater distances and without regard for the constraints of time.

Yet pretty much everywhere the space of the networks and flows of the global continues to subsist with economic, cultural and political architectures characteristic of territorial spaces and the identities tied to them. So the danger lies in treating transnational networks as modal phenomena, rather than as just intimations of what Timothy Luke has called "third nature" (1996), and in whose functioning Ulrich Beck has already divined a politics based upon "global mutualities " (1994, 1996). While the rise of transnational interest groups or transnational social movements, such as Greenpeace or Amnesty International, may be seen as going beyond mere interconnectivity to fashion both a cognitive and a global moral density, and even to constitute new solidaries, communal ties and collective frames of reference, a proper social – scientific caution is necessary. Sidney Tarrow's recent discussion of transnational collective action (1996) is a pertinent reminder of the pitfalls in conflating what are actually different forms and generalities of collective action. Tarrow suggests that what are rather airily discussed as transnational social movements are often instances of the diffusion of nationally-based collective action, forms of transnational political exchange between actors fully rooted in national contexts, or transnational issue networks. Tarrow's strictures are helpful in establishing a useful typology of collective action, but less so on what for me are the key issues of how and with what effects do active agents (in this case transnational networks as collective actors) engage with institutions and rules of greater generality, to constitute and perhaps transform themselves and the conditions for their action? To begin to address this question, I will now outline a structurationist approach to globalization.

## 3 A STRUCTURATIONIST PERSPECTIVE ON GLOBALIZATION AND TRANSNATIONAL NETWORKS

To reiterate, transnational networks are becoming ubiquitous features of a globalizing world, although they are not its only expression. At the very least networks are contributing to a process of growing interconnection and exchange between individuals, groups, businesses and movements across borders. While this gloss is unexceptionable, it is also pretty anodyne. The real burden attached to the idea of transnational networks as collective actors is that they are, or can be, coherent discursive entities, even communities, active in the construction of their own world, where that includes its transformation as well as its reproduction, rather than being implicated in those processes simply by being there, or in effect. For example, the activities of human rights activists in INGOs instantiates a politics of rights not governed by the imperatives of national actors (Boli and Thomas, 1997), while through strategic networking self-consciously "global " managers interact with each other and with "environmental" constraints, to imagine "global" companies. Both bear witness to the reflexive relationships between actors and the conditions of action.

From a structurationist perspective agency and structure are mutually constitutive (Giddens, 1990, 1992). This is not a conflation of agency and structure, because while agents engage with structures through reflexive interaction, structures themselves are often scripts of great social and cultural power which carry rules, resources and meanings for agents, thereby contextualising and legitimating their actions. The part played by agency in the reproduction and transformation of structure can be seen in the ways in which social institutions(rules) as frameworks for action are initiated, legitimated and diffused by the practice of actors routinely and where there is co-presence, and through more conscious and even "distanced" interventions, for example as members of transnational networks. In the global circumstance, the power of agency to confront rules which are not local in origin or scope may seem limited, but transnational collective action can expand the sphere of agency in a world where co-presence is increasingly rare. From the point of view of the power relationships involved, the key issue is less the spatial scale of the relationships and more how agents use the available rules and resources to reproduce themselves and to reproduce or transform contexts which supply meaning.

My purpose in offering what might otherwise appear as a highly abstract schematic for the understanding of how global social relations may be configured, and what part transnational networks play in those configurations, is to suggest that the scope for effective agency may be enlarged because of the growing complexity and globalization of modern life. Now, agents are faced not just by a dominant set of structural properties, largely based on the foundational principle of territoriality, but by intersecting, overlapping and sometimes contradictory sets where institutional scripts – local, national, inter and supra-national, gender, welfare and so on-cross-cut (Axford, 1995, pp 86-93). Multiple sources of authority and meaning in the "external" world may be matched (perhaps through autopoeisis) by internal ambiguity and tension, as actors variously imagine and enact the global circumstance, informed by rapidly changing conditions. One of the effects of these changes is to problematise what constitutes a political sphere or a cultural order and who are to be allotted roles as legitimate and competent actors in them. Globalization has relativized the world and identities in it by penetrating and dissolving the boundaries of previously closed systems, sometimes of a communal or ethnic variety, creating inter-societal and supra-territorial discursive spaces and networks of relationships along the time-space edges of existence. On the way, various transformations are in train, including reconceptualisations of existing categories of social stratification, and of key signifiers such as race, ethnicity, locality, class, gender and sexual preference, along with key associations such as citizenship and nationality. Is the outcome a rearranged social space where networked social actors (perhaps only convenient summaries of shifting identities) predominate and identities can be constructed out of place and out of time?

## 4 THE DIALECTIC OF BORDERS AND GLOBALIZATION

Globalization involves variable shifts in the spatial reach and ordering of networks and the stretching of social relationships across time and space, but it also involves changes in consciousness, as individual and collective actors embrace, oppose, or are in some way "constrained to identify" (Roberston, 1992) with the global condition. Borders – to taste and imagination as well as to the seminal modernist script of territoriality – are being redefined. This at least is the strong position on globalization; how does it stack up? Historically, globalizing forces produced global systems which were of limited extent spatially, and in which the density of social relations established across borders and time, varied greatly. As we approach the millennium, it is clear that through various media – the exponential capacity of electronic communications to compress both time and space, changes in technology which are allowing production and culture to be divorced from space, capital's ceaseless and inventive search for accumulation, the pervasiveness of ideologies on subjects such as the environment and gender equality, and of course, recent seismic shifts in the world's geo-political demeanour – the world is now thoroughly, if contentiously, globalized.

The strong position on this undoubted shift in territorial dynamics has it that territorial borders are becoming increasingly irrelevant to the real flows and actual patterns of much economic, political and even cultural activity. Kenichi Ohmae's vision of a borderless world paints a picture in which the order of national and societal territories is increasingly moribund and is being replaced by a glocalized networked cultural economy of production and consumption (see also Burton, 1997). In a state of the art comment laced with a dash of polemic on the ways in which information and communications technologies (ICTs) are bringing about major alterations of social space and in modes of association, Geroid O'Tuathail counsels that "territoriality is being eclipsed by telemetricality" (1998, 6). This may be too glib, and I will return to the ways in which new technologies are altering the frame of social agency and how they may be rendering traditional territorialities and subjectivities ambiguous, drawing upon the limited empirical work to date on this facet of globalization. For all this, territoriality remains a durable institution, and seen from a structurationist perspective, both its obduracy and its fragility are understandable.

Actors reproduce structures through their routine interaction with sets of institutionalized rules. Constitutive rules such as territoriality, provide powerful meaning frameworks for action and for securing identity, validating the ontological status of actors by providing broad cultural contexts for social action (Barrett, 1992, but see also Boli and Thomas). So that while it may be appropriate to describe national sovereignty and territoriality as no more than "discursive structures" or intersubjective phenomena rather than material ones, as Wendt notes,worlds defined intersubjectively are not necessarily malleable, and certainly not as much as they would be in postmodernist discourse. At the same time structures have themselves to be reproduced by actors through both routine and dramatic interventions. Even powerful constitutive rules like territoriality have to be practised in order to remain universal frameworks for action. Where the identity securing power of structures is challenged or vitiated through various media: a deterritorialized currency such as the Euro; by glocal production and global communication flows, and by the difffusion of global cultural commodities such as Oscar- winning movies, it becomes less likely that they will be able to suggest to people how they should live, think and, above all imagine. When actors such as transnational social movements make conscious and in Giddens' (1990) sense "distanced" interventions in, for example, the issue of the human rights record of notionally sovereign states, or their track record on immigration and refugees, the secureness of terrritorial representations of space and of territorial boundaries around a status such as citizenship is called into question (Soysal, 1994; Wiener, 1997). The modern "geopolitical imagination," sold on the isomorphism of people, culture and territory (Collins, 1990) looks much more threadbare, and the opportunities to redraw boundaries as legal and cultural markers between people more bullish.

And yet, while such changes in imagination open up possibilities for new forms of structuration, they can also serve to intensify homogenisation in individual and collective constructions of the world. While the autonomy of local and national boundaries and meaning systems is relativised by a host of transnational networks – formal and informal, interdiscursive, economic, religious, democratic – the resilience of the inside-outside dialectic, discussed by Connolly (1991) and the fear of flying immanent in its removal still vitiates the possibility of many forms of "radical interdependence" across borders (Campbell, 1996, and see Slater, 1995).

To a condiderable extent this is a matter of consciousness and affect, rather than (just) a question of resources. Embracing the networks and flows of the global is experienced by some actors as a disabling loss of identity and culture. Hybridised identities, bruited as the hallmark of an interpenetrated world, or "habitats of meaning" (Bauman, 1992, 190) which owe more to Sony than soil, are sometimes taken to defile sacred or civilizational scripts. Even more prosaic examples of global fare in the form of meat patties, leisure wear, or Blockbuster rental videos, may be treated as incursions from a globalised culture that is by definition, protean, depthless and therefore inauthentic, to say nothing of threatening. Such responses can and sometimes do fortify existing boundaries, or lead to nostalgia for previous ones,as well as mobilising a politics fed on such sentiment. On the other hand, as Ohmae says, one of the features of a borderless world has to be growing consumer indifference to the national origins of products, except where these carry some sort of cache, or if the Sunday Times is to be believed, if they are automobiles. (May, 1998). Just how far French people (as opposed to French cultural elites, or politicians with an eye for publicity) experience Disney's Hercules, or Marks and Spencer's sandwiches as diminutions of Frenchness, is open to question. Perhaps less open to question is their continued attachment to the symbols of French democracy and the particular esprit of French political culture.

Challenges or perceived challenges to local and national practices, and thus to the jurisdictional boundaries and cultural walls which isolated and insulated them, seldom go uncontested. The sort of politics which results can be relatively benign, or more visceral. In Algeria, Islamist opposition to western secular values and cultural commodities like satellite dishes, not only presents difficulties for modernising (Westernizing) elites in the form of the quasi-socialist and military regimes that have ruled there over the past few decades, but also (and this is another possible dynamic of a globalized world) fuels the demonology of those who see the flip side of a globalized liberalism as being a regrettable slide into primitivism and fanaticism (Huntington, 1996; Rodrik, 1997).

To add to this soup, retrenchment is not, or need not be, just a response to perceived globalizing threats to territory, identity and culture. The dissolving of a trans-territorial hegemony in the form of the Soviet world-empire, has contributed to a pluralization of conflict in which national, regional, ethnic and civilizational strains are apparent. Ethno-territorial conflicts precipitate an increase, rather than a decrease in the number of land boundaries and territorial claims which configure the world map, and claims to be acting in the national interest are still the stock-in-trade of jobbing politicians. At the time of writing this piece, news bulletins are reporting further fighting in what is descibed as the breakaway region of Abkhazia in the Russian Federation and Pakistan's foreign minister rallies his people in face of world opprobrium at Islamabad's tit-for-tat response to India's testing of nuclear devices, by invoking the mantra of national defence and the protection of contested boundaries. So what is the message? In a globalized world borders matter, for how could we be deceived into thinking anything else in face of the growing commitment to orthodoxies that celebrate exclusion and nurture dreams of a savage past, or appeal to the ideal of a closed community against the depradations of any number of demonised Others or mere strangers? Frontiers too often remain landscapes of bitter contention; between Arab and Jew, and between Jew and Jew in the West bank, and between Indian and Pakistani over Kashmir. Only in the heritage cultures of some post-historical societies has the visceral symbolism of landscapes and nature been educated out of the collective consciousness. The world remains a patchwork of frontiers, often peopled by those willing to defend them.

And yet there are significant intimations of a post-territorial world polity. In Europe, the construction of a non- state citizenship (Wiener, 1997, Soysal, 1995) through EU policy and treaty provisions, proceeds, albeit at a snail-like pace. There has also been what Sidney Tarrow (1995) calls a marked "Europeanization" of conflict through the agency of Euro-groups and transnational movements, where the locus of conflict and of conflict resolution is shifted upwards to the Community level. In Italy at the moment, growing concern with North African immigration is perceived as a European, rather than an Italian problem, stemming from EU policy interventions that have turned Europe into a world space. Reactions to this, in Italy and elsewhere in Europe, range from a willingness to celebrate mobility and hybridity to brutish affirmations of difference. Still within the EU, the scope for forms of "private interest governance" in the shape of transnational policy networks and communities is also mightily enhanced through the willingness of corporate and other associational actors to engage with European institutions as major allocators of value. How far this engagement Europeanises actors, or exactly what this means, as opposed to simply altering their behaviour, remains in doubt.

Transcendance and reaffirmation of boundaries are all part of the dialectic of globalization. When William Connolly talks about the need to transcend the borders of democracy through a politics of non-territorial democratization of global issues (usually the environment, human rights and gender equality, but also Third World debt and poverty), we can point to the now established politics of non-state transnational actors whose interventions have at least problematised thinking about the spaces of democracy and accountablity and, where human rights are concerned, created a truly global discourse (Boli and Bennett, 1998). At the same time the continued attraction of what Shapairo (1998) calls the "Neo-Tocquevillian gaze" – with its penchant for democratic civil societies organised as territorial states, and with the world beyond these enclaves seen as untamed wilderness, liminal and only potenially redeemable – bears witness to the continued power of the liberal discourse on democracy. On the wilder shores of reflection the sheer exuberance of claims to discern an anarchic yet fructive "contra-governmentality" (Luke, 1996, pace Foucault, 1984) amid the spatial re-orderings generated by the collapse of state socialism and the various "scapes" of dis-organised capitalism (Appdurai, 1990; Lash and Urry, 1994) is intellectually liberating, once again provided that due regard is taken of the resilience of "mythic liberal categories, identities and narratives".

Luke's schema (see 1994, 6 and 7) offers the whole postmodern package and then some. In a powerful anti-realist diatribe, he argues a profound de-territorialization of world politics in which new anti-statal, transnational and extraterritorial social forces proliferate – both sub and supranational in origin and scope – and where territories "branch into fractal nets". This is a global field on which anyone can play, or so it seems, as long as the effect of their interventions is to undo statist territories and the discourse of territoriality. Balkan ultra-nationalists, Baltic nationalists, Islamicists, friends of Friends, virtual communities in cyberspace, in short, anything or anybody which encourages contragovernmentality and which "rewrights," yes rewrights, people as different kinds of denationalized agents are part of the creation of "neo-world orders" (1995) made up from rearranged glocal space. The upshot is a more dynamic, more interconnected, more interdependent, yet more fragmented and certainly more fluid milieu for enacting authority, playing out roles and managing flows of influence from multiple sources than can be contained by the Euclidean geometry and identity spaces of territorialized modernity. As Fritz the Cat once said, "heavy traffic," but can this sort of networked globalized world be discerned, if not in full, then in part, and where?

## 5 THE NETWORK METAPHOR AND TRANSNATIONALIZATION

Processes of globalization move through the negotiated and often contingent articulation between local subjects and more encompassing global flows and structures. The growing complexity of these articulations intimates the possibility of disorder, rather than functional closure, since the connections reveal new sites for potential conflict and new opportunites for structuration and transformation. William Robinson (1996,13) certainly no globalization groupie says that "globalization is redefining all the fundamental reference points of human society and social analysis," while Luke has it that " Moving from place to flow, terrains to streams, introduces non-perspectival, anti-hierarchical and disorganisational elements into traditional spatial/industrial/ national notions of sovereignty" (1995, 127). So notions of the world as a single place, an ecumene of interconnectedness do not, can not describe a featureless, anodyne global field; despite, as McGrew, says a sameness in the "surface appearance of social and political life across the globe" (1992). Rather, we can discern multiple configurations in a globalized world (Axford, 1999) which overlap with, but also confront each other.

Briefly, these configurations encompass a world which is little more than a map of variable tastes; one in which processes of relativization and indigenization are both characteristic demeanours of actors coming to terms with global pressures; a world in which whole cultures and identities are becoming "impure and intermingled" (Rushdie, 1991) and one in which local resistance to global scripts challenges hybridity and the dissolution of borders.

Transnationalization is a feature of all these configurations and is expressed through various kinds of linkages. It is seen particularly in the growing reach and density of networks and flows-of goods between nations, through migration, businesss and tourism, (Ash, 1998) as well as in the post- national politics of INGOs and the cyborg cultures of "organisationless" transnational coprorations which, through strategic networking, show a "single face" to the world. Such interconnections globalize the world in a measurable way, but do so more profoundly because they are redefining the experiences and perceptions of more and more actors. Thus, the taxonomic status of a global company may lie more in its management style and corporate culture than it does in objective measures of globality, such as the proportion of its operations and employees abroad. At all events, the global now becomes the cognitive frame of reference for many actors in many domains, although (as I have suggested above) it remains much less so in matters of culture and morality.

The globalized world created out of the intersection and entwining of these multiple congfigurations is likely to be disordered, chaotic in the sense suggested by Jonathan Friedman (1992, 94, 97). In it ontological certainties are themselves relativized and as I have argued, constitutive rules, even hegemonic scripts are increasingly challenged through the transformative capacities of agency. As a metaphor for such a world, the imagery of transnational networks is entirely appropriate. From my structurationist perspective the advantages of network analysis are obvious. For one thing, it affords a more systematic picture of the organisation of global social relations than is possible in any postmodernist account, where only the discursive practices of individual actors are deemed relevant. In network analysis, both the frames of meaning used by actors and the circumstances in and on which they act are admissable. This admissability involves understanding the reflexive relationships between the actor and a notionally external world which is both natural and social. I say "notional" to emphasise the point that actors enact their environments, but as suggested above, this does not mean that the external world is simply a mirror of "internal" identity or consciousness, as in autopoietic systems.

Hannerz says that the global ecumene is a network of networks where individuals and groups are drawn into "a more globalised existence " (1992, 47) and the morphology of networks facilitates this shift. In the first place, networks can be intra and inter as well as trans-organisational, and can cut across more conventional units of analysis to clarify lnkages which exist between different personal and institutional domains

(Axford, 1995, 78-82). Most appropriate to the global setting, networks can structure social relationships without constraint of place or the need for co-presence. Much of the work done by cultural anthropologists addresses the ways in which local and global social relationships are articulated and either reproduced or transformed by sustained or fleeting encounters. By contrast, in the field of International Relations the interest in networks, most pronounced in the study of international regimes, has stemmed largely from a concern with the problems of cooperation in a world still governed by the rational anarchy of the international system of states. More recent and theoretically impertinent work does look to explore the ways in which global instabilities are challenging the bordered world of states, having regard for the burgeoning number of "postnational mobilizations" (Shapiro and Alker, 1995) that are both the product of that instability and which subvent it.

The network perspective draws attention to those increasingly widespread and diverse forms of transnational mobilization found in networks – of business men and women, of exchange students, of pen pals and diasporas – whose relationships (pace Hannerz) may be either long-distance or involve a mixture of presence and absence, of coming together and moving apart, of brief encounters on the telephone, or extended dialogues, or many-to-many exchanges on the Net. The strength of the network metaphor is that it captures the openness of social relationships which do not involve only economic or market exchanges, and are not just governed by administrative rules, the systematic use of power, or the constraints of place. In this it shares some of the anti-categorical fervour of postmodernist positions. The network idea, perhaps I should say the network ideal, stresses complementarity and commitment, as well as accommodation between participants, in which the key "entanglements" are reciprocity and trust (Powell, 1991, 272). This does not mean that power and conflict are absent from networked relations, which are unlikely to be pacific. Doreen Massey (1995) cautions the need to be aware of the power-geometry present in de-spatialised social relations, and this is a pertinent reminder that the "organisation of diversity" in the global ecumene, is often quite brutal, attesting to great asymmetries of power. This noted, the network metaphor affords insights into a world becoming more integrated, while acknowledging that the processes of global integration are "more pluralistic, decentralized and mutable" (Marcus and Fisher, quoted in Hannerz, 1992, 36) than is often assumed. Network analysis portrays a looseness and diversity which go some way to capture the inchoate character of current globalization, and offers a glimpse of the diverse contexts through which a more acute consciousness of the world is occurring for many people.

The very looseness and inchoateness of the globalized, post-hegemonic world itself accelerates the dissolution of bounded and autonmous nation-states and territorial geopolitics. The postmodern feel of this liminal environment is palpable, as the borders between the domestic and the international implode, to reveal "configurations of people, place and heritage (which) lose all sense of isomorphism," to quote Appadurai (1996, 46). Geography, as Latour (1997) has opined, now becomes a matter of association and connectivity, not space. For Latour the globalized world is made up of "actor-networks" consisting of collectives of humans, cyborgs and technologies, which quite confound received wisdom about territories and the subjects and objects under their dominion.

This is good knockabout stuff, and useful for its uncompromising embrace of new ways of imagining global space and new forms of representation. But in such a world there are only networks and everything else "melts into air," to borrow a phrase. Even in Hannerz's more cautious arguments there is a sense that considerations of place are often secondary to the transnational reach of a network, and for some social relationships this has to be true. For networks of commodity dealers in world markets, place has meaning only to the extent that local factors impinge on the functioning of the market, through civil war, change of regime, earthquake or famine. Yet these same dealers may also enact intense and visceral identities as locals, and in other aspects of their non-working lives, continue to behave as though "real" culture is fully the property of particular territories. Networks often carry highly specialist discourses of a technical variety, and their "thinness" in this respect makes it hard for some commentators (Smith, 1995) to accept that they can be firm or authentic contexts for identity formation. In the case of diasporas, whose raison d'etre is the myth of return to a particular territory, the growing sophistication of electronic communications which link members of the diaspora, may be no more than a convenient instrumentality. On the other hand, it might be argued that the ease with which cultures of "real virtuality" (Castells, 1996) can be sustained on the Net, as well as by fax and telephone , could vitiate the appeal of returning, though the "ingathering" of Jews to Israel from the former Soviet Republics continues apace. My point here is that in discussing the relative potency of networks as opposed to places as the repositories of firm or thick identities, we should not reduce place (localities, any territories) to a space through which meanings flow, nor should we assume that networks are immanently fragile, perhaps unworkable contexts for identity formation. Of course, in a thoroughly postmodern world there would be no solid referential contexts or identities, and no need for them, but the world is not (or not yet) like that. Even Silvio Berlusconi, prophet of the networked "videocracy," was moved to ground his popularity in appeals to the foundational principles of Italian life, at the same time as his actions as media mogul were serving to erode what Paul Rabinow has called the "traditional spaces within a culture" (1993).

## 6 THE NETWORK METAPHOR: SOME KEY ISSUES

In other respects the network metaphor as a means of addressing the transformative qualities of globalization needs some fine-tuning. Before turning to an examination of different forms of transnational practice, I want just to deal briefly with three issues: The first is the question of technological determinism; the second concerns networks and power, where that refers to questions of inclusion and exclusion rather than the power of networks as such; and the third is the matter of where to locate transnational networks in the morphology of the globalized world.

*6.1*: Discussion of transnational networks often, and rightly, puts stress on the space and time devouring capacities of various forms of electronic communications and associated technologies. It is quite common to find arguments to the effect that these technologies have, in and of themselves, remade the "bonds, boundaries and subjectivities of actors, societies and polities, as they have unfolded across global space" (O'Tuathail, 1998, 6). Castells's powerful exegesis of the "network society" is perhaps the most complete statement of the significance of information technologies in the spread of networks throughout the entire social structures of bounded societies and beyond (1996). He argues that networks "constitute the new social morphology of our societies" (469) making new sorts of spatial practices possible. Being part of a network is vital to the exercise of power in the information age. Now much of this is unexceptionable, but, and clearly this is not Castells's intention, it does rather smack of determinism. From what I have said above, it is the potential for both re-structuration and re-trenchment that resides in globalizing forces that is its most disturbing and challenging characteristic. In structurationist terms, new technologies have to be seen as new cultural scripts in relation to which agents adopt reflexive strategies of accommodation and resistance.

*6.2*: Networks transcend and may even destroy borders. On the face of it they might seem like ecumenical forms of social organisation, quite free from the trammels and divisions that characterise modern imaginaries: universal and particular; insider and outsider; powerful and powerless; and of course, centre and periphery. However, it is important to guard against the vision of the networked world as being bloodless, anodyne and benign. If networks dissolve certain kinds of boundaries and walls, they inscribe others. Questions of inclusion and exclusion remain significant, partly because of the uneven distribution of resources and skills available, partly because networks are almost always specialist discourses, more discriminating of membership/inclusion than the amorphous social categories they may be replacing. In other respects, networks may serve to entrench existing inequalities or centre-periphery relations, or to reproduce them in another form whose spatial reach reflects existing geo-politics or geo-economics as north-north and south-south networks. Research into the use made of computer-mediated communications by men and women (Herring, 1996) found that "electronic speech" often replicated the sex differences found in face-to-face communication. Castells says that in the network society, the key power-brokers are always the "switchers" who connect the nodes of the network, while Doreen Massey (1995, 146-56) reminds us of the power geometry found in different networks and flows, often populated by those who are not "in charge". Migrants and refugees are not in charge in her usage, while members of an executive club of business travellers are. An elderly person eating a TV dinner-for-one while watching an American film on B.SKY. B is just a passive recipient of global fare – a description of the consumer and of the audience which is contestable – whereas virtual travellers on the Internet are conscious and probably willing participants in the compression of their own world (Axford, 1997, 490).

*6.3*: Received models of territorial societies and bounded states depict them as the containers of both thick and thin identities. By "thick" I intend a notion which is closer to the idea of community (Gemeinschaft), perhaps even of "habitus," though without its more brutish overtones. Here the idea of "us" refers to palpable communites and the jumble of meanings that bind people to particular places and to the past (Lash and Urry, 1994, 316). Thick identities constitute a group of people, closing the gaps between them. By "thin" I imply more apparent instrumentality in relationships and an emphasis on procedures which open up spaces for and between people as individuals, thereby respecting their autonomy. In some measure, but only loosely, this notion is akin to the established concept of Gesellschaft. Now clearly, what constitutes a community in a globalized world is open to debate. Referring to the possibility of transnational cultures, Hannerz (1996, 98) says that the idea of "transnational communities is not a contradiction in terms," because what is personal, primary and has the feeling of intimacy is not always restricted in space. In other words the spatial reach of networks is, in itself, no barrier to their "thickness". Of course one of the problems with conceptualising transnational networks as thick in the sense used here, is that thick cultures are seen as providing the basis for a cohesive, and probably exclusive form of community, while thin constructs seem to owe more to the observance of a common set or rules or protocols, which overlay or disguise more elemental attachments. Thick communities have the feel of wholeness, they are overarching and primary, while thin networks are partial, convenient, secondary or ephemeral, except in postmodern discourses where the distinction is meaningless. To some extent this imagery demonstrates the continued power of the territorial narrative and the continued appeal of "real" places. Like Monty Python, we all know implicitly what we mean when we say that the extension of social relationships across space and across borders is likely to produce only thin networks of capital, production, communication, INGOs and epistemic communities. In this imagination, firm or thick cultures are found in localities, in bounded nations, in ethnies, in tribes and in criminal gangs. Where exceptions are made, as in the case of cults and diasporas, it is because they are vivified by transcendent and all-subsuming spirituality, by love of particular places, and occasionally, as in the case of some transnational social movements, by ideology or some powerful expressive motivation which augments mere connection. Imagery apart, it seems to me that the de-centring of the nation-state and of territorial identities still has to be addressed through the growing spatial reach of transnational networks, the increasing density of their actions and interactions in different domains, and the changing consciousness of networked actors. At this point in the contested transformation of territoriality, the thickness or thinness of their ontologies is perhaps less crucial than the fact that their appearance is discommoding to this order, though their character remains crucial to the sort of world that is emerging.

## 7 TRANSNATIONAL NETWORKS IN PRACTICE

In the final section of the paper I want to look at different forms of transnational network practice in different domains. I will do this by examining i) recent work on transnational networks and movements, which either adopts a world society problematic, or else is located as part of a discussion of the "geographies of resistance" (Pile and Keith, 1997), ii) by discussing some forms of what I call radical connectivity, applied both to virtual networks and to those which now routinely use information and communcations technology to compress the world, and iii) through a consideration of different ways of conceptualising European unity in the spaces and flows of the European Information Society.

*7.1*: Transnational networks are part of the changing logic of collective action in the globalized world (Cerny, 1995), but the "radical interdependence" across borders that they exemplify and foster (Campbell, 1996, 96) is nowhere near modal, although it is increasingly dense and visible. As Michael Mann says (1998, 187) however we choose to define transnational networks, there has been a huge increase in the shift away from local networks of interaction, to the national, the international and the transnational, and of course to the global. One index of this development is the growth of international non-governmental organisations (INGOs) over the last one hundred years or so. As part of a study to demonstrate the roles played by INGOs in shaping world culture and impacting upon states and inter-statist organisations, Boli and Bennett (1997) chart the increase in active cross-border organisations from a base of 200 at the turn of the century to 800 in 1930, to 4000 in 1980. Their argument is part of a strong case for transnationality, tempered by the recognition that territorial states and their offshoots still exercise great power in the world polity. In this hybrid world INGOs as transnational actors in areas like population policy, the environment, the status and role of women and technical standardization, "employ limited resources to make rules, set standards, propagate principles and broadly represent "humanity" vis-a-vis states and other actors" (1997, 172). Related evidence on the impact of transnational INGO activity on the policies of national states can be found in Jakobsen's account of the way in which transnational dynamics affected the policy of Brazil and India on climate change (1997). In like vein, Mato (1996) seeks to reveal the manner in which transnational networks, and what he terms other "global agents" have been instrumental in the reconstruction of civil societies in Latin America.

On a more cautious note, Sidney Tarrow (1996) is agnostic on the question of whether a transnational civil society is being constructed out of the many cases of diffusion, political exchange, issue networks and social movements, all spawn of the globalization of the world economy and the greater density of transnational ties (1996, 14). He is aware that notionally objective conditions – economic and geo-political flux – are not enough in themselves to trigger collective action, just as a sense of common identity or a more diffuse awareness of shared interests may not be sufficient to produce action. Questions of transaction costs and other resource considerations are also critical in turning potential into actual mobilization. Tarrow acknowledges that there are important forms of transnational collective action, but insists that most of what is defined as transnational collective action, or more narrowly as transnational social movements are not actually cases of unified movements which cross national boundaries at all, but forms of action which, on the face of it, are more in keeping with the world as it is, being largely national or international in scope and character. This is quite a powerful critique, but in key respects misses the point, which lies less in the taxonomic status of networked actors, and more in the kind of politics which their existence opens up, and the challenges they pose to the script of nationality and national definitions of value, even where their remit may be thoroughly local and their actions confined to particular places. Terrains of resistance, as Paul Routledge says, comprise a "multiplicity of possibilities and movements" (1996, 526) and can refer to any site where contestation between hegemonic and counter-hegemonic powers and discourses takes place (1996, 516).

In all this activity there is not and probably never can be any uniformity of purpose or organisational style. Local resistors meet with their transnational counterparts only on the site of contestation that is the territory and the representational forms of the nation-state, or maybe in opposition to the ideology and practices of global neo-liberalism or unaccountable government. Even where they consciously challenge globalization, they are often implicated in it, and, as Castells says (1997, 70) are themselves "symptoms of our societies," impacting upon social structures and cultures with variable intensities and outcomes. Which view is not too distanced from the more assertive and up-beat formulation offered by Ulrich Beck in his discussion of the "sub-politics" of an emerging cosmopolitan world society (1996). Like Castells, Beck argues that transnational networks are symptoms of the current disorder, which in his case is the advent of a global "risk society". Beck insists that the contingent qualities of the world risk society promote intense reflexivity and open up the prospects for a cosmopolitan society made up of "global mutualities," cooperative global institutions and forms of "sub-politics" which give shape to what he calls the "world public". Sub-politics constitutes a form of globalization from below in that its appearance through new transnational actors, such as Greenpeace, establishes a politics which is outside and beyond the representative institutions of the political system of nation-states (1996, 18). Critically, he suggests that "sub-politics sets politics free by changing the rules and boundaries of the political" (1996, 18). In all these accounts of transnational networks, the importance of information and communications technologies (ICTs) is seen as critical.

*7.2*: The key role of ICTs in at least facilitating the formation and work of transnational networks is acknowledged widely. Castells writes that new technologies are critical to the survival of social movements, especially where they are oppositional. Referring to the "Zapatistas" in Mexico, he opines that without the aid of fax, Internet and alternative media they might have remained an isolated and localized guerrilla force (1997, 107). In an aside to a more thorough-going examination of transnational migrant communities and the nation-state, John Rex muses that "ethnicity today often operates by e-mail" (Rex, 1998, 73). But aside from their obvious instrumental uses in promoting "long-distance nationalism" (Anderson, 1993) and other, seemingly more respectable kinds of social movement, there is often some reluctance to treat with networks actually constituted by electronic communications as authentic, despite the fact that they must be a expression of a globalized world par excellence. In this respect Tarrow's sentiments are typical. He worries lest the growing web of virtual networks – e-mail conferences; gossip-swaps and so on – are proving so seductive in terms of their ability to reduce transaction costs and afford "visibility" that they blind participants to the real social costs incurred. These are that such networks do not, indeed can not deliver the same "crystallization of mutual trust and collective identity" (1996, 14), the same thickness, as the interpersonal ties seen for example among the founders of nineteenth century socialism or Islamic fundamentalism. Here once again is a clear rehearsal of the points I raised above. Electronic networks are by definition, inauthentic, incapable of being either subject or context. These sentiments echo the debate about the impact of media cultures on the stock of social capital in the United States (Puttnam, 1995) and are part of a neo-Tocquevillian romanticism about the propriety of certain political forms and practices relative to others. Part of the problem with countering these claims is that there is dearth of empirical evidence on the construction and functioning of electronic networks. Prescription and perhaps hyperbole abound. Appadurai (1996) waxes lyrical about the profusion of "diasporic public spheres" effected through the mediascapes and technoscapes of a deterritorializing globality, but we know little about the actual working of these, because the more lumpen reality is that to date there is a lack of the kind of ethnographic studies of electronic networks which are now commonplace for other transnational communities and transnational networks (see Basch, 1994; but see the proposals under the UK/s ESRC Programme on Transnational Communities). And yet "global communications spaces" (Schlesinger, 1992) as well as Appadurai's mediascapes are obvious sites for the examination of communities entirely reliant upon electronic mediation, even if this has to be conceptualised as the study of diverse audiences. Mediascapes offer large and complex repertoires of images, narratives and ethnoscapes for audiences throughout the world (Uncapher, 1994). As sharers in a mediated culture, these audiences "experience themselves as a complicated and interconnected repertoire of print, celluloid, electronic screens and billboards" (Uncapher, 1994, 21). Too slick? Possibly, but most assuredly these developments bear strongly on questions of meaning and identity. But when the opportunity arises for the creation of new transnational, borderless environments in cyberspace, the convention is that by far the most durable are those which allow people to interact in a shared place where they can feel secure. The attempt to construct actor-networks which are more than "thread-like, wiry and stringy" to quote Latour (1997) and to analogise properties of the "real – world" – from bills of rights to the virtual mansion as a meeting place – demonstrates just how strong our older fictions are.

*7.3*: In the European Union many of the issues that I have raised here are being played out in the most audacious experiment in regional integration seen in the modern world. Current interest in the integrative process centres on whether the EU is to be understood as some kind of superstate, an exercise in advanced intergovernmentalism, or, as is now fashionable, sui generis, a unique, multi-level polity and exemplar of the "new governance" (for a summary of these positions, see Hix, 1998). In the new Europe of the 1990's all sorts of boundaries are being redefined (Axford and Huggins, 1998), partly by dint of the liberal ideology of deregulation which has driven the Single Market process, partly because of the collapse of state socialism, and also through the space and time devouring capacities of electronic communications. Along with global markets, digital technologies are attenuating the territorial state's claims to autonomy and its status as the sole locus and guarantor of the "imagined community of the nation". For all this, confusion over the way to conceptualise the EU polity, the official version of constructing Europe owes much to a "conceptual grid" (Caporaso, 1996) which converts what are really questions about transnational governance into the niceties of territorial government, thereby suggesting that uniting Europe is, or can be, a process akin to that of nation-building. But the EU does not fit easily into any accepted category of government, and its lack of legitimacy among national populations in member states makes it difficult to conceive of it as an imagined community. To consolidate the integration process, the Commission has given prominence to the idea of a European identity as a key building block in the integration process (Laffan, 1996). But the "inarticulate major premises" (Ruggie, 1992) governing the ideals of territorial rule and ways of legitimating it culturally, seem at odds with the more postmodern concept of Europe as "space of flows," which Ruggie also puts forward, and which is the rationale of the internal market process (though not of Maastricht). Now to some extent, the EU has already addressed the fact that the idea of "a" Europe is in reality only a pot-pourri of local, regional, national, ethnic and even global identity claims. So pluralism of sorts is already part of its wish-list for a viable "united" Europe.

If Europe is a space of flows, even a loosely articulated multi-level polity, then it is possible to imagine Europe as a network polity and civil society, as a space created and reproduced through transnational, regional and local networks of interaction – cultural, commercial, scientific, military and educational – rather than, or as well as a territory to be governed or regulated in the usual sense of these terms. This is clearly Castells's intention in his discussion of the network state in Europe, (1997b) and it informs Michael Mann's insistence (1998, 205) that "Euro" is an ecumene of interaction networks, composed of multiple, overlapping and intersecting networks: of specialists, Euromanagers, Socrates exchange students and so on. However, as I have suggested, this mildly postmodern interpretation runs up against the imagining of those seeking European cultural integration and *a* European identity. These conflicting visions of Europe collide in the policy space of the European Information Society Project (ISPO).

Overall the idea of a European Information Society offers a general prescription for a virtual Europe made up of transnational networks (Bangemann 1994; High Level Group of Experts, 1997; Bangemann, 1997). At the same time, it is influenced by two strands of thinking about culture as an integrative force and about the role of ICTs as the chosen means of cultural production and delivery. The first strand interprets culture as a discourse which transcends national societies and expresses a genuinely European heritage. In this strand, ICTs are integral in mapping a post-national cultural space, which not only affects the ways in which people interact with each other across borders, but also changes their perceptions through the representation of existing culture, through the ways in which cultural goods are produced and disseminated, and thus through the ability of people to understand the traditions and cultures of the past. ICTs are thus the gateway to the representation of a new European cultural metanarrative.

By contrast, the second strand emphasises the role of ICTs in reviving local cultures, or the cultural survival of spatial communities of various kinds. Here the EU is mindful of the "space annihilating nature" of information technologies, while it also holds out the prospect of new non-spatial "communities of interest," that is, specialist discourses, which presumably subist in (rather than transcend) the wrack of local cultures and fit alongside the transcendental discourse of European culture. Leaving aside the functionalist use of culture on offer in Euro policy statements, this collision of different imaginings of Europe looks quite fruitful and properly inchoate, though it results in a good deal of policy confusion. The increasing reliance on transnational networks and communities of interest to initiate and deliver programmes under the ISPO remit represents a significant institutional innovation and a re-imagining of policy space. In addition it problematises what is meant by community. Both Mann and

Anthony Smith (1998; 1995) wish to distinguish any form of European network identity or symbolic community from national sentiments which are embedded in communities of ritual and emotion. Smith goes so far as to argue that it is impossible to create an authentic European identity in the absence of real European signifiers, but in the absence of much hard evidence it is wiser to be less dogmatic. My structurationist, and mildly postmodern position is that the networks and flows of the European information society, open up new possibilities for the articulation of spatial and virtual communities and new ways of imagining European unity.

## 8 CONCLUSION

The role of transnational networks, both thick and thin, in remaking the world's social, political and cultural geographies is widely acknowledged, but in key areas pertaining to their formation and functioning, and in relation to their ontologies as collective actors, much empirical research still has to be done. To adapt William Connolly (1991) the radical changes which we usually refer to as globalization are still falling through the gaps between disciplines with different rules and agendas. My argument here has been that a modified structurationist approach to the ways in which these "new" actors both reproduce and transform the conditions for action will yield important insights, despite the claims that structurationism is difficult to use in empirical investigation. As to the thesis that transnational networks are contributing to a radical deterritorialization of social relationships and identities, the evidence is mixed, some of it confirming the thesis, the rest pointing to the continued vitality of states as actors and particular places as the repository of firm identities and traditions. This is not, or not yet a borderless world, but how could it be otherwise? As my brief discussion of the European case suggests, the world being made through the multiple intesections of and sometimes the conflicts between transnational networks, which stretch social relationships; and between them and other versions of social organization which traffic ideas about world order still rooted in territory (sometimes super-territories) and tradition. For all this I do not subscribe to the view that transnational networks are by definition "thin," if by that is meant in some way inauthentic, or incapable of sustaining identities. To argue thus, without the benefit of detailed empirical investigation is the worst kind of a-priori reasoning. In the case of European unity, study of transnational networks can reveal a rather different vision of that process and of the outcome than is possible in either intergovernmentalist or conventionally integrationist positions. It trades on the recogniton that transnational networks and communities of affect and interest ought to be understood as what Featherstone (1990) calls "third cultures," which all afford opportunities for new allegiances and identities, but (and this is significant) without the necessary concomitant of the destruction of older ones, because (where ISPO is concerned) of their location in the hyperspace and cyberspace of European flows. This picture of a hybridized European ecumene in a globalized world seems to me to reflect current circumstances, and may be paradigmatic. Transnational networks are re-ordering the world "from below" as it were, and we should beware of responding to this either through reflex hand-wringing about the world we are losing, or ritual hand-clapping about the joys to come.

## REFERENCES


Agnew Jonathan and Steven Corbridge (1995): *Mastering Space*, (London, Routledge).

Agnew Jonathan (1994): "The Territorial Trap: The Geographical Assumptions of International Relations Theory, " *Review of International Political Economy*, 1, pp. 53-80.

Albrow Martin (1996): *The Global Age*, (Cambridge, Polity Press).

Amin Ash (1997): "Tracing Globalization," *Theory, Culture and Society*, 14: pp. 2, 123-37.

Appadurai Arjun (1990): "Disjuncture and Difference in the Global Cultural Economy," *Global Culture*: Nationalism, Globalization and Modernity, (in M. Featherstone, ed.), (London: Sage).

— Appadurai Arjun (1996): *Modernity at Large: Cultural Dimensions of Globalization*, (University of Minnesota Press, Minneapolis).

Arrighi Giovanni (1997): "Globalization, State Sovereignty, and the 'Endless' Accumulation of Capital," delivered to the conference on "States and Sovereignty in the World Economy," University of California, Irvine, Feb. p. 21-3.

Axford Barrie and Richard Huggins (1998): "European Identity and the Infomation Society," F. Brinkhuis and S. Talmor (eds), *Memory History and Critique: European Identities at the Millennium*, (New haven, MIT Press/ISSEI).

— (1996): "Media Without Boundaries: Fear and Loathing on the Road to Eurotrash or Transformation in the European Cultural Economy?" *Innovation*: the European Journal of Social Science, 9,2, pp. 175-185.

Axford Barrie (1999): "Globalization," G. Browning et al (eds) *Theory and Society: Understanding the Present*, (forthcoming, Sage, London).

— (1997): "The Processes of Globalization," B. Axford et al *Politics*: An Introduction, (Routledge, London).

— (1995): *The Global System*: Economics, Politics and Culture, (Polity Press, Cambridge).

Bangemann Martin (1997): "Europe and the Information Society: the Policy Response to Globalization and Convergence," *Speech*, Venice, 18 September.

Barber Benjamin (1996): *Jihad vs McWorld*, (Ballantine, New York).

Barrett Deborah (1996): *Reproducing People as a Public Concern*, Phd. Thesis, Stanford University.

Bauman Zygmunt (1992): *Intimations of Postmodernity*, (London: Routledge).

Beck Ulrich (1996): "World Risk-Society as Cosmopolitan Society: Ecological Questions in a Framework of Manufactured Uncertainties," *Theory, Culture and Society*, 13,4, pp. 1-32.

Boli John and George Thomas (1997): "World Culture in the World Polity: A Century of International Non - Governmental Organization" *American Sociological Review*, 62, April, pp. 191-90.

Burton David (1997): "The Brave New Wired World," *Foreign Policy*, 106, pp. 23-38.

Campbell David (1995): "Political Prosaics, Transversal Politics and the Anarchical World," M. Shapiro and H. Alker (eds, op.cit.).

Caporaso James (1996): "The European Union and Forms of State," *Journal of Common Market Studies*, 34, 1, pp. 29-52.

Castells Manuel (1997b): *End of Millennium*, (Oxford, Blackwell).

— (1997a): *The Power of Identity*, (Oxford, Blackwell).

— (1996): *The Rise of the Network Society*, (Oxford: Blackwell).

Cerny Philip (1995): "Globalization and the Changing Logic of Collective Action," *International Organization*, 49, 4, pp. 595-625.

Collins Richie (1990): "National Culture: A Contradiction in Terms?" R. Collins, ed, *Television, Policy and Culture* (London, Unwin-Hyman).

Connolly William (1991): *Identity and Difference; Democratic Negotiations of Political Paradox*, (Ithaca, Cornell University Press).

Eriksen Thomas Hylland (1996): "Walls: Vanishing Boundaries of Social Anthropology," *Anthropological Notebooks*.

Featherstone Mike (1990): *Global Culture*, (London: Sage).

Friedman Jonathan (1996): "Transnationalization, Socio-Political Disorder and Ethnification As Expressions of Declining Global Hegemony," http://creepy.soc.lu.se/ san/papers/ transnateth.html

Giddens Anthony (1990): *The Consequences of Modernity*, (Cambridge: Polity).

Hannerz Ulf (1992): "The Global Ecumene as a Network of Networks," A. Kuper ed, *Conceptualising Society*, (London, Routledge).

— (1996): *Transnational Connections*, (London: Routledge).

Herring Susan (1996): "Gender and Democracy in Computer-Mediated Communication," R. Kling ed, *Computerisation and Controversy: Value Conflicts and Social Choices*, 2nd ed, (San Diego, Academic Press).

Hix Simon (1998): "The Study of the European Union 11: the "New Governance" Agenda and its Rival," *Journal of European Public Policy*, 5, 1 pp. 38-65).

Huntington Samuel P. (1996): *The Clash of Civilizations and the Remaking of World Order*, (New York: Simon and Schuster).

Inglis Fred (1996): "Review of John Fiske's Media Matters," *Sociological Review*, 2, pp. 154-6.

Jakobsen Suzanne (1997): "Transnational NGO Activity, International Opinion, and Science: Crucial Dynamics of Developing Country Policy-Making on Climate (draft)," to the Conference on Non-State Actors and Authority in the Global System, Warwick University, November.

Jakobson Harold (1984): *Networks of Interdependence: International Organizations and the Global political System*, 2nd ed, (New York, Knopf).

Keohane Robert (1986): *Neorealism and Its Critics*, (New York, Columbia University Press).

Kroeber A. L (1945): "The Ancient Oikumene as an Historic Culture Aggregate," *Journal of the Royal Anthropological Institute*, 75, pp. 9-20.

Laffan Bridget (1996): "The Politics of Identity and Political Order in Europe," *Journal of Common Market Studies*, 34, 1, pp. 80-102.

Lash Scott and John Urry (1994): *Economies of Signs and Space*, (London, Sage).

Latour Bruno (1997): "On Actor-Network Theory: a Few Clarifications," http://www.keele.cstt.cstt.latour.html.

— (1993): *We Have Never Been Modern*, translated by C. Porter (Cambridge, Mass, Harvard University Press).

Lefebvre Henri (1974 /1991): *The Production of Space*, translated by D. Nicholson-Smith, (Oxford, Blackwell).

Luke Timothy (1996): "Governmentality and Contragovernmentality: Rethinking Sovereignty and Territoriality after the Cold War," *Political Geography*, 15,6/7, pp. 491-507.

— (1995): "New World Order or neo-World Order: Power, Politics and Ideology in Informationalizing Glocalities," M. Featherstone, ed *Global Moderenities*, ( London, Sage).

Mann Michael (1998): "Is there a Society Called Euro?" in R. Axtmann ed: *Globalization and Europe*, (London, Pinter).

— (1996): "Neither Nation-State nor Globalism," *Environment and Planning A*, 28, 1960-64.

Massey Doreen (1995): "A Global Sense of Place,"D. Massey Ed, *Space, Place and Gender*, (Cambridge, Polity Press).

Mato Daniel (1997): "A Research Based Framework for Analyzing Processes of Reconstruction of Civil Societies in the Age of Globalization," to the International Conference on Media and Politics, Brussels, March.

McGrew Anthony (1992): "Conceptualizing Global Politics," A. G McGrew et al (eds) *Global Politics*, (Cambridge: Polity).

Meyer John W. et. al. (1997): "World Society and the Nation State," *American Journal of Sociology*, 67, 4.

O'Tuathail Geroid (1998); *Re-Thinking Geopolitics*, (London: Routledge).

Ohmae Kenichi (1990): *Borderless World: Power and Strategy in the Interlinked Economy*, (London: Harper Collins).

Pile Steve and Michael Keith, eds. (1997): *Geographies of Resistance*, (London, Routledge).

Puttnam Robert (1995): "Bowling Alone: America's Declining Social Capital," *Journal of Democracy*, 6, 1, 65-78.

Rabinow Paul (1993): "A Critical Curiosity: Reflections of Hypermodern Place," to the Conference on The Uses of Knowledge: Global and Local Relations, St Catherine's College, Oxford, July.

Reich Michael (1991): *The Work of Nations*, (New York, Knopf).

Rex John (1998): "Transnational Migrant Communities and the Modern Nation-State," R. Axtmann, ed *Globalization and Europe* (London, Pinter).

Robertson Roland (1992): *Globalization: Social Theory and Global Culture*, (London: Sage).

Robinson William (1996): "Globalization: Nine Theses on our Epoch," *Race and Class*, 38,2, pp. 13- 31.

Rodrik David (1997): "Sense and Nonsense in the Globalization Debate," *Foreign Policy*, 107, pp. 19-37.

Rosenau Pauline and Harry Bredemeier (1993): "Modern and Postmodern Conceptions of Social Order," *Social Research*, 62,2, pp. 337-62.

Routledge Paul (1996): "Critical Geopolitics and Terrains of Resistance, " *Political Geography*, 15,6/7, pp. 509-31.

Ruggie John (1993): "Territoriality and Beyond: Problematising Modernity in International Relations" *International Organization*, 47, 1, pp. 149-74.

Rushdie Salman (1991): *Imaginary Homelands*, (London: Granta).

Schlesinger Philip (1994): "Europe's Contradictory Communications Space," *Daedalus*, 123, 2, pp. 25-53.

Shapiro Michael and Hayward Alker ed. (1995): *Challenging Boundaries: Global Flows, Territorial Identities*, (Minneapolis, University of Minnesota Press).

Shapiro Michael (1997): *Bowling Blind: Post Liberal Civil Society and the Worlds of Neo- Tocquevillian Social Theory*, (Baltimore, Johns Hopkins University Press).

Slater David (1997): "Spatial Politics/Social Movements: Questions of (B)orders and Resistance in Global Times, " S. Pile and M. Keith eds, *Geographies of Resistance*, (London, Routledge).

Smith Anthony D. (1995): *Nations and Nationalism in the Global Era*, (Cambridge: Polity).

Soysal Yaesmin (1994): *The Limits of Citizenship in the Contemporary Nation-State System*, (Chicago, U. Of Chicago Press).

Tarrow Sidney (1995): "The Europeanization of Conflict: Reflections from a Social Movement perspective, " *West European politics*, 18,2, pp. 223-51.

Tarrow Sidney (March 1996): *Fishnets, Internets and Catnets: Globalization and Transnational Collective Action*, Estudios Working Paper 1996/78.

Uncapher Willard (1994): *Between Local and Global: Placing Mediascape in the Transnational Cultural Flow*, (mimeo).

Wallerstein Immanuel (1996): "The Rise and Future Demise of World-Systems Analysis," delivered to the 91st Annual Meeting of the American Sociological Association, New York, August.

Waters Malcolm (1994): *Globalization*, (London, Routledge).

Wendt Alexander (1992): "Anarchy is What States make of it,: Social Condtruction of Power Politics, " *International Organization*, 46, 2, pp. 329-425.

Wiener Antje (1997): *"European" Citizenship Practice: Building Institutions of a Non-State*, (New York, Harper Collins).

MATHIAS BÖS

# IMMIGRATION AND THE OPEN SOCIETY

## The Normative Patterns of Membership in the Nation State[1]

*As a collectivity; it [the societal community] displays a patterned conception of membership which distinguishes between those individuals who do and do not belong. Problems involving the 'jurisdiction' of the normative system may make impossible an exact coincidence between the status of 'coming under' normative obligations and the status of membership...*
*Parsons, 1969, p. 11*

### 1 INTRODUCTION

Immigration is increasingly seen as a problem for open societies. The "exploding numbers" and the "decline in quality" of immigration are common themes. Mass media are depicting a world full of poor people sitting on their suitcases waiting for a chance to come to the prosperous centers of our global economy. Potential immigrants are pictured as eager to take "our" homes and jobs or even worse, profit from "our" welfare system without having to contribute to it – in other words immigrants are suspected of craving for an easy life on "our" costs.

Many migration researchers point out that all this is either an extreme exaggeration, or simply wrong. But this is not the whole story. My main argument is, that considering the reality of immigration and the presence of ethnic minorities the balanced normative patterns of the majority are called into question. Normative patterns, which thus threatened, are these articulated in the structure of membership definitions. This creates paradoxes[2] in the interaction between the government, the legal system and the majority of the people. The concept of society, which describes what is at stake, is the Parsonian notion of societal community.

To unfold my argument I use two starting points. The first point is the increasing differentiation of immigration flows into western industrial societies: this is linked with an intensifying of poly-ethnicity and a stabilization of ethnic-identities within these societies. The second point is the term open society: it refers to the institutional setting



*G. Preyer, M. Bös (eds.), Borderlines in a Globalized World, 125-140.*

of democratic nationally constituted societies, especially epitomizing rational-legal authority.

Constitutional and legal norms of the open society regulate who belongs to a society and what is expected from each individual. In the second part of the paper I describe how the definitions of membership in the open society produce paradoxes under the presence of poly-ethnicity.

The paradoxes blur the clear-cut membership definitions in the open society. In the last part of the paper I show that these paradoxes refer to the normative aspects of the collectivity which Parsons called the societal community.

## 2 INCREASING POLY-ETHNICITY AND THE OPEN SOCIETY

### *2.1 Immigration and Poly-Ethnicity in Open Societies*

To place my argument in the context of immigration, some short remarks on immigration and the increasing poly-ethnicity in present day societies will be in order. The structure of migration flows in Europe has changed since the end of the 1980's. The collapse of the Soviet Union, preceded by that of the GDR, but also the civil war and ethnic conflict in Bosnia-Herzegovina exposed Germany to new flows of refugees: although they might be not as large as those in Africa or Asia, they nevertheless put new challenges to national immigration policies. This goes together with European unification that means implementation of new regulations concerning migration within the EU (Heinelt 1994, p. 7). In North America, changes in immigration flows are accompanied by attempts of regional integration at least between Mexico and the United States within the NAFTA (Simons, 1996, p. 9). To sum up an increase in the ethnic[3] diversification is visible in these highly industrialized countries.

In general the diversification of immigration flows is higher in the USA than in Germany or France (see table 1[4]). All three countries show a considerable decrease in European countries of origin. In 1990 in France the main countries of origin were Portugal (18%), Algeria (17%) and Marocco (16%); in Germany the main inflow came from Turkey (32%) followed by the inflow from former Yugoslavia (12%); the overwhelming part of US-immigration comes from Mexico (32%), followed by a highly diverse inflow from Latin America and Asia.

Concerning the foreign population within each country France faced the strongest decline in the proportion of foreigners of European origin (88% in 1962 – 41% in 1990), immigrants from Africa constitute now nearly halve of the foreign population. In Germany the main increase lies in the Turkish immigration, whereas the USA has the sharpest increase in South American and Asian foreign population (see table 2).

The increasing poly-ethnicity concerning the inflows and the foreign population within each country goes together with the stabilization of ethnic identities. The main factors for that are: (1) better chances for traveling (to the countries of origin); (2) more chances to get products and information from the home country; (3) and an improvement of the protection of minorities. (4) Furthermore it is getting more and more important – for every individual and community – to define itself in the worldwide game of identity-definitions, which is characterized by an increasing nationalization and ethnisation.

### *2.2 Normative Patterns in Open Societies*

Open society has been a metaphor depicting democracy. The image that the open society is open for all kinds of ideas, goods and human beings and hence unable to protect its borders efficiently, is obviously nothing more than a distorted image of the concept that was put forward by Sir Karl Popper in his "open society and its enemies". Popper's main concerns were not the external or territorial borders of societies, but the internal structure of modern democratic societies.[5] Important in this context is the main argument of Popper's book. Open does not mean a society without borders or regulations. An open society always implies a specific institutional setting, which ensures the ability of a society to learn – or more precisely the ability of a society to organize controlled social change.

Popper developed his notion of the open society during his exile in New Zealand. Under the impression of Nazi-Germany he tries do develop a social-philosophical basis for a democratic society. In his analysis of Plato, Hegel and Marx he developed his critique on historicism. Every utopia is in principle fallible therefore every society has to have the ability to correct mistakes. To elect a new government, with new political ideas without the necessity to kill and/or to make a revolution is the main mechanism to prevent tyranny.

Free choice as the main feature of the open society has many implications. The freedom to chose is the burden, which has to be carried by every member of the open society. Every individual has to act as rational as possible and has to take responsibility for others. Freedom, rationality and responsibility are safeguarded by the legal system of the open society. This is done by the assumed equality of all human beings, by the protection of individual rights and by the demand of solidarity.

In Popper's notion of the open society immigration and poly-ethnicity simply does not exist. Considering the fact most people stay most of the time of their lives within the territorial boundaries of their home society, this might be not very problematic. Even today where international migration reaches new heights, only about 2% of the world population do not live in their country of origin. Nevertheless immigration – the process of passing the external boundaries of the open society – is a common feature for all western industrialized societies.

### 2.3 *Immigration and the Legal Construction of Membership in Open Societies*

Immigration forces the open society to give rules who belong to society and who not. Concerning immigration open societies developed an institutional setting of three different policies of membership: immigration policies, nationality laws and citizenship policies.

Immigration laws regulate who is allowed to enter the country and who is not. This is not congruent with the distinction who falls under regulation of the legal system and who not. For example illegal immigrants were not allowed to enter the country, but are treated according the legal norms of the country they entered. Besides illegal immigration open societies have developed four selection corridors in which immigrants were labeled according to different criteria: (1) the increasing important category of family reunification, (2) the equally increasing class of refugees and asylum seekers, (3) settlers and economic immigrants like entrepreneurs, investors and guest workers, (4) and last not least 'ethnic' immigrants. These four categories correspond with types of membership. Family reunification reflects the importance of households and families as a basic collectivity in the normative structure of open societies. The category of settlers and economic immigrants is today largely influenced by economic considerations, in order to provide the economic system with sufficient 'input' to fulfil its function. Refugees and asylum seekers are defined by the idea of natural rights of every human being. This category is not so much influenced by international treatise like the declaration of human rights or the Geneva convention but by the human rights defined in the constitution of every open society of all human beings regardless their nationality or – more general – their membership status. As refugees are the expression of universal elements in every constitution, ethnic immigrants are defined by the particularistic criteria which are as well inbuild in the moral economy of every open society (for the process of ethnisation see e.g. Bös 1997).

Nationality laws are largely developed with reference to the political system. Today nationality mainly means the right to vote and right to be elected. Different criteria are used to define nationality. These criteria are place of birth and descent. Both criteria can be easily derived from "'socialization,' the whole complex of processes by which persons become members of the societal community and maintain that status" (Parsons, 1969, p. 13). As how important socialization is considered, is for example demonstrated by the regulation that the president of the United States must be born within the United States. Besides descent and place of birth criteria like gender, marital status, the principle of docile, 'cultural affiliation,' and of course belonging to another nation were used to determine ones nationality.

Analytical separated from nationality is the concept of citizenship; it refers to full membership in the society. It embraces a whole set of different ideas on the relation between the individual and the legal, political, and economic subsystems of society.

These forms of membership could be easily paralleled to the notion of civil, political and social citizenship. Social citizenship in this case is somehow a Janus-faced concept, on the one hand many aspects of the welfare state are linked to economic membership, on the other hand some basic regulations of the welfare state are explicitly developed in order to separate economic performance of an individual from his or her minimal standard of living. Or as Marshall pointed out, in the last century participation in welfare programmes led to the abolition of political rights, whereas today economic success is no more a necessary requisite of political participation.

All these three areas – immigration, nationality, citizenship – are combined in the complex of membership definitions within open societies. Further on I will try to pinpoint more precisely on the different paradoxes this complex produces in respect to immigration and poly-ethnicity in the open society.

## 3 THE PARADOXES OF MEMBERSHIP

Membership definitions have to answer two questions the first question is: Who is a member and who not? And the second question is: How should a member of the collectivity behave? The first question refers to the external border-structures of the open society and the second question refers to internal border-structures.

### *3.1 Paradoxes of the External Border-Structure*

#### *3.1.1 The Refugee Paradox*

The first paradox one may call the 'universal rights of particularistic citizens' or the refugee paradox. Basically it points to a contradiction in the constitution of every open society. On the one hand every human being has a whole set of rights that every state has to accept, e.g. the right to life. On the other hand the nation state is not responsible for those who do not belong to the nation state and by definition not all human beings belong to one nation state.

As an example, how the reaction on the increasing number of refugees poses new problems to legitimize international inequality may serve what happened in Canada during the last decades. As human rights concepts became more and more a part of political culture or law, it became more and more difficult to distinguish between irregular and regular immigrants. For example in Canada irregular immigrants were given the right to take a lawyer and take his or her case to the Supreme Court of Canada, which resulted in a total breakdown of the immigration control system. So Canada blocked entry by refusing to led into Canada anyone who had not already established his or her refugee status and had obtained permission to enter from Canadian authorities (Caldwell 1994). A quite similar process took place in the case of Germany concerning the increasing number of asylum seekers.

*3.1.2 The Paradox of Citizens without Nationality*

Besides the problem to distinguish between regular and irregular immigration, it is increasingly difficult to distinguish between an immigrant and a citizen. Those who have earned the status and assumed the responsibilities of citizenship (officially recognized by granting nationality) are increasingly frustrated to see the same rights and privileges extended to those who have done neither. This again refers not so much to 'real' obligations between the individual and the state. In most industrialized countries immigrants get a whole bunch of social and civil rights together with many obligations, e.g. they have to pay taxes or they are constantly in danger to be deported by committing a crime. In fact granting of nationality today means more or less the granting of political rights and only a few obligations are accompanied e.g. sometimes military service. All this is not reflected in the social construction of nationality, which equates nationality and citizenship. Citizenship is the concept that links individual and states through a genuine link together with rights and obligations (Brubaker 1989). Non-citizens or citizens without nationality are seen as not in the same way reliable as full members of the open society – even if they pay their taxes as accurate as everyone (Robert 1994).

*3.1.3 The Paradox of Nationals without Citizenship*

The third paradox refers to people who are by definition belong to the people of a country but were neither born nor socialized on the territory of the nation state. This problem arises in the de-colonization process. In Great Britain the British construction of nationality as 'British subject' which owes 'allegiance to the crown' led to the definition of the 'citizen of the United Kingdom and Colonies' (Dummett/Nicol 1990), this, in turn, led to an increasing immigration from the colonies into post-war Britain. In 1962 a regulation was implemented that only British subjects with parents or grand parents born in Britain were allowed to enter the country. Similar problems arose in France after the Algerian war, were Algerians who fought on French side were naturalized but largely considered as foreigners because of their skin color.

This paradox is as well exemplified in 'ethnic immigration'. The 'Ausiedler' in Germany has been increasingly seen as a problem after 1989. By law many of them has the right to get German nationality but because their totally different cultural background, they were considered as foreigners regardless their nationality status. To solve these problems quotas were introduced in the nineteen's, which implies the paradox situation that people who has the right to get German nationality were not allowed to enter the country.

### *3.2 Paradoxes of the Internal Border-structure*

#### *3.2.1 The Paradox of Freedom*

The paradox of freedom concerns the relation of collective and individual rights in the open society. Freedom means individual freedom. Public welfare and individual freedom is very strongly linked in USA. Freedom means to be responsible for one's own life, this is the same for migrants. Individual assimilation took place by economic success – for members of ethnic groups this means: 'to move upward, is to move outward'. The problem lies here in the collective discrimination of immigrants, or in the refusal of migrants to follow the ideal of individual freedom.

For example at the beginning of the century some states in the USA prohibited to teach children between 8 and 16 foreign languages. This law was largely aimed against a supposed ethnisation of children in German Schools. After a few years these laws were suspended by the Supreme Court, not because of the discrimination of ethnic minorities, but because of the right of every individual to learn languages. The most influential norm in the American legal system, the protection of individual rights, makes it possible to stabilize ethnic communities.

Even more important is that the organization of ethnic communities led to a demand of political measures to compensate disadvantages of these minorities. Having different kinds of affirmative action is nothing more than the legal recognition of ascribed characteristics in order to distribute transfers. This might be inline with the rational of social citizenship but contributes to a stabilization of ethnic cleavages.

#### *3.2.2 The Paradox of Equality*

The paradox of equality arises, because equality in the open society means equality of all according to universal criteria. This universal equality is institutionalized in the separation of the public and the private sphere. France may serve as an example for the mediation of the individual and the societal community through equality. Neither status nor religion affiliation should interfere with public concerns. All French citizens are equal because they choose to be a member in the democratic French nation (see Renan 1882). This is exemplified in the naturalization of Thomas Paine in 1792 because of his affiliation to democratic ideas and his defense of the French Revolution. Maybe it was exactly because of this democratic affiliation that he was sent to a French prison one year later.

Universal rules establish equality in the public sphere, difference is seen as something private. The problem concerning immigrants is clear: as private defined, ethnic differences must not break through in the public sphere, every demand of unequal treatment in the public sphere questions the separation of the private and the public sphere.

One can see this at the 'veil-affair' in France. The veil or hijab – originally worn in school by four Maghrebian young women in the outskirts of Paris – was seen as a provocation of the laicism and the typical relation of the individual and the state in France. The wearing of a hijab was interpreted as a sign of the 're-tribalisation' of the French society. That exactly this kind of reaction could also be seen as the tribalisation – or better ethnisation – of the French society as a whole was ignored. Needless to say that despite the fact that the wearing of the hijab in French schools is now more or less forbidden, the 'Front National' had its greatest success in the elections directly after this affair.

*3.3.3 The Paradox of Socialization without Being Socialized*

To become a member of a society means usually to be socialized within a given society. This socialization process produces the loyalty to the whole collectivity and therefore produces trust in the reciprocity of solidarity.[6] By this way to define solidarity within the open society, solidarity means the internalization of public interests and public welfare (Gemeinwohl). In Germany the emphasis on this kind of connection between the individual and the society is wide spread. This leads to an extensive discourse on responsibility of everyone for the whole society. The internalization process of public interest is largely seen as an outcome of the socialization process in the family and in school. So the immigrant – by definition not socialized in Germany – is always under the suspicion that she or he only acts according to her or his interests and that he or she is not loyal enough. Only a kind of 'cultural turncoat' is regarded as able to have enough solidarity. This can be easily seen at the criteria of naturalization in Germany and at the arguments on double citizenship. Nevertheless, as Parsons (1969, p. 51) rightfully pointed out, contributes the development of the institutions of citizenship to a new basis of societal solidarity.

The first group of paradoxes is related to the membership/non-membership distinction: because of the universalistic norms in every constitution and the inclusiveness of the open society it becomes more and more difficult to distinguish between human being and citizen. The institutional structure of citizenship creates inclusion processes regardless to the nationality status, so that the distinction between citizens and non-citizens is blurred. On the other hand provides the inclusiveness of particularistic definitions of nationality rights for people, who are not integrated in the institutions of citizenship. More problems arise in the normative structure of the open society when it comes to normative patterns of membership in the open society: individual rights vs. collective rights, public sphere vs. private sphere, public interest vs. individual interest. The normative structure and institutionalization of these dimensions evolved in the historical development of the open society. Minorities who question these specific constellations are seen as a threat for the majority.

## 5 THE SOCIETAL COMMUNITY OF THE OPEN SOCIETY

### *5.1 Poly-Ethnicity and the Paradoxes of the Open Society*

Increasing immigration, poly-ethnicity, and stabilization of ethnic identities is a common trait for all western societies. This kind of diversity is not recognized in the notion of the open society. A notion, which is based on the assumed equality of all human beings, on the protection of individual rights and on the demand of solidarity. Increasing poly-ethnicity forces the political system of the open society to give rules who belong to society and who not. This is institutionalized in a setting of three different policies of membership: immigration policies, nationality laws and citizenship policies. With the implementation of these policies different paradoxes arise.

The paradoxes of external border-structures are of special importance because they blur the member/non-member distinction of the open society. The refugee paradox arises because the jurisdiction applies legal norms to all people on the territory of the open society. Universal human rights, a basic constitutional element of open societies, apply to them. That leads to the fact that the open society give rights to every member of the human kind but only if these individuals are on the territory of the nation state. Every individual – even people who illegally entered the country – has some basic civil rights. Every individual which stays legally on the territory of open societies acquires certain civil, political and social rights regardless of its nationality status. This leads to the paradox of the citizenship without nationality. On the other hand the legal systems apply in some special cases legal regulation to people which do not live on the territory. The paradox of nationals without citizenship bases on the fact that people living outside the territory of the nation state are defined as nationals by nationality law without any clear citizenship status.

Other paradoxes arise when we look at the normative definitions of membership within the open society. What I call the paradox of individual freedom, derives from the mechanism that the legal implementation of the norms of personal freedom contributes to a stabilization of ethnic subcollectivities in societies. The cultural definition of what is considered as private or public, serves as a basis for the equality in the public sphere. The definition of the universal criteria of equality rely on the definition of differences as something private. These separation of public and private is called into question when ethnic groups want to symbolize there differences in the public sphere. One of the basic ideas within the normative system of the open society is the idea of solidarity. The trust in the reciprocity of solidarity relies on the process of socialization, which not applies – by definition – to foreigners. But socialization is a mechanism that ensures that the collectivity as such is valued by the individual. Belonging to the societal community implies to belong not because of self-interest, but because of a shared interest in the entire society.

Open societies developed a complex structure of membership definitions. Immigration laws are designed to control the external member/non-member distinction in relation to the territoriality of the open society, whereas citizenship defines internal normative structures of membership as full membership in the open society. Nationality produces an internal membership/non-membership distinction in reference to the political system. The member/non-member-definition and the normative definition of membership form institutional setting that is the outcome of a historical process of the last two hundred years. Poly-ethnicity reminds the majority of all the contradictions and paradoxes in the normative patterns of this institutional setting. And minorities are blamed for that, like in former times the messenger was killed for the bad news he brought.

### *5.2 The Societal Community and the Political System*

From a sociological view we can go one step further in describing these paradoxes. As pointed out above the main mechanism to gain membership in a collectivity is socialization. Socialization ensures two important aspects of membership in a collectivity. The first aspect is the assumption that each member acts according the normative expectations within the collectivity. The second aspect is that each member sees a value in the collectivity as such, or in more Parsonian terms, that each member is loyal to the collectivity. A third aspect is that every collectivity has to ensure the member / non-member distinction. These are general characteristics of every collectivity. This aspects can be used to analyze the paradoxes as a product of the interaction between the collectivity of the open society and its political system. Talcott Parsons calls this collectivity 'societal community'.

The societal community is characterized by a set of universalistic and particularistic norms. The universalistic norm of individual freedom is accompanied by particularistic ideas, which are considered as belonging to the individual freedom. The universalistic norms of equality are institutionalized in the context of a particularistic separation of public and private. The universalistic norm to help those in need is implemented by the particularistic definition of solidarity with those who belong to the collectivity.

Socialization is the main process to produce full members in the societal community. Full membership generates the loyalty of each member to the society to which he or she belongs. If members of a collectivity can not assume that all members are fully socialized, trust in the reciprocity of solidarity weakens. The normative patterns of the distinction between public and private are blurred. Furthermore the trust in the loyalty of the other to the society as a whole breaks down.

The problem of loyalty is so important because modern societies consist of a large number of different collectivities. The "societal community is a complex network of interpenetrating collectivities and collective loyalties, a system of units characterized by both functional differentiation and segmentation" (Parsons, 1969, p. 42). This complex structure consists of systems of norms: these reconcile legitimate values, world views and images of the members of each society, while they consider themselves equal in terms of this membership.[7] Such systems are neither fully coherent nor do they lack contradictions or paradoxes but they provide a basis for solidarity in the respective society.

The most obvious problem for individuals is to deal with all the different loyalties to religious groups, to ethnic groups, or to the family. If loyalty to the societal community and to the political system as whole weakens, the solidarity between different collectivities weakens as well. In this case the typical membership pluralism in open society becomes a threat for the open society itself. "The institutions of citizenship and nationality can nevertheless render the societal community vulnerable if the bases of pluralism are exacerbated into sharply structured cleavages. ... This is particularly true when regional cleavages coincide with ethnic and/or religious division". (Parsons, 1969, p. 51)

This leads to the last point Parsons mentioned as a central problem for the societal community: territoriality. "[T]he most obvious discrepancy derives from the territorial basis of society. Territorial jurisdiction requires that normative control apply to some extent independently of actual membership in the societal community". (Parsons, 1969, p. 49). All the paradoxes of the external border-structure are linked to the problem of territoriality. Refugees are by definition people who flee one territory and enter another, and it is simply this process of entering which produces high difficulties to apply the member/non-member distinction. Furthermore staying legally on a territory inevitably produces some kind of membership, this leads to the paradox of the citizens without nationality. The flip side of that, the legal definition of a member regardless of the territory, leads as well to problems, exemplified in the paradox of nationals without citizenship.

By talking about the normative patterns of majority one has to keep in mind that, "[t]he constitution of a societal community is never static, but constantly changing over time". (Parsons, 1969, p. 263) The momentum towards the strengthening of individual rights in the USA did not only lead to a stabilization of ethnic cleavages, as for example the civil rights acts of 1964 and 1965 showed. It can as well lead to a change in the normative patterns in the whole societal community towards more universalism (Parsons, 1969, p. 262). The awareness of cultural differences in the public sphere may cause a stabilization of the ethnic identity of the minority. In turn it is equally possible to redefine what is public and what is private as the example of turban wearing Sikhs police officer in Canada shows. Even the distrust in cultural different socialization processes can turn into legal arrangements of co-existence as the example of the Danish and Sorb minorities in Germany shows.

Central for this kind of institutional change is the institutional setting of citizenship. Citizenship itself produces loyalty and societal solidarity. Only the normative structure of the complex of citizenship ensures that conflicting loyalties – for example to ethnic groups – do not become dominant. Or as Talcott Parsons put it: "In fully modern societies, there can be diversity on each basis, religious, ethnic, and territorial, because the common status of citizenship provides a sufficient foundation for national solidarity". (1969, p. 51)

*Table 1: Main National Origins of the Foreign[a] Population as per cent of the Total Foreign Population, 1960-1990*

| | France | | | | | | Germany | | | | | | U.S. | | | |
|---|---|---|---|---|---|---|---|---|---|---|---|---|---|---|---|---|
| Year, 19: | 60 | 70 | 75 | 82 | 85 | 90 | 61 | 70 | 75 | 80 | 85 | 90 | 60 | 70 | 80 | 90 |
| Nationality/ Nativity | (%) | (%) | (%) | (%) | (%) | (%) | (%a) | (%) | (%) | (%) | (%) | (%) | (%) | (%) | (%) | (%) |
| Portugal | - | - | 22 | 21 | 20 | 18 | - | - | - | - | - | - | - | - | - | - |
| Algeria | - | - | 21 | 22 | 22 | 17 | - | - | - | - | - | - | - | - | - | - |
| Spain | - | - | 14 | 9 | 7 | 6 | 9 | 8 | 6 | 4 | 4 | 3 | - | - | - | - |
| Italy | - | - | 13 | 9 | 7 | 7 | 33 | 19 | 15 | 14 | 12 | 10 | 13 | 10 | 6 | 3 |
| Marocco | - | - | 8 | 12 | 14 | 16 | - | - | - | - | - | - | - | - | - | - |
| Tunisia | - | - | 4 | 5 | 5 | 6 | - | - | - | - | - | - | - | - | - | - |
| Turkey | - | - | - | 3 | 4 | 6 | - | 16 | 26 | 33 | 32 | 32 | - | - | - | - |
| Netherlands | - | - | - | - | - | - | 10 | - | - | - | 3 | - | - | - | - | - |
| Greece | - | - | - | - | - | - | 8 | 12 | 9 | 7 | 6 | 6 | - | - | - | - |
| France | - | - | - | - | - | - | 3 | - | - | - | - | - | - | - | - | - |
| Yugoslavia | - | - | - | - | - | - | 2 | 17 | 17 | 14 | 14 | 12 | - | - | - | - |
| Austria | - | - | - | - | - | - | - | - | - | - | 4 | - | 3 | 2 | - | - |
| Poland | - | - | - | - | - | - | - | - | - | - | - | 5 | 8 | 6 | 3 | 2 |
| UK | - | - | - | - | - | - | - | - | - | - | - | - | 9 | 7 | 5 | 3 |
| USSR | - | - | - | - | - | - | - | - | - | - | - | - | 7 | 5 | 3 | - |
| Germany | - | - | - | - | - | - | - | - | - | - | - | - | 10 | 9 | 6 | 4 |
| Hungary | - | - | - | - | - | - | - | - | - | - | - | - | 3 | - | - | - |
| Vietnam | - | - | - | - | - | - | - | - | - | - | - | - | - | - | 2 | 3 |
| Canada | - | - | - | - | - | - | - | - | - | - | - | - | 10 | 8 | 6 | 4 |
| Mexico | - | - | - | - | - | - | - | - | - | - | - | - | 6 | 8 | 16 | 22 |
| Ireland | - | - | - | - | - | - | - | - | - | - | - | - | 3 | 3 | - | - |
| Cuba | - | - | - | - | - | - | - | - | - | - | - | - | - | 5 | 4 | 4 |
| Philippines | - | - | - | - | - | - | - | - | - | - | - | - | - | - | 4 | 5 |
| Korea | - | - | - | - | - | - | - | - | - | - | - | - | - | - | 2 | 3 |
| China | - | - | - | - | - | - | - | - | - | - | - | - | - | - | 2 | 3 |
| Japan | - | - | - | - | - | - | - | - | - | - | - | - | - | - | 2 | - |
| El Salvador | - | - | - | - | - | - | - | - | - | - | - | - | - | - | - | 2 |
| India | - | - | - | - | - | - | - | - | - | - | - | - | - | - | - | 2 |
| Total[b] (%) | - | - | 82 | 80 | 79 | 76 | 64 | 72 | 73 | 72 | 70 | 68 | 71 | 63 | 59 | 59 |

*a* U.S., foreign-born; France and Germany, foreign nationals.

*b* Total of main origins shown, as % of each state's foreign inflow. Rounded independently, and so the sum of individual entries may differ slightly from the total shown. Source: France: Thränhardt, 1992:31; Romero, 1990:182; Coleman, 1995:163; Germany: Hammar, 1985:171; Hoffman-Nowotny, 1978:94; Booth, 1992: 222; Romero, 1990:182; Coleman, 1995:163; United States: Census of Population, 1960:I:1:366; Statistical Abstract 1994: Table 55; 1992: Table 46; 1979: Table 43. See Bahr, Bös, Caldwell et al. 1997, table 3.

*Table 2: Continental Origins of the Foreign[a] Population, as per cent of the Total Foreign Population, 1960-1990/94*

| Country, year | Europe (incl. USSR) (%) | Asia (incl. Turkey) (%) | Africa (%) | America (%) | other (%) | Total (%) | Total (1000s) |
|---|---|---|---|---|---|---|---|
| *France* | | | | | | | |
| 1962 | 88 | 2 | 4 | 5 | 1 | 100 | 1819 |
| 1968 | 73 | 2 | 25 | 1 | - | 101 | 2664 |
| 1975 | 61 | 3 | 35 | 1 | - | 100 | 3442 |
| 1982 | 48 | 8 | 43 | 1 | - | 100 | 3714 |
| 1990 | 41 | 12 | 45 | 2 | - | 100 | 3597 |
| *Germany (W)* | | | | | | | |
| 1961 | 77 | 4 | 1 | 3 | 15 | 100 | 686 |
| 1967 | 78 | 13 | 1 | 4 | 4 | 100 | 1807 |
| 1970 | 76 | 18 | 1 | 3 | 2 | 100 | 2976 |
| 1975 | 64 | 29 | 2 | 3 | 2 | 100 | 4090 |
| 1980 | 56 | 38 | 2 | 3 | 1 | 100 | 4453 |
| 1982 | 54 | 39 | 3 | 3 | 1 | 100 | 4667 |
| 1985 | 54 | 39 | 3 | 3 | 1 | 100 | 4379 |
| 1990 | 52 | 41 | 4 | 3 | 1 | 101 | 5343 |
| 1994b | 55 | 38 | 4 | 3 | 1 | 101 | 6991 |
| *United States* | | | | | | | |
| 1960 | - | - | - | - | - | - | - |
| 1970 | 59 | 9 | - | 27 | 5 | 100 | 9619 |
| 1980 | 39 | 19 | 2 | 40 | 1 | 101 | 13182 |
| 1990 | 25 | 26 | 2 | 46 | 1 | 100 | 20699 |

*a* Foreigners represented here are defined as follows. France: persons of foreign nationality enumerated in censuses; Germany: persons of foreign nationality; United States: the foreign-born enumerated in censuses.

*b* Unified Germany. Source: France: computed from Tribalat, 1985:135, as reported in Kubat, 1993:166; OECD; Germany: Statistiches Bundesamt; United States: Statistical Abstract 1992:42; 1979:37. See Bahr, Bös, Caldwell et al. 1997, table 4

## NOTES

1 I would like to thank Uta Gerhardt, Birgitta Hohenester, and Uwe Wenzel for their comments on an earlier draft of this paper.

2 A paradox means more than a simple contradiction. A paradoxon is defined in three ways: "1. A statement which seems contradictory but is true. 2. A statement which seems true, but is contradictory. 3 A logical chain of proof, which leads to a contradiction". (Falletta, 1985, p. 9, translation by M.B.).

3 It is not the place to report the extensive discussion of the concept of ethnicity in the frame work of the nation state (see as two different examples Floya Anthias / Nira Yuval Davis 1992 and Athony D. Smith 1992). I refer here to the definition Max Weber 1922 put forwards: "Wir wollen solche Menschengruppen, welche aufgrund der Ähnlichkeit des äußeren Habitus oder der Sitte oder beider oder von Erinnerung an

Kolonisation und Wanderung einen subjektiven Glauben an eine Abstammungsgemeinschaft hegen, daß dieser für die Propagierung von Vergemeinschaftung wichtig wird..., ethnische Gruppen nennen". (Weber, 1985, p. 237).

4 Only immigrant flows with a proportion higher than 2 percent are shown in table 1.

5 Despite the fact that Popper has only some rough suggestions on how his main ideas could be realized in the institutional setting of the modern nation state, his book serves as a reference point for many liberal economists and sociologists (Albert, Dahrendorf, Hayek). These approaches have many more implications and assumptions than Popper's initial work, even if they carry the spirit of critical rationalism. The main argument against Popper's idea is, that the epistemological assumptions of Popper imply a form of discourse which might be useful in a scientific context but is incompatible with the structure of the political discourse. For a more careful critique on Popper see for example Becker 1989.

6 This is only one aspect of solidarity, one of the most important forms of social relations within modern societies, for a closer examination see Hondrich / Koch-Arzberger 1992.

7 These shared norms and values, like the identification with different cultural patterns, are not necessarily congruent with borders of the nation state. This is exemplified in the increasing density of the shared value- system in Western Europe as well as on the global level in the declaration of the human rights or the rules of free trade.

## REFERENCES

Alonso, William (1987): *Population in an Interacting World*, (Cambrige, Mass. / London: Harvard University Press).

Anderson, Benedict (1983): *Imagined Communities*, (London: Verso).

Anthias, Floya/Yuval-Davis, Nira (1992): *Racialized Boundaries – Race, Nation, Gender, Colour and Class and the Anti-racist Struggle*, (London: Routledge & Kegan Paul).

Bahr, Howard M., Mathias Bös, Gary Caldwell and Laura Alipranti (1997): "International Migration and Inequlity," Unpublished Manuscript prepared for the 16th Conference of Comparative Charting of Social Change, Bordeaux.

Becker, W. (1989): "Kritischer Rationalismus oder Kritizismus," pp. 203-20, K. Salamun (Hg.): *K. R. Popper und die Philosophie des kritischen Rationalismus* (Amsterdam/Atlanta: Rodopi).

Birnbaum, Pierre (1997): "Citoyenneré et Identité: de T.H. Marshall à Talcott Parsons," *Citizenship Studies* 1, p. 133-151.

Booth, Heather (1992): *The Migration Process in Britain and West Germany: Two Demographic Studies of Migrant Populations*, (Aldershot: Avebury).

Bös, Mathias (1993): "Die Ethnisierung des Rechts: Der Wandel der Staatsbürgerschaft in Frankreich, Deutschland, Groß-Britannien und den USA." *Kölner Zeitschrift für Soziologie und Sozialpsychologie* 45 / 4: pp. 619-643.

— (1997): *Migration als Problem offener Gesellschaften*, (Opladen: Leske + Budrich).

Brubaker, Williams Rogers (ed.) (1989): *Immigration and the Politics of Citizenship in Europe and North America*, (Lanham: University Press of America).

Caldwell, Gary (1993): "Migration in Quebec 1960-1990," Unpublished Manuscript.

Caplow, Theodore/Bahr, Howard M./Modell, John/Chadwick, Bruce A. (1991): *Recent Social Trends in the United States 1960-1990* (Frankfurt am Main / Montreal & Kingston: Campus Verlag/McGill-Queen's University Press).

Coleman, D.A. (1995): "International Migration: Demographic and Socioeconomic Consequences in the United Kingdom and Europe," *International Migration Review* 29 (Spring): pp. 155-206.

Dummett, A. und A. Nicol (1990): *Subjects, Citizens, Aliens and Others: Nationality and Immigration Law*, (London: Weidenfeld and Nicolson).

Falletta, Nicholas (1985): *Paradoxon*, (München: Hugendubel).

Forsé, Michel/Jaslin, Jean-Pierre/Lemel, Yannick/Mendras, Henri/Stoclet, Denis/Déchauy, Jean-Hugues (1993): *Recent Social Trends in France 1960-1990*, (Frankfurt am Main / Montreal & Kingston: Campus Verlag/McGill-Queen's University Press).

Glatzer, Wolfgang/Hondrich, Karl Otto/Noll, Heinz-Herbert/Stiehr, Karin/Wörndl, Barbara (1992): *Recent Social Trends in West Germany 1960-1990*, (Frankfurt am Main / Montreal & Kingston: Campus Verlag/McGill-Queen's University Press).

Hammar, Tomas (1985): *European Immigration Policy: A Comparative Study*, (Cambridge: Cambridge University Press).

Heinelt, Hubert, (ed.) (1994): *Zuwanderungspolitik in Europa*, (Opladen: Leske + Budrich).

Hoffmann-Nowotny, Hans-Joachim (1978): "European Migration after World War II," pp. 85-105, William H. McNeill / Ruth S. Adams, (eds): *Human Migration*: Patterns and Policies, (Bloomington & London: Indiana University Press).

Hondrich, Karl Otto/Koch-Arzberger, Claudia (1992): *Solidarität in der modernen Gesellschaft*, (Frankfurt/Main: Fischer).

Horowitz, Donald L. (1992): "Immigration and Group Relations in France and America," pp 3-38 in: Donald L. Horowitz, Gérard Noiriel (eds.): *Immigrants in two Democracies, French and American Experience*, (New York: New York University Press).

Kritz, Mary M./Lim, Lin Lean/Zlotnik, Hania (ed.) (1992): *International Migration Systems*. (Oxford: Clarendon Press).

Kubat, Daniel (1993): "France: Balancing Demographic and Cultural Nationalism," pp. 164-187 Daniel Kubat, (ed.): *The Politics of Migration Policies: Settlement and Integration: The First World into the 1990s* (New York: Center for Migration Studies).

Langlois, Simon / Baillatgon, Jean-Paul / Caldwell, Gary / Fréchet, Guy / Gauthier, Madeleine / Simard, Jaen-Pierre (1992): *Recent Social Trends in Québec 1960-1990*, (Frankfurt am Main / Montreal & Kingston: Campus Verlag/McGill-Queen's University Press).

Marshall, Thomas Humphrey (1950): *Citizenship and Social Class and Other Essays*, (Cambrige: Cambrige University Press).

McNeill, William H. (1986): *Polyethnicity and National Unity in World History* (Toronto: University of Toronto Press).

OECD (ed.), (1992): *Trends in International Migration 1992*: Continuous Reporting System on Migration (SOPEMI), Paris: OECD.

OECD (ed.) (1993): *The Changing Course of International Migration*, Paris: OECD.

Parsons, Talcott (1969): *Politics and Social Structure*, (New York: Free Press).

— (1972): *Das System moderner Gesellschaften* (München: Juventa).

Popper, K.R. (1980): *Die offene Gesellschaft und ihre Feinde* I+II, (Tübingen: Francke).

Renan, Ernest (1993 [1882]): "Was ist eine Nation?" pp. 290-311, Jeismann, Michael / Ritter, Henning: *Grenzfälle: Über alten und neuen Nationalismus*, (Leipzig: Reclam Leipzig).

Roberts, Bryan (1994/5): "Socially Expected Durations and the Economic Adjustment of Immigrants," A. Portes (ed.), forthcoming: *The Economic Sociology of Immigration*, (New York: Russel Sage).

Romero, Frederico (1990): "Cross-border Population Movements," pp. 171-191, William Wallace, (ed.): *The Dynamics of European Integration*, (London: Pinter).

Schiffauer, Werner (1993): "Die civil society und der Fremde – Grenzmarkierungen in vier politischen Kulturen," pp 185-199, Friedrich Balke, Rebekka Habermas, Patrizia Nanz, Peter Sillem (ed.), *Schwierige Fremdheit – Über Integration und Ausgrenzung in Einwanderungsländern*, (Frankfurt: Fischer).

Silverman, Maxim (1992): *Deconstructing the Nation – Immigration, Racism and Citizenship in Modern France*, (London: Routledge & Kegan Paul).

Simmons, Alan B. (1996): "Resaerch and Policy Issues in the Field of International Migration and American Economic Integration," pp. 1-27, Simmons, Alan B. (ed.): *International Refugge Flows and Human Rights in North America*, (New York: Center for Migration Studies).

Thränhardt, Dietrich (1992): "Europe: A New Immigration Continent: Policies and Politics in Comparative Perspective," pp. 15-74, Dietrich Thränhardt, (ed.): *Europe: A New Immigration Continent*, (Münster: Lit Verlag).

Tilly, Charles (1990): "Transplanted Networks," Virginia Yons-McLaughlin (ed.): *Immigration Reconsidered*, (New York: Oxford University Press).

U.S. Bureau of the Census (1994): *Statistical Abstract of the United States*, Washington, D.C.: Government Printing Office. Annual. Abbreviated SA.

Weber, Max (1985): *Wirtschaft und Gesellschaft*. Tübingen: J.C.B. Mohr , 5. Aufl.

Zolberg, Aristide et al. (1989): *Escape from Violence: Conflict and the Refugee Crises in the Developing World*, (Oxford: Oxford University Press).

UTA GERHARDT, BIRGITTA HOHENESTER

# A TRANSFORMATION OF NATIONAL IDENTITY?

## Refugees and German Society after World War II[1]

### 1 INTRODUCTION: A FALLACY IN THE CURRENT DEBATE

In 1989/1991, when the division between an Eastern block and a Western world ended in unprecedented oneness of the globe, a new era obviously began. In sociology, this new age has been characterized under two equally tentative labels. One is globalization, and the other is civil society.

Globalization, to be sure, comes under two separate but related perspectives. One is that in the wake of his warning against unanticipated consequences of high-technology systems in post-modern world-wide risk society, Ulrich Beck[2] distinguishes between givenness of globality in the labour market or mass communication etc., on the one hand, and dangers of globalization for political and societal structures, on the other hand. He warns of surreptitious increase of mafia-like power structures in the globalized world that tend to neutralize improvements of the quality of life of the masses. Although improvement of life-chances obviously followed the recent collapse of former totalitarianisms, he ventures, new sources of chaos loom large due to the uncontrollability of sheer globality.

The other view on globalization is that it is but a *mode de parler*. To name but three among many similar voices, Martin Albrow welcomes the *Global Age* that began after World War II but finds that nationalism still prevails where it ought to be replaced by universal negotiable identities that should be independent of group membership status(es)[3]; Roland Robertson sees national labour markets and commodity consumption patterns that are only linked to globalized firms or worldwide trade networks[4]; and Martin Ferguson emphasizes that globalization is but a matter of discourse, even a mere communication formula, when it is mistaken to indicate changes of world-wide impact.[5] These views contain a pledge for universalism as they criticize a creed in the oneness of the world when global discourse signifies only particularism writ large.

Although analytical accounts of globalization frequently date its beginning in the 1940s or earlier when postmodernism replaced modernity or globalization overcame nationalisms, serendipity of this analytical viewpoint only emerged with the end of the Cold War. When the Iron Curtain came down at the end of the 1980s and successive



*G. Preyer, M. Bös (eds.), Borderlines in a Globalized World, 141-172.*

"velvet revolutions" triggered by the fall of the Berlin wall suggested a millennium of worldwide democracy, ideas of a universal world became apparently urgent for social-science analysis. The dream predating the era of Cold War, "One World[6]," apparently could at last be reactivated. However, authors analyzing globalization warn, in the spirit of relief and hope when distinctions between the communist-block in-group and capitalist-world out-group, or *vice versa,* suddenly became obsolete, too much optimism surfaced too indiscriminately. Ethnocentrism which now is being newly recognized as a phenomenon, and nationalism analyzed as a reality, they find more deeply rooted in the very fabric of the social world than hitherto has been realized. Whereas identities could now become multiple formations as they reflect globalization, they warn, obsolete identification which nation or race give could easily spoil the prospects of the "one-world" future.

The other line of recent discussion focuses on civil society; its two lines of thought conceptualize the political and "bodily" dimension of membership. In the light of inequality in the traditional ("bourgeois") society, Jean Cohen and Andrew Arato[7], in their exhaustive review of contemporary theories – ranging from Gramsci to Habermas – , endorse the perspective of a "self-reflective and self-limiting utopia of civil society".[8] They proclaim an ideal of cultural heterogeneity, engendering freedom of self-realization particularly for minorities such as women, blacks, or other disadvantaged groups. They suggest that political self-expression which typically spurs voluntary associations and social movements should become the major driving force facilitating worldwide civil society.

The other view sees civil society related to citizenship. In the triple meaning given it by T.H. Marshall, some authors suggest, citizenship provides a long underestimated answer to the modern question how the state can serve rather than dominate its citizens.[9] However, other authors disregard Marshall when they discuss political or societal aspects of citizenship. William Brubaker[10] distinguishes two types of attribution of citizenship, Jus Sanguinis and Jus Solis, and he shows that the ease or difficulty of immigrants to be allowed to become citizens is related to cultural traditions but also political expediencies of interpretation of the two principles in various countries. Other authors reject Marshall's conception outright since to them it is too closely linked with the nation-state. In this vein, Bryan S. Turner[11] argues that the nation-state is doomed as a political framework for civil society and therefore cannot serve as a model of citizenship in our current age of globalization. A theory of social rights, he suggests, should replace sociology's notion of citizenship. Turner argues that men's basic characteristic is that humans have bodies. This, he suggests, should be the principle of equality and set social rights. Through such "new" importance of bodies, he feels, limitations of classical sociological theory could be overcome which obfuscate proper conceptualization of membership in the globalized world.

These two views of civil society entail different principles. Whereas Cohen/Arato endorse universal politicization that makes an extended public sphere an arena of expression for individual wants and needs, Turner, endorsing citizenship, proclaims "social rights" derived from "human frailty and the precariousness of institutions".[12] Whereas Cohen/Arato suggest a world of activist social movements, Turner endorses "a system of mutual protection" for individuals based on the fact that their social rights derive from their having a body.[13]

Theorems discussing globalization and civil society delineate a new agenda for sociology subsequent to the collapse of the East-West divide. These theorems re-interpret theories discussed worldwide since the 1970s, such as, for instance, those of Jürgen Habermas or Niklas Luhmann, but they also create new concepts or conceptions when they search for suitable answers to emergent world problems. Nevertheless, no matter how convincing these theorems look, and how innovative they find their endeavours beyond classical theory, they share what can be called a conspicuous fallacy.

Approaches analyzing globalization mostly do not rely on detailed evidence of historical processes or population structures when they propose social theory that is meant to explain (post)modernity in present-day world society.[14] Neither the conception of risk society nor the conjecture that globalization is a mode of discourse have been grounded in systematically comparative, empirical analysis. None of the analytical approaches to globalization appear to place their concepts in a classical framework of social theory such as that of Max Weber. These approaches frequently analyze arenas of continent-wide conditions or century-wide structural processes (as did Immanual Wallerstein who might even be regarded as the very first analyst of globalization[15]), but their empirical data serve the purpose merely of illustration, not systematic proof of hypotheses ventured or conclusions drawn.

Similarly, literature on civil society aims to develop new lines of thought but fails to give credit to classical theory's well-established arguments. Even though this literature shares the view of Weberian or Parsonian sociology that social conditions should be such that a maximum of individual freedom and an optimum of humanism in society are possible, neither Cohen/Arato nor Bryan Turner endorse the conceptual foundations established by theories such as those of Max Weber or Talcott Parsons. Instead, Cohen/Arato opt for more individualistically minded theory such as that of Habermas, and their postulate is that civil society means freedom from domination of the individual irrespective of the question of what are the political conditions of a stable social order. Turner adopts the institutionally minded approach of Arnold Gehlen, but inadvertently adopts the latter's philosophy which proclaimed social darwinism at least until 1945 before Gehlen declared himself a sociologist after World War II. Gehlen's idea that to be human means that a person has/is a body, Turner takes as a baseline for defining the social right of citizenship; but he fails to take account of the fact that Gehlen disregards individual freedom of choice when he sees human nature lodged with constraints as they prevail in social institutions.

The fallacy in this current debate may follow inadvertently from these authors' good intentions. To be sure, these approaches are concerned with what political solution could help to solve the problems of the post-Cold War world. But they overlook that politics should not be confused with scientific sociology. If findings are to be valid proof, Weber warned in 1904 and 1917, science must refrain from taking sides.[16] In Weberian terms, much of present-day analysis of globalization and civil society represents a political standpoint. Therefore, it might best be called a prolegomenon to scientific analysis. Although value-neutrality defines sociology as a science, no doubt, a scientist as a political person may engage himself in contemporary politics as a citizen. Weber, in this vein, participated in the creation of the Weimar Constitution. However, in the debate on globalization and civil society, self-styled humanistic views may bear witness to sociologists' good intentions but violate their claim to scientific relevance.

From this vantage point, a limited-scope topic may be a suitable starting point for sociological discussion of global themes. If globalization and civil society, even the question of what could hold together a globalized "one-world" society or societies, are at issue, theoretical ideas must nevertheless be discussed using small-scale, paradigmatic, empirical material. Moreover, we believe, Weber's requirement that value-neutrality affords a *sine-ira-et-studio* attitude might be fulfilled more easily if the sociological topic discussed is taken from a past era of social history. Of course, such topic should be compatible with problems that prevail in and are urgent for our world today.

Our topic is how citizenship is gained through national (and possibly even international) identification in a world of changing borders encompassing changing populations.[17] We wish to analyze citizenship as it is important in our decade when we discuss a chapter of the history of (national) identification of Germans. Citizenship, for us, serves as a model that may epitomize national identity, when we analyze evidence from a historical era of Germany when some eight million refugees arrived in Western Germany. These refugees came from previously German as well as non-German regions East of Germany, whose revised borders had been established at the Potsdam Conference in July/August 1945 subsequent to World War II. More specifically, in our case, most of the millions of refugees arriving in West Germany came from former parts of "Greater Germany" that had ceased to exist when this country had been defeated in a war of its own criminal making. Our main theme is transformation, that is, extension of membership in a country or nation to a group or category of citizens previously belonging to another country, society, or nation.

Our theoretical baseline is phenomenological sociology, especially the work of Alfred Schütz and Georg Simmel. Our first reason for choosing this relatively unusual framework for our analytical account is that these two authors have concerned themselves with the topic of "The Stranger" in two equally famous essays. The theme of the stranger, connected with its sociological recognition by Schütz and Simmel, moreover, has given rise to discussions of inclusion and exclusion in structures of social action in some recent texts on citizenship.[18] Simmel's and Schütz's essays, in our view, witness that classical sociology had a vital interest in issues of citizenship.

The second reason for choosing Schütz and Simmel as theoretical foundation of our argument is that both these theories were intricately linked with that of Max Weber. Whereas Simmel was a predecessor and reference person for Weber with regard to the conceptualization of social relations, typification, etc., Schütz managed to elaborate on Weber's action theory such that it could recognize the complicated differentiation between the subjective and the objective social worlds.[19] In this latter vein, Schütz took up most themes of Weber's social theory developing them in a direction better suited to the taken-for-granted world of the actor than Weber's notions had been. In our particular context, Schütz in the middle 1950s analyzed the action dimension involved in typificatory processes constituting social equality – realizing that a policy like that of the United Nations' refugee program meant equality but, at the same time, allowed for a certain scope of freedom through inequality. This is the main point constituting our theoretical baseline.

## 2 A BASELINE FOR SOCIAL THEORY OF CITIZENSHIP: ANALYSIS OF TRANSFORMATION AS TRANSLATION OF TYPIFICATIONS

In 1944, five years after his arrival in New York (at the New School for Social Research) as a refugee from Europe most of which had come under Nazi domination, Viennese philosopher cum sociologist Alfred Schütz published an essay entitled "The Stranger".[20] It analyzed the transformation from one culture to another as an exchange or translation of taken-for-granted social worlds. Its main point was to distinguish between two phases of acculturation, namely crisis and assimilation. Intent upon assimilation, the stranger in the culture of refuge experienced his taken-for-granted expectations related to the "new" culture to be inadequate in as much as they represented merely remainders from his "old" world's typifications of what then und there had been a foreign land. In this situation, Schütz found, the actor underwent a personal crisis. None of the actor's typifications, building blocks of any reliable social world, continued to work in his new surroundings. It added to the actor's confusion that everybody else around him functioned on the basis of taken-for-granted assumptions which he failed to share: "He becomes essentially the man who has to place in question nearly everything that seems to be unquestionable to the members of the approached group".[21]

In another essay published some ten years later, Schütz returned to the topic of personal crisis.[22] His main interest was now equality. He discussed how equality could be established between actors whose racial, national, political, or ideological differences constituted the divided, even compartmentalized social meaning structure prevailing in most modern societies. He stated that the taken-for-granted worlds of the actors in social groups were structured in in-group typifications. They were distinct from typificatory categorizations of out-group races, nations, religions, etc., which, by that very token, were frequently deemed inferior or outright hostile. The ethnocentric structure of group-related typifications stabilized individuals' taken-for-granted worlds. This, however, lasted only as long as the individuals managed to continue to live in their cultures or taken-for-granted worlds. If, for whatever reason, a person had to change allegiance such that a previous out-group would become his new in-group, personal crisis ensued. "For example," he reported, "Jewish immigrants from Iraq have considerable difficulty in understanding that their practices of polygamy and child marriage are not permitted by the laws of Israel, their national home".[23] Worse still, personal crisis could result from external definitions of the social type being imposed on a person who was made to belong to a previous out-group against his will. "To cite just a few examples:" – wrote Schütz – "persons who believed themselves to be good Germans and had severed all allegiance to Judaism found themselves declared Jews by Hitler's Nuremberg laws and treated as such on the ground of a grandparent's origin, a fact up to that time entirely irrelevant. Refugees from Europe, who believed they had found a haven in the United States, discovered themselves placed, after Pearl Harbor, in the category of enemy aliens, by reason of the very nationality they wanted to abandon".[24] Subsuming this experience under "imposed typification," he explained: "It is submitted that the feeling of degradation caused by the identification of the whole, or broad layers, of the individual's personality with the imposed typified trait is one of the basic motives for the subjective experience of discrimination". [25]

The wholesale nature of the label of stranger, as it meant discrimination, had been explained by Georg Simmel in another famous essay entitled "The Stranger"[26]. In 1908, when he composed his *major opus,* "Soziologie," from mostly previously published parts but also added thirteen newly-written so-called "notes" ("Exkurse"), Simmel inserted the "Note on the Stranger" into the chapter entitled "Space and the Spatial Orders of Society". Unlike Schütz, he located the stranger as a social type within society's boundaries; that is, for Simmel the stranger was a fully-fledged member albeit a second-class citizen at best. "The stranger will thus not be considered here in the usual sense of the term, as the wanderer who comes today and goes tomorrow, but rather as the man who comes today and stays tomorrow," he clarified.[27] Three aspects of the social type were important. One was the stranger's actual or potential mobility which made him less identified with kinship, locality, or occupation. Another was objectivity, that is, his being seen and seeing himself as impartial observer rather than partisan participant. Most important, however, was the third aspect, namely, a certain generality of the social category which, in turn, rendered relatively abstract any social relationship established thereby. "With the stranger one has only certain *more general* qualities in common," Simmel realized (as translated by Donald Levine), "whereas the relation with organically connected persons is based on the similarity of just those specific traits which differentiate them from the merely universal".[28] In other words, the stranger was an impersonal category epitomized by, for instance, Jew or foreigner – denying its incumbent those qualities of personal individuality that could instigate feelings of personal closeness in indigenous, ordinary members of the society. In this vein, the worst case was that the stranger would not be regarded even as human in the same way as were his compatriots, Simmel observed: "The relation of the Greeks to the barbarians is a typical example. ... The relation with him is a non-relation; he is not what we have been discussing here: the stranger as a member of the group itself".[29]

It emerges from Simmel's thoughts, supplementing Schütz's observations, that to be a stranger means that a person is treated as, and behaves as, a member of an out-group. Such typification is valid irrespective of whether or not the person in question, in fact, is a bona-fide citizen of a society and therefore ought to be treated as belonging to its in-group(s). The difference between in-group and out-group, no doubt, is that these life-worlds are separate realms kept apart by systematic exclusion or veritable discrimination. Indeed, such separation can amount to virtual non-relations as in the case of the Greeks discriminating against the barbarians.

These distinctions are sociologically important because typifications actually constitute social roles. This is evident from Schütz's understanding where he writes: "What the sociologist calls 'system,' 'role,' 'status,' 'role expectation,' 'situation,' 'institutionalization,' is experienced by the individual actor on the social scene in ... a network of typifications – typifications of human individuals, of their course-of-action patterns, of their motives and goals, or the sociocultural products which originated in their action".[30] The crucial point is that roles as typification schemes are the social forms through which scarce resources such as money, power, or prestige are channeled and distributed within a social structure. Roles as typification schemes function on three levels of generality of abstraction, namely, status, position, and situation[31]: They institutionalize the resources and reciprocity relations contained in, for instance, statuses connected with ethnicity, culture, or nationality. In a given society, status roles mean more or less limited opportunity structures opening up more or less limited ranges of position roles, e.g. allowing for occupational or educational achievement in varying degrees linked to a given ethnic or other status incumbency. To give an example of historically well-remembered exclusion, women until 1908 were not usually permitted to take part in lectures or seminars as students at German (Prussian) universities. To cite a more drastic limitation, the closure of German society to Jewishness defined as an imposed status role of non-relation by National Socialism meant that

Jews – allegedly being of a Jewish race – were denied even the most elementary rights of citizenship. Eventually, this related even to the right to live which was denied to Jews through the Nazi arbitrary interpretation that their's was an out-group status role tied to so-called Jewish race which was anathema. To be sure, typifications are institutionalized also in democratic societies. In general, typificatory distinctions between in-group(s) and out-group(s) delineate role structures which, in turn, regulate life-chances.

From this perspective, boundaries between in-group and out-group often mean privilege on the side of the in-group in contrast with discrimination, or in extreme circumstance even persecution, directed at and experienced by the out-group. In this dualist set-up, typifications stipulate that a certain in-group comprises a certain realm of members who are defined through characteristics not shared by out-group(s) who merely become strangers or non-members. (Schütz, to be sure, ventured that a member of an in-group who becomes typified as belonging to a subgroup that is an out-group does not automatically belong to the out-group in the eyes of the out-group's members since the latter judge him from the perspective of their own in-group typifications). Our main point is that nationality means inclusion in a dominant category of a society. Our hypothesis is that national identity is connected with privileges extended to in-groups, whereas non-nationals might become targets for exclusion being more or less drastic in different types of society. In the worst case, non-nationality would define a pariah status connected with a role of severe deprivation or degradation.

Schütz, whose treatise on equality was concerned with the problem of how cleavages in the social meaning structures might be overcome, distinguished between an in-group universe of typificatory meanings and a separate out-group realm of meanings. He juxtaposed these in the fashion of mirror images under the proviso that in-group membership and out-group status are mutually exclusive but are parallel to each other. His aim was to think about how an immigrant could be transformed from a stranger (non-member) to a member – losing his out-group membership in due course. What was needed, he ventured, was "a formula of transformation ... which permits the translation of the system of relevances and typifications prevailing in the group under consideration into that of the home-group".[32]

## 3 REFUGEES IN POST-WAR GERMANY: PARIAHS TO GERMAN IDENTITY?

After World War II, due to the Potsdam Conference in 1945, millions of expellees from Eastern Europe and refugees from Eastern Germany were forced to go West, which means that they entered what later became Western Germany, and had to find a place to live there. Two main groups may be differentiated: Between 1944 and 1950, about eight million expellees from Eastern territories, some of them formerly German (e.g., coming from Silesia or Pomerania), fled to the Western Zones, or West Germany respectively.[33] From 1945 onwards, culminating between 1951 and 1961, about 2.5 million refugees left Eastern Germany and settled in the West.[34] Many among them, to be sure, may have crossed a border more than once: After they had been expelled from Eastern territories formerly German and fled into what became the German Democratic Republic, an unknown number of at least two million fled a second time, now into one of the Western zones, which after 1949 became the Federal Republic of Germany. These refugees might even have been among the at least one million who had been compelled to leave their original homes in former Eastern Poland when the Nazi administration had relocated German-speaking populations from there into more Western parts of their *Grossdeutsches Reich* in the wake of the Hitler-Stalin Pact of 1939.[35] When expellees/refugees[36] arrived in Western Germany after 1945, they frequently owned only what they had been able or allowed to carry. Often they had nowhere to go, and were distributed more or less at random to places of residence (preferably villages or small country towns) where they either had to live in make-shift camps or were sent to local families who had to take them into their homes.

By definition these people were not foreigners. Indeed – they were Germans by origin and/or nationality. But coming from a different part of Germany, representing a different cultural background, and frequently speaking dialects uncommon in Germany's Western regions, they appeared to belong – in Schützean terms – to an "out-group" in the eyes of the "in-group".

This situation may be pictured vividly by accounts given by (former) expellees remembering their arrival in research interviews conducted by sociologists in the 1980s.[37] For instance, one interviewee remembered that he had been among a group of refugees taken to a small town by lorry, and the lorrydriver had dropped them somewhere in a street and had disappeared pretending he did not know the location of the town hall where the mayor's office was.

> On the other side of the road was blacksmith Ruhnke' remembered the interviewee' he stood in front of his house and stared at us. I went over and said: 'Excuse me, can you tell me where we can find the town hall where the mayor's office is?' He said: 'I don't know where it is'. He thought, if I don't tell them they will go elsewhere, maybe they go to the next village. ... Nobody wanted us. We were Germans, but nobody wanted us. And today, if Poles come here and want to work illegally for three months, they are welcomed eagerly[38]

The same interviewee told another story about a mother and child:

> Mrs. Lahn had little Agnes, who was two years old. She had hurt herself badly during the train journey. When we arrived, they were sent to live in the pastor's house. How did they get in? Through the police. They needed police protection to be taken in by the pastor. When we went in – I helped to carry things – the pastor's sister went through the house and locked all doors[39]

In a newspaper article in "Neue Württembergische Zeitung" of August 4, 1946, which has been reprinted in a collection of documents issued by the Baden-Württemberg Ministry of the Interior in the 1990s, an expellee complained about discrimination against the newcomers in housing and at the work place. He wrote:

> We were and are keen to adapt to the routines of life here, and we have been fully aware of the fact that we have to be modest in every respect and cannot ask from the local population that they welcome refugees who are imposed on them in their homes. On the other hand, everybody will agree that it is not our fault that we were driven away from our homes and land and now have to roam the country as beggars and are a burden on other people. ... At work we often encounter lack of symphathy or egoism, which seem particularly inappropriate with regard to the refugees. While refugees, even those who are sick, have lost a limb, are old, or are in poor physical condition, are made to work very hard indeed with shovel and pick on road-work sites, local dodgers are tolerated who not only have secured for themselves less strenuous posts or types of work but are often those who do as little work as possible, even young people[40]

A report compiled in the spring of 1946 by the Refugee Ombudsman of Württemberg-Baden on Filderstadt, a small town, stated that occupants of houses frequently were extremely hostile to refugees placed in their homes; in fact, the report said, many refused to take them in, and while local helpers were on the stairs helping with the refugees' luggage, home owners or residenttenants would throw it out of the window into the street again:

> On the occasion of a recent arrival[41] of some 45 refugees conflicts arose. The authorities had failed to notify in advance the owners of housing when the refugees arrived. A flood of abuse and hate was poured over them. They were even called scum or gipsies or pack. In one case they were told, 'rather shoot than let a refugee in my house'[42]

A photograph taken in the late 1940s and now reprinted on the cover of a book on the topic shows two carnival-dressed men carrying a placard saying about the region of Baden in Southern Germany: "Baden's most terrible threat the new refugee treck !!".[43]

American Military Government was alarmed about the situation. The "Information Control Division" (ICD) of the Office of Military Government of the United States in Germany (OMGUS) conducted research to understand what was going on. Using random samples, over one hundred surveys investigated social and political issues in postwar Germany; they were analyzed in nearly two hundred reports on specific problems over the time period until September, 1949. These surveys show how hostile the reception was which expellees received by local Germans. Indeed, a deep societal cleavage developed between this out-group and the in-group of natives in the years 1945-1948. Three reports whose data were collected in 1946 dealt with the expellee/refugee situation specifically.

ICD-Report No. 14A published in July 1946 and based on data collected in March of that year investigated "German Attitudes Toward the Expulsion of German Nationals from Neighboring Countries".[44] It reported on the following findings:

Among expellees, at that time about one half said that they expected to get along with the resident German population. The report clarified: "Whereas about six in ten thought they would get along with the resident German population, one-fourth of the expellees said they did not expect to do so. But when the thoughts in this direction were probed, it was apparent that some of the confidence in good relations was merely a reflection of determination to get along rather than a founded appreciation of how this was possible. ... One in eight was already discouraged saying, 'These are another kind of people and do not understand us evacuees'".[45]

In contradistinction, two thirds of the resident German population had not even as much as spoken with an expellee:

> Fully a third (35%) of the resident population said they had already spoken with an evacuee. ... Those who had spoken with the evacuees were also asked what impression these strangers had made upon them. About one in eight resident Germans said that the impression they had gotten was 'good'. ... A group of about the same size said that they were unfavorably impressed with the evacuees, that at least a part of them made a 'bad' impression.[46]

Among resident Germans, 26 percent felt that they were not ready to give political equality to expellees, and 19 percent did not wish to extend equal economic opportunities to them. Even worse,

> About two in three Germans estimated that both food and housing would be adequate to provide for the evacuees. ... Only about one in three people thought that jobs would not be plentiful enough to provide work for the evacuees.[47]

In November 1946, another report was published based only on data collected in the Land Württemberg-Baden in Southern Germany. Its title was "An Investigation To Determine Any Changes in Attitudes of Native Germans Toward the Expellees in Wuerttemberg-Baden".[48] This report which witnessed a worsening of relationships between the two parts of the population culminated in its anonymous author's comment at the end of the summary given on the front page:

"The presence of the expellees in German society furnishes this society with a potential scapegoat. The possible assimilation of the expellees depend(s) on favorable economic conditions, absent in Germany of today".[49] What were the findings reported?

Among expellees, the report said, "three out of five ... stated that they were satisfied with their reception in Amzon. ... Further probing reveals that this proportion of the expellees consider themselves as German citizens (*Deutsche Staatsbuerger*)".[50] In other words, 40 percent did not consider themselves as German citizens. In more detail, "Two out of five of the expellees ... stated that the native Germans did not regard them as Germans and considered them as human beings of inferior value, as foreigners or as beggars. This same proportion of the expellees did not classify themselves as German citizens and claimed Hungary, Czechoslovakia and other countries as their native states. One in ten of the expellees considered themselves as stateless. Further probing reveals that one in ten of the expellees cannot speak German".[51]

In reverse, over one quarter of native Germans considered the expellees foreigners, and only one half considered them to be German citizens – which leaves about another quarter who obviously chose not to answer the question.[52]

Regarding where expellees belonged and whether they would stay in (Western) Germany, the one half of the Germans who, as the report said, "believe that the expellee will eventually return to the land of his birth, half explained their statement by saying that the expellees want to return. ... One fourth of the group who believed that the expellees will return formed their opinion on the basis that the Land will not be able to support their continued presence".[53]

About one quarter of native Germans would not extend equal rights to expellees, which the report qualified as follows: "Approximately three of four of the people questioned believed that the Expellee should have equal political rights. Of the minority (17%) who believed that they should not have equals rights, almost half (40%) stated that the expellees are not Germans and do not think as Germans".[54]

In the light of such depressing findings, the author of the report closed it with a comparison between postwar Germany and the U.S.:

> The presence of this minority (the expellees as a whole) constitutes a potential scape goat. There is a strong tendency of the entrenched native group in any society to regard the recent arrival, even after a generation or more of residence as 'foreigners' (e.g., the native white American considering the Ytalo-American (sic) or the Polish-American as a 'foreign element'). This is almost a truism in Europe where small ethnic elements preserve their identity for generations, viz., the Basques of Spain, the Balts, the Sudeten Germans, etc. Furthermore, the assimilation of immigrant groups into American society has been aided by a frontier economy, i.e., open lands, shortage of labor, a fluid society, etc., characteristics absent in the present situation of Germany. To prevent any organized resistance to the expellees demands either rigid control or else the alleviation of any economic distress within the Zone which can be ascribed to their presence – a task of years duration[55]

On February 20, 1947, another report was published entitled "Opinions on the Expellee Problem" (No. 47).[56] It was based on data collected in the last two weeks of November 1946. It reported a worsening of the overall situation in the following main findings:

Fewer expellees than before were satisfied with the treatment given to them by the local population; the percentage had been 78 in March 1946 and now had dropped to

52 percent. Dissatisfaction had risen from 7 percent to 35 percent, and "no opinion" had decreased from 15 percent to 3 percent.

As regarded the question of citizenship, "almost nine out of ten (88%) of the expellees in the American zone consider themselves to be German. ... But Germans or not, most expellees (84%) desire to return to their homeland. The full measure of discontent of these uprooted people is seen in their replies to this question: 'If you were permitted to in the future, would you return to your home?' Emphatic Yes: Bavaria 59%, Hesse 68%, Wtb Baden 77%"[57] (to which had to be added between 5% and 24% Yes answers in the various Länder, yielding an average of 84 percent wishing to return "home").

Among native Germans, still not more than one half expected that they and the expellees would ever get along with each other.

Only just over half native Germans considered expellees German citizens. Therefore, nearly one half (45%) either did not consider them German citizens or refrained from having an opinion on the matter.

Finally, native Germans were even less prepared than expellees themselves to see the latter as permanent residents in the Länder of the American zone. The report stated:

> Native Germans almost approach unanimity in the opinion that the expellees will return to their homeland when and if they are given the opportunity. The vote on this (91%) is larger than that of the expellees themselves (84% – 64% emphatic Yes) ... in fact it is so large that it looks rather like speeding the departure of the unloved guest, though it may also be in part a reflection of the expellees' own thoughts on the matter. There is also a remarkable concurrence of opinion here – the three Laender, hamlets and cities (even Berlin), PG's and non-PG's, educated and uneducated, old and young are almost as one in thinking that the expellees will want to return home[58]

Eventually, the anonymous author of the report again warned against the dangers of "public discontent and dissatisfaction": "Clearly apparent from these findings is that potential, if not actual trouble lies in the expellee problem. The almost unanimous opinion that the expulsions were not just, that the expellees should return home, plus the increasing tendency to shift the burden of their support away from the Germans and onto the expelling countries certainly does not make for harmony. When viewed against the backdrop of bombed-out houses with consequent crowded living quarters and economic disequilibrium, it may be dangerous".[59]

To sum up what has been illustrated through contemporaneous sources so far: Refugees arriving by the million from former Eastern regions of Germany as well as countries East of Germany were not welcomed by native Germans in the Western zones. A large proportion of these expellees did not consider themselves Germans until 1946 or later while an even larger part of the native population denied them recognition as German citizens. An overwhelming majority of local residents were not willing to accept these Silesians, East Prussians, etc., as native Germans with whom they had to get along and who would live in their midst from then on. Hostile exclusion of expellees/refugees meant that about one fourth of native Germans stated in public opinion surveys that they were not prepared to extend economic and political equality to these newcomers. In other words: These German refugees were regarded as foreigners by a considerable part of local German residents. Despite the fact that many of these refugees had "lost everything," as the saying went, their new beginning in "the West" was made even more difficult by the fact that they were frequently treated as foreigners and were not welcomed to stay. In fact, until the end of 1946 most of them had no intention themselves to stay in the Western regions – if only they had been allowed to return "home".

## 4 IN-GROUP AND OUT-GROUP DIFFERENCES IN THE TYPIFICATION OF NATIONAL IDENTITY

The relationship between refugees and locals may be described as one of in-group and out-group in Schütz' terms. This perspective helps to reinterpret the data collected by ICD as indicating how deep the cleavage was which emerged between the two groups of the population in the years immediately after World War II.

Upon arrival at their places of destination, expellees frequently experienced that local residents were extremely hostile. As quoted above, one former expellee remembered how he was refused even the information where the town hall was – a piece of taken-for-granted knowledge presumably shared by every local inhabitant. Many locals not only refused to open their doors to the expellees but one pastor's sister was observed busily locking doors from them. Such hostile behavior was experienced by an overwhelming majority of newcomers. Even forty years later Lehmann's interviewees frequently had neither forgotten nor forgiven how upon their arrival in their new "home" city, town, or village they had been treated like unwelcome guests, beggars, or even thieves.

The three ICD reports whose data were collected between March and November 1946 document that in-group and out-group typifications between expellees and locals were so different that the warnings expressed by the anonymous authors of the reports may appear highly justified.

Expellees consisted of a majority who felt as an out-group and deplored the obvious segregation with which they were treated by the local in-group, a minority who saw no similarities with locals and had given up hope ever to be integrated, and a minority who felt that reconciliation between out-group and in-group would eventually by successful. In more detail: In March 1946, over one half of expellees saw themselves as an out-group willing to be incorporated into the in-group of locals whereas one fourth saw no chance for such integration. One eighth (some 14 percent), however, had accepted that the two categories would never merge: "These are another kind of people and do not understand us". The latter group was an emergent pariah population who no longer made efforts to be accepted by locals. Three months later, in July, 60 percent expellees considered themselves Germans but 40 percent did not. In November, nearly 90 percent felt they were Germans but, at the same time, only some 15 percent were prepared to stay. 84 percent would have returned "home" if only they could, at least some 60 percent wanting this emphatically.[60]

In other words: From the perspective of expellees, a growing awareness of their being German – which they had in common with local residents – was paralleled by an equally overwhelming desire to return to their homeland whenever it would be possible. In this vein, the vast majority who considered themselves Germans may have felt to be *different Germans* than the locals in Germany's Western zones. At the lowest end of the scale, to be sure, were 15 percent expellees who had become socialized into a pariah status. At the other end of the scale were some 15 percent expellees who were willing to become integrated into the local in-group, which may be learned from the fact that they said they did not wish to return "home".

In contradistinction, locals consisted of a growing majority who considered expellees as foreigners or people who could not be regarded as German citizens, a minority of a fifth or a fourth who wished to actively discriminate against expellees in the political and economic realms, and a possibly diminishing minority who felt that expellees were German citizens who were to be integrated into social life in the Western zones. In more detail: In March, at least the two thirds of locals who never had spoken with an expellee may have regarded them as not fully belonging to the German population, or outright foreigners. The same proportion felt that there was not enough food and housing to provide for the expellees in the same way as for locals. A quarter of locals were against extending equal political rights to expellees, and some 20 percent wanted to deny them economic equality. In short, more than half regarded expellees as foreigner-like out-group members whom they were prepared to exclude from equal access to food, housing, or – to a lesser extent – jobs. About a quarter felt that expellees should be given second-class citizen status. Four months later, at least one quarter and possibly up to one half of native Germans considered the expellees foreigners, or at any rate did not wish to accept them as German citizens. Again, about one quarter desired to see them degraded to second-class citizen status. Another four months on, somewhat under one half of natives either felt that expellees were no German citizens or expressed no opinion on the matter. Not more than one half expected that the two groups of the population would ever so much as get along with each other. A full over 90 percent felt that expellees belonged to their homelands and should return there whenever they could.

In other words: Among locals, a large majority did not consider expellees potential local Germans; this group grew from about half to over nine tenths in the time period between March and November, 1946. Among them was a minority of about one quarter who favored an inferior political and economic status for expellees. In this vein, nearly the entire local population endorsed more or less sharp segregation between themselves as in-group and expellees as out-group. In fact, only a minority of some ten percent felt that expellees should not return to their homelands, and this group may also have welcomed gradual assimilation.

To analyze this kind of ethnocentric exclusion, Schütz coined the term of "imposed typification". Applied to the situation after World War II, it meant, for one, that Silesians, East Prussians, Sudeten Germans, Balts, and others from many other cultural backgrounds or geographical origins were lumped together under the wholesale label of "refugee," which was used both by locals and expellees. The label, to be sure, was discriminatory inasmuch as it accrued generalized traits – including characterizations such as "beggar," "scrounger," or foreigner – to the newcomers who were treated as if they were no individualized persons. Therefore, Simmels worst-case-scenario of the situation of stranger – that of the non-relation as it divided ancient Greeks from "barbarians" – came true for the relations between German locals and refugees in the immediate post-war period.

The second side of "imposed typification," following Schütz, is that such generalization of typifications produces a "feeling of degradation" in those who are being typified in this consummatory way. "Identification ... of the individual's personality with the imposed typified trait is one of the basic motives for the subjective experience of discrimination," Schütz explains.[61] In the case of expellees in Germany after World War II, no doubt, such feelings of degradation were not wholly unjustified. About one quarter of locals openly advocated in public opinion surveys that expellees be reduced to political and economic second-class citizen status. At the same time, expellees themselves voiced their feelings of being discriminated against in such documents as the newspaper article quoted above expressing *resentment* against locals. While expellees, irrespective of whether disabled or not, were given the hardest work to do, stated an expellee-author who signed with his initials, local dodgers ("Drückeberger"[62]) had the least strenuous jobs and did "as little work as possible, even young people".[63]

What was Schütz' answer to the question of how "imposed typification" that could result in hostile segregation between in-group and out-group could eventually be overcome? In 1944, he proposed assimilation. That is, he advocated that the stranger whose out-group status pervaded his typifications even of in-group practices which he perceived in the new surroundings should abandon his original world view and turn into a fully-fledged member of the (new) in-group. By this process of assimilation, the stranger turning member would acquire the taken-for-granted world-views and role behaviors of group members to an extent that eventually only faint feelings of habitual uncertainty might remind him of his past.

In 1955, however, Schütz was more specific how such inclusion could function. Equality between former in-group and out-group members had to be achieved through sameness of their structures of relevances, he now observed. Despite the fact that some of the relevances of those who now were recognized as belonging to the same category of person might otherwise be vastly different, the point was that members with previously different systems of relevances would now have to become the same. In other words, the in-group's and also the out-group's self-interpretations of the world taken for granted by them were to disappear as separate entities, and merge into one taken-for-granted world interpreted by heterogeneous members. In this "one" world, homogeneous domains of relevance would apply constituting equality as it, in turn, facilitated inequality. This meant that individuality resulted from equality, as Schütz maintained on the basis of an argument quoted from Simmel: "Wherever an attempt is made at effecting equalization, the individual's striving to surpass others comes to the fore in all possible forms on a newly reached stage. But, says Simmel, it makes a characteristic difference whether this attempt at winning cherished values is to be obtained by means of abolishing what he calls the 'sociological form' (and what we should call the prevailing system of relevances and their order) or whether it is to be obtained *within* this form, which is thereby preserved".[64] What mattered was that equality of opportunity opened up, in fact, a chance for individuals to become unequal in their respective individualized selves or roles. An increase of such scope for potential individualization, to be sure, could only be achieved if members of a group that overcame in-group/out-group segregation were aware of their equality of opportunity. Only if they could act on the basis that their chances were the same, and all members had equal opportunities to reach important goals or values, members could attempt self-realization through differentiation within the (in)group's system of relevances. Schütz, considering the problem how equality could mean individualization when it united different groups rather than distinguishing them, had this to say about the individual's "chance given to him, as a likelihood of attaining his goals in terms of his private definition of his situation within the group": "This subjective chance exists ..., from the subjective viewpoint of the objectively qualified individual, only under certain conditions: 1. the individual has to be aware of the existence of such a chance; 2. the chance has to be within his reach, compatible with his private system of relevances, and has to fit into his situation as defined by him; 3. the objectively defined typifications or role expectations have to be, if not congruent, then at least consistent with the individual's self-typification, in other words, he has to be convinced that he can live up to the requirements of his position; 4. the role for which the individual is eligible has to be compatible with all the other social roles in which he is involved with a part of his personality".[65]

It was here that Schütz spoke not only of a "translation of typification" but even of a "formula of transformation" which had to be found. Only through such translation eased by what he called a "formula of transformation" could it be avoided in the relationship between an in-group and an out-group that their typifications (including role behaviors) "remain ... ununderstandable" to each other. The latter, he added, frequently was 'facilitated' in the cases where "they are considered to be of minor value and inferior".[66]

Our hypothesis is that American Military Government "found" the "formula of transformation" when it treated locals and expellees strictly alike as "Germans". Against considerable resistance from German authorities and also local populations, American Military Government insisted that equal rights applied to all Germans and that segregation would not be tolerated. With the "absolute power" which Military Government enjoyed as occupying force, it decreed consistently and persistently that no differences were to be tolerated between the two parts of the population from the very beginning of the occupation regime. Only in the years 1947-8, on the basis of advice given it by visiting experts who had been inspecting the American zone to judge the severity of the refugee problem, OMGUS revised its policy and allowed cultivation of cultural heritage of Silesians, East Prussians, etc., in the interest of its firm and unchanged aim, namely, to prevent emergence of a pariah population among Germans.

## 5 AMERICAN MILITARY GOVERNMENT POLICY AGAINST DISCRIMINATION OF REFUGEES

The post-war social meaning structure among Germans in Germany was characterized by a tendency expressed by local authorities in the newly created Laender and even the Laenderrat to prefer administrative measures or legal regulations discriminating against refugees. Germans in the immediate post-war era generally felt that peaceful cooperation of groups was an illusion – which, to be sure, might have been a belated remainder of their previous Nazi mentality. Primarily interested in the well-being of long-standing residents, local and Land administrations wanted to avoid problems when they tended to discriminate against refugees; since shortage of jobs and housing appeared to make life difficult enough even for the indigenous population, they did not wish to further aggravate a difficult situation. Ministers as well as mayors attempted to keep the number of refugees as low as possible for whom they had to provide housing, schooling, jobs, etc. German authorities, in general, were less than keen to care for expellees and often openly discriminated against them. Their politics strengthened negative typification schemes that emerged in the population at large.

How did American Military Government change this situation? Two types of measures were destined to deny that there was a difference between the two groups of Germans; such denial, on the one hand, was to indirectly put pressure on German authorities that they secure equal rights for expellees, and, on the other hand, eventually to entice locals to realize that expellees were Germans just like themselves. The two types of measures were, first, orders or demands that German legislation secure equality and, second, programs that encouraged expellees/refugees to preserve their cultural heritage in non-political realms.

### *5.1 Political and Economic Citizenship Rights*

The main purpose of American Military Government was to establish equal rights for expellees on a basic citizenship level, that is, equality concerning the right to live, work, vote etc. Every administrative measure enacted by the Germans had to be confirmed by Military Government, and the latter staunchly refused to give permission to programs discriminatory in any way against expellees. The following letter by William W. Dawson, Military Governor of Wuerttemberg-Baden, addressed to Prime Minister Reinhold Maier, dated 22 June 1946, shows how criticism of and comment on a plan submitted to Military Government for approval could act as instigation for change:

> 1. The plan for German expellees and refugees presented 11 May 1946 by the cabinet of Ministers to Military Government Wuerttemberg-Baden appears: a. Inadequate to achieve the objectives of Military Government. b. To be organized without close reference to the basic principles approved by Military Government. 2. Basically it is the purpose of Military Government to have these German expellees and refugees absorbed by the present population and accepted, so far as possible, on an equal basis without prejudice or discrimination. The plan submitted 11 May 1946 is an emergency plan only, providing for the primary reception and distribution of the expellees and refugees, but it lacks an affirmative long range program that will accomplish the purpose of Military Government. 3. The organization as outlined in the plan submitted, appears to be built somewhat on the principles of separation: separate budgets, separate staff, separate schools, separate societies (sic) of settlers, separate industries. The basic principle approved by Military Government is one of assimilation, not separation. (...) 4. No part of the plan should establish a special category within the population. It is recommended that there be no special registration of expellee by the land[67]

The memoirs of Lucius D. Clay bear witness to the intensity with which equality between expellees and locals was pursued by Military Government. In 1950 when Clay wrote his memoirs, he remembered that he even had put pressure on the Minister Presidents of the three Laender to make them abstain from discriminatory measures:

> We became distressed over the treatment being accorded to the expellees which came in part from wishful thinking that their stay in Germany was temporary. Therefore, in February 1947, the minister-presidents were advised of our concern in the words: 'These people are with you. They must be absorbed and your good citizenship in the future depends on the manner in which you absorb them. If it continues as at present, you will be establishing a minority group fostering

> hatred and hostility for years. You should know the difficulties that minority groups have caused in the past'. On several occasions it was necessary to insist on improved food collections as a requisite to continued American aid[68]

The quotation states that the Minister Presidents apparently were told that distribution of food which at the time was being imported from the U.S. to ameliorate hunger in the German Laender might be made dependent on the latters' policies in the expellee question. The Laenderrat's reaction was prompt. On explicit suggestion of Military Government, in 1947, it passed a law regulating admission and naturalization of refugees "which guaranteed their political rights and equal opportunities for welfare assistance and employment. They became citizens with full rights in German economic and political life. State legislative bodies set up advisory boards for refugees with half their members expellees".[69]

Another example is the following "Draft of Directives for caring of Refugees and Expellees" which was authored by the Office of Military Government of Wuerttenberg-Baden (OMGWB) and has been preserved among documents detailing the latter's work (the political use of these directives is unclear, however). Among the ten drafted requirements for caring for refugees and expellees in the Land were the following:

> *§ 4. Educational Institutions:* 1. The general educational institutions are at the disposal of the refugees and expellees according to the prescriptions valid for their use. 2. The general obligatory schooling is also applicable to them.
>
> *§ 5. Taking part in Associations:* 1. The refugees and expellees can take part in the same manner as the old time residents in political, socio-political, cultural, religious, social and economical associations which have been approved by Military Government. (...)
>
> *§ 6. Taking part in Economic Life:* The free exercising of a profession appertains to the refugees and expellees in the same manner as to the old time residents according to the laws and the provisions issued by Military Government. (...)
>
> *§ 8. Membership with Social Insurance:* 1. Commensurate with their occupation the refugees and expellees are liable to insurance in the same manner as the old time residents. They take part in the same manner in the earnings of the bearers of the insurance. 2. The claims acquired by the refugees and expellees will be maintained to the issued special regulations[70]

To avoid political conflict between privileged locals and disadvantaged expellees/refugees, and to speed up their cooperation in the political arena, expellees were allowed neither their own pressure groups nor political parties. No separate press representing their interests was to be established. It was only as late as 1948 that an organized interest group speaking for "expellees and the disinherited" ("Heimatvertriebene und Entrechtete") was established which, in 1949, when Military Government ended, was transformed into a political party.

Military Government was concerned that expellees should have the same economic rights as locals. The latter, however, were far from keen to extend such rights to the newcomers. In fact, since firms usually belonged to local owners, locals had a far better chance than expellees/refugees to find jobs on the tight labour market. When expellees/refugees attempted to open up their own firms, they were discouraged by local authorities who put all sorts of difficulties into their way in order to keep them from becoming competitors to local firms. Local government in cities and towns systematically excluded expellees/refugees when trade licenses were being issued which were required for setting up new commercial enterprises. Locals preferred to hold on to a Nazi regulation that gave local employers a right to decide whether or not new enterprises were needed in the special field where a trade license was being sought. Only after the currency reform of June 1948, American Military Government decreed – against vigorous protest from the Laender who refused to enact the necessary laws – that freedom of trade was to be established in all parts of the American Zone from January 10, 1949 onwards. Within a matter of months, the number of trade licenses multiplied spectacularly: Due to the large proportion of expellees/refugees who at last could now start their businesses, between January and April, 1949, in Hesse, the number of new registrations rose from 5,240 to 20,703, in Wuerttemberg-Baden from 6,598 to 16,505, and in Bavaria from 1,940 to 55,791. For American Military Government, to be sure, this meant establishment of the "right to economic self-determination" which Clay and his staff considered a vital prerequisite for a democratic society which they promoted for Germany.[71]

### *5.2 Cultural Citizenship Rights*

Additional to securing equal political and economical rights for expellees, American Military Government decided from about 1948 onwards that successful integration meant cultural identification. In order to see their policies evaluated but also be advised on what line to take regarding these issues, Military Government invited three "visiting experts"[72] to prepare memoranda on present problems and future policies. These experts proposed that cultural identity be encouraged, on other than political fields: "The most difficult, but one of the most important aspects of assimilation is that of cultural integration into German communities," wrote Jane Carey a New-York based expert.[73] A central hypothesis of these memoranda was that the new citizens could enrich the culture of the local in-group by practicing their own distinctive folkway traditions.[74] The experts were especially interested in specific technical skills rooted in traditional industries which refugees had brought with them from their native regions or countries. The experts' advice was to preserve and protect such indigenous skills or industries of Silesians, Sudeten Germans etc. against discrimination from local inhabitants. Carey in her report wrote: "The development of expellee industries should become an integral part of a general plan of development, if possible, for the whole of western Germany".[75]

Another recommendation was that folklore groups and similar associations could help preserve the cultural heritage of regions of former Germany and East-Central Europe that had been home to the expellees. Indeed, a study carried out in the 1980s documented retrospectively that such group meetings helped expellees/refugees to cope with their often traumatic experiences connected with their expulsion und flight.[76] Another of the "visiting experts," London School of Economics professor Julius Isaac, advised Military Government to support cultural associations because they helped with integration into the new surroundings and could curtail feelings of isolation. This, in turn, could help rebuild a social and cultural identity of expellees, he recommended, who would thus be able to cope with the exigencies of their new beginning:

> There is, therefore, little point in discouraging newcomers from forming local associations with a view to maintaining social contacts, giving mutual aid and preserving the traditions of their country of origin. On the contrary, it may be worthwhile to support such associations; they have an important function to fulfill during the period of transition, they give greater self-confidence to the individual who otherwise would feel isolated in a foreign world and they can be the source of invaluable advice for him in his attempts to adjust himself to his new environment[77]

Furthermore, he felt, on a local level cultural gatherings might improve reciprocal acceptance between old and new residents. Isaac advocated an "education for assimilation," as a step of a "reunion-program" which would accomplish some kind of "education for citizenship":

> Education for assimilation should be an essential part of the program of education for citizenship. Indeed, good citizenship implies readiness to understand each other and to cooperate for the common weal. Greater efforts should and probably could be made to bring old and new citizens socially together, to give the newcomers a fair share not only in the rights, but also in the duties of citizenship. Open meetings at which all topics of interest to the community could be freely discussed with representatives of MG and German administration have proved a success in Wuerttemberg and should be arranged on a broader basis in the whole zone[78]

From 1949 onwards, under the High Commission of the United States in Germany (HICOG) which replaced Military Government, a new institution was created whose task was to mediate between locals and expellees, among other similar objectives. "Kreis-Residence-Officers" organized "town-hall-meetings" whose aim was to bring together all inhabitants, locals and refugees, to discuss problems of common concern. These occasions became public forums to voice opinions, not always free from conflict, but they were an enormously successful arena for discovering and discussing misunderstandings as well as joint interests.[79] Disputes frequently were frustrating – but step by step over a time period of some three years natives and newcomers came to listen to each other at these meetings.

How much American Military Government came to care about cultural citizenship rights for the expellee population may be learned from the speech given by Military Governor of Wuerttemberg-Baden, Charles M. LaFollette, at the first cultural festival for expellees in Stuttgart-Bad Cannstatt in October, 1948. With support from Military Government, expellees could display their cultural heritage (dance, theater, handicraft etc.) as they were to become one and the same with local Germans, LaFollette said in his opening speech:

> Today no thinking person can deny that the new citizens have been absolutely essential to the rebuilding of this state. They have taken up the tools and the tasks of those who have fallen and those who have not been able to return. And only the new citizens can provide the labor necessary to rebuild and expand your cities, rebuild your roads, your railroads and your economy. And tomorrow? As the new citizens take their place alongside the old citizens during the coming years of hard work necessary for the new Germany, the 'alt' and the 'neu' before the buerger will gradually disappear. Heinz Schmidt, 'the Neubuerger from Karlsbad,' will become Hans (sic) Schmidt, 'my friend on the Betriebsrat'. All citizens must work together if there is to be a free and prosperous Germany. But the alt and the neu must work together for perhaps a more important reason. It is horribly evident from the tremendous destruction and suffering during this past war that the only hope for a peaceful world is for closer economic and cultural relations among all peoples than ever before (...)[80]

## 6 THE TRANSFORMATION OF GERMAN SOCIETY

Schütz postulated a "formula of transformation" that could help merge two realms of typification into one. Previously more or less irreconcilable typifications, he suggested, could be incorporated into one and the same meaning structure through a process which allowed typifications to be translated into each other, or become one realm of differentiated orientations.

In the time period subsequent to World War II, separate realms of typification first came to develop in West Germany. Expellees/refugees who arrived by the million were not welcomed by the native population but were mainly treated as if they were intruders, even foreigners. Surveys conducted by the Information Control Division Survey Analysis Branch discovered that a sharp segregation developed between locals and expellees/refugees who began to treat each other as out-groups. Indeed, over the year of 1946 the proportion grew both of expellees/refugees and locals who did not even see that the newcomers attempted to be assimilated into the local in-group, and each group increasingly developed into an in-group who saw and treated the other as an out-group.

In this situation, Military Government provided a "formula of transformation" by its program of inadvertent integration of expellees/refugees through policies which were strictly opposed to any (further) segregation. This "formula of transformation" was based on the notion that refugees were inhabitants like locals who had the same national (German) identity. Therefore no differences between old and new residents were allowed with regard to central citizenship rights, especially concerning political and economic self-realization (despite the fact that realization of these rights was frequently denied to refugees through obstruction by locals). In 1948, following the advice of "visiting experts" who had been asked to evaluate the situation, Military Government somewhat changed its "formula of transformation"; from now on, the principle of equal political and economic rights for all Germans was supplemented with a policy of encouraging preservation of expellees/refugees' cultural heritage of folklore or trade. Under HICOG, this policy of reconciliation was continued, among other programs, by the extremely constructive work done by the "Kreis Residence Officers".

To be sure, Military Government policy was designed to convince rather than coerce the Germans. Re-Education aiming at Germany's (re)democratization meant to induce or encourage German practices in "clear" or "sound" areas of their behavior where Germans themselves could overcome their previous totalitarian structures.[81] In this vein, re-education sought to bring out in Germans indigenous forces which the psychologist Kurt Lewin, in 1943, had addressed as those of "self-reeducation".[82] Following a principle borrowed from psychiatry where re-education meant rehabilitation (recovery),[83] re-education practiced by Military Government had the purpose of making Germans learn to live in a democratic society of their own making. Military Government rather than imposing on Germans democratic attitudes wished to cajole Germans to see for themselves that only a democratic society was viable.[84]

From this vantage point, social change transforming Germany from dictatorship to democracy benefitted from Military Government's "formula of transformation" as it was related to refugees. Indeed, that separated groups of locals and expellees/refugees developed during the first years of the postwar period might have been a belated expression of Nazi-type mentality. No doubt, until 1945, a deep cleavage had existed between first-class Aryan citizens and second-class non-Aryan citizens, distinguishing further between an array of categories of population endowed with more or less restricted rights to income, power, prestige, or even life itself. In this situation, a "formula of transformation" that stemmed the tide of a return of Nazi-like exclusionary ethnocentric prejudices against refugees was badly needed; that it worked, no doubt, was due to the fact that it was not just a formula but a new mentality and even nationality that helped to integrate the millions of newcomers into the society of what was a defeated, devastated country.

Transformation, in Germany after World War II, was more than mere application of a "formula of transformation" helping to unite the separate parts of the population. What happened after World War II in Germany was transformation of an entire society; it led from charismatic-traditional to rational-legal authority, to use Max Weber's terms as they were applied by Parsons.[85]

No doubt, when Schütz in 1955 proposed a "formula of transformation," he did not think of Germany, not even post-war Germany, but he was concerned with the task of the United Nations who had published two memoranda on its refugee policy. Most certainly, Schütz could not envisage at the time the peaceful world-wide transformation of entire societies which, after forty years of Cold War, would produce a series of "velvet revolutions" between 1989 and 1994. In West Germany after the end of the Second World War, however, events occurred that could have informed Schütz of another arena of translation of typifications, leading up to a type of system transformation not unlike the change of entire societies in our own contemporary world in, for instance, Rumania, Poland, Russia, or South Africa today. What happened in Germany after World War II, we suggest, can serve as a model depicting paradigmatic processes of translation of typifications from heterogeneous to homogeneous categories. What Schütz discussed in his essay can serve as epitome of how citizenship is being extended beyond the borders of territorial or ethnic entities.

West Germany, the one democratic state and society on German soil between 1945 and 1989, underwent transformation – to paraphrase Hans-Peter Schwartz[86] – *from Reich to Federal Republic*. Until 1955, it regained (limited) sovereignty, passing through successive stages of economic recovery when it was one of the Marshall Plan recipient countries and eventually became a member of the European Community at its creation in 1958. West Germany, therefore, not only regained parliamentary democracy but gained a degree of democratization of social institutions unparalleled in its entire previous history.[87] In this vein, a new West-German national identity emerged after 1945. This identity replaced whatever remained of previous Germandom, and it was an effective alternative to nationalistic Nazi identity dominant in the so-called *Grossdeutsches Reich*. The new and different Germany, the Federal Republic as a state and society, had to abandon its traditional authoritarian tendencies before it could eventually settle with its – in the immediate post-war period, tentative – democratic way of life.

Concerning the refugee problem this meant that unity between refugees and locals grew when both were treated and acted as Germans in a German society adopting democratic institutions in a Western world of democracies. On the one hand, the defeated Nazi world had to be transformed into a democratic post-war world. Overcoming the Nazi type tendency to distinguish between first-class and second-class citizens, Germans had to accept democracy's legal, political, and social equality. This meant for Germans that they had to build from scratch what Talcott Parsons termed "societal community" of democratic societies – a community characterized by solidarity and mutual identification of its members.[88] In other words: German society became transformed into a democratic nation state, and this affected both old and new citizens alike who had to overcome Nazism and start from zero to build their post-war world of democratic institutions. Only through this thorough reconstitution of Germany's entire regime could national identity of West German citizenship develop. That is, integration of locals and refugees "worked" because both had to change; those who previously had been locals no longer were a privileged in-group, and equally those who were refugees now had to become West Germans like everyone else. Their new identity could make them equal because together they had to transform into one newly established community with democratic institutions.

Seen from a "Schützian Perspective," therefore, transformation meant that both groups, old and new German citizens, developed the same typification scheme(s) of membership in the societal community. These typification schemes were not related to geographical or political boundaries since everybody had to acquire a completely new – non-Nazi – German identity. Our empirical data picturing the post-war situation of refugees in Western Germany demonstrate how integration in the developing post-war German society had a bad start on both sides of the divide between refugees and locals. The most difficult boundary was the one established upon arrival of the newcomers who were treated as an out-group by the local in-group. The boundary meant hostile discriminatory typifications that had to be translated into unprejudiced judgments. Democratization of German society by Military Government, especially protection of basic rights of refugees in the first years after the war, was the most important step toward eventual sameness of West Germans. Reduction of inequality-producing boundaries between hostile groups subsided when all West Germans learned their new identity, every one shedding his or her previous Nazi-prone, discriminatorily nationalistic Germandom.

What does this entail for current debates on globalization and civil society? Our obvious conclusion derives from our baseline of social theory. Schütz' and also Simmel's observations on "The Stranger" incurring typification as a mechanism for distinction between in-group and out-group, may help to understand that equality means sameness of typification. Sameness of typification, however, does not usually develop automatically or easily. Schütz took care to point out that since typifications tend to distinguish between in-groups and out-groups, they frequently may lead to mutual classification between opposing groups as inferior or may hostile. Only a "formula of transformation," Schütz thought, can help to break down these barriers. "Translation of typifications," he suggested, is the first step toward an eventual merger between different groups or categories.

Germany's experience after World War II may help to envisage what route is most promising toward an eventual "one world" universalist civil society today. Total transformation of the identity of the out-group into that of the in-group is not required. Assimilation is not always the best answer to the question how borders and barriers can be overcome. At the same time, however, multi-culturalism may represent an even less viable solution because it tends to multiply social worlds (in-groups) in a way that could aggravate tensions between a growing number of in-groups looking at each other as – even hostile – out-groups. Like Schütz, we think that sameness of system of relevances allows all members to categorize each other as the same with respect to one important identification or identity, e.g., nationality or, for instance in the European Community, "Europeanness". Equal opportunities may serve as shared typification schemes defining commitments of membership.

To sum up: The more generalized and universalized democratic values are, the more particularistic and differentiated individual self-fulfilment may become. The two-step integration program of American Military Government in Germany after World War II for German refugees – establishing social equality but facilitating cultural diversity – was effective because it contained the "formula of transformation" for the entire German society from dictatorship to democracy. In the emerging Federal Republic of Germany, an entire society transformed through social change made possible by Military Government policies fostering new (West) German national identity internalized by locals and refugees alike. Together they became the inhabitants of Western Germany; today, the distinction between locals and refugees has long become utterly irrelevant for German citizenship.

## NOTES

1 We wish to thank Mathias Bös for his patience while this paper slowly took shape, and his helpful comments all along.

2 Ulrich Beck (1986): *Risikogesellschaft. Auf dem Weg in eine andere Moderne* (Suhrkamp, Frankfurt/Main); idem (1997): *Was ist Globalisierung?* (Suhrkamp, Frankfurt/Main).

3 Martin Albrow (1996): *The Global Age* (Polity, Cambridge); Albrow (1998): *Abschied von der Heimat.* Gesellschaft in der globalen Ära (Suhrkamp, Frankfurt/Main).

4 Roland Robertson insists that global and local structures merge into what he addresses as glocalization, an apparent link of global enterprises with local cultural scenarios which, in turn, situate worldviews in different parts of a fragmentized rather than unitary world; cf. Roland Robertson (1992): "Glocalization: Time-Space and Homogeneity – Heterogeneity;" Mike Featherstone/Scott Lash/Roland Robertson (eds.): *Globalization – Social Theory and Global Culture* (Sage, London) pp. 25- 44.

5 Martin Ferguson (1992): "The Mythology about Globalization," *European Journal of Communication* , Vol. 7, pp. 69-93.

6 In 1943, when World War II was still ongoing, Wendell Willkies's book *One World* signaled a future of humankind subsequent to the end of the most terrible of all wars. Willkies's book which sold over two million copies in the first weeks after publication alone, was the Republican Senate Leader's report on a trip around the world which he undertook on a war-related presidential mission. "If I had ever had any doubts that the world has become small and completely interdependent, this trip would have dispelled them altogether", he began, judging globalization to have become viable: "There are no distant points in the world any longer. ... Our thinking in the future must be world-wide " (pp. 5,6). As to America's rôle in such future "one world", he rejected isolationism ("narrow nationalism") or "international imperialism"

but endorsed "the creation of a world in which there shall be an equality of opportunity for every race and every nation" (p. 202). The road to choose, he recommended, was designated along the lines where America represented "a reservoir of good will" (Chapter 10). The latter fostered internationalism, not only as a political accomplishment but also as economic internationalism, that is, free trade supplemented by aid for the weak nations in the interest of welfare for entire humankind. In this scenario, the idea of liberation, replacing that of political domination or economic autarchy, creating a world of active solidarity was, for him, what made the Second World War worth fighting for (Chapter 11). That Russia, in a postwar future world order, would be a power and nation that America had to learn to live with, and that the Russian people despite even Stalin's government were a forceful source of humane strength, was, for Willkie, a lasting lesson learnt from his trip. It goes without saying that his suggestion for the post-war world was that Americans avoid the post-World War I mistake of retreat to isolationism, and go forward instead with their war-time allies to form a United Nations globalized structure of interdependent free countries. To be sure, much of Willkie's judgment on what he encountered in late 1942 does, in fact, appear amazingly familiar in the present-day situation labeled global. Cf., Wendell Willkie (1943): *One World* (New York, Simon and Schuster).

[7] Jean Cohen/Andrew Arato (1992): *Civil Society and Political Theory* (MIT Press, Cambridge).

[8] Ibid., p. 451.

[9] E.g., Elmar Rieger (ed.) (1992): *Bürgerrechte und soziale Klassen: Zur Soziologie des Wohlfahrtsstaates/ Thomas H. Marshall* (Campus, Frankfurt/Main/New York).

[10] William R. Brubaker (1989): "Citizenship and Naturalization: Policies and Politics," idem, (ed.), *Immigration and the Politics of Citizenship in Europe and North America* (University Press of America, Lanham) pp. 99 – 128.

[11] Bryan S. Turner (1993): "Contemporary Problems in the Theory of Citizenship," idem (ed.), *Citizenship and Social Theory* (Sage, London) pp. 1 – 18.

[12] Turner: "Outline of the Theory of Human Rights," idem (ed.), *Citizenship and Social Theory*, op. cit., p. 186.

[13] Ibid., pp. 179ff.

[14] To be sure, such criticism does not hold for, e.g., Saskia Sassen (1991): *The Global City – New York, London, Tokyo* (Princeton University Press, Princeton), or idem (1995): *Cities in a World Economy* (Pine Forge Press, Thousand Oaks) whose more focused argument is based on systematic interpretation of extensive statistical material.

[15] Immanuel Wallerstein (1974-1989): *The Modern World System I – III* (Academic Press, New York). Wallerstein based his conception of a world system on the hypothesis that a world capitalist system emerged which failed to be challenged by political revolutions in the 18th and 19th centuries. While Wallerstein thus took a globalization stance, he also embraced a Marxist baseline what reveals his detailed analysis nevertheless as a deterministic account of economic forces in history which he followed between the 16th and the 19th centuries.

[16] Max Weber (1968): "Die 'Objektivität' sozialwissenschaftlicher und sozialpolitischer Erkenntnis (1904)," idem, *Gesammelte Schriften zur Wissenschaftslehre*, 3rd ed., ed. Johannes Winckelmann (Mohr, Tübingen), pp. 146-214, and "Der Sinn der 'Wertfreiheit," der soziologischen und ökonomischen Wissenschaften (1917)," ibid., pp. 489 – 540.

[17] See also, Birgitta Hohenester/Uta Gerhardt: "Identität durch Integration. Vertriebene, Flüchtlinge und die Entstehung der deutschen Gesellschaftsgemeinschaft in der ersten Nachkriegszeit". To be published: Alois Hahn/Herbert Willems (eds.), *Identität und Moderne* (Suhrkamp, Frankfurt/Main).

[18] For references to Simmel quoted merely as a witness to the early history of the idea of inclusion/exclusion, cf., e.g., Ann Game: "Time, Space, Memory, with Reference to Bachelard," Mike Featherstone et al. (eds), *Global Modernities*, esp. p. 207, or Ulrich Beck (1996): "Wie aus Nachbarn Juden wurden," Max Miller/ Hans-Georg Soeffner (eds): *Modernität und Barbarei* (Suhrkamp, Frankfurt/Main) esp. p. 323; for a comprehensive study using Simmel's as well as Schütz's viewpoints as a point of departure, see Lesley D. Harman (1988): *The Modern Stranger. On Language and Membership* (Mouton de Gruyter, Berlin etc.). Harman recognizes that Simmel conceived of the stranger as an ideal type and cites related images in American sociology such as that of the marginal man, and he appreciates Schütz's conception as related

to language. "Where Schütz stopped, however, and where this inquiry must begin, he writes, is with the notion that membership competence *can be achieved* " (p. 38). "This book is an attempt to free the stranger from being an outsider," he clarifies his intention to show that membership means that in the midst of a community are all sorts of strangers that are keen to become or want to be full-fledged members. Indeed. Harman suggests, society consists of "a world of strangers" where "the modern stranger is engaged in an ongoing quest for membership *from within*" (p. 44). "With modernity has come the need on behalf of the modern stranger to *recognize* community with potential others and *negotiate* membership on the basis of minimal indicators of commonality" (p. 127). In this, Harman holds against Simmel and Schütz that they presumed an "inner-directed" individual who either does or does not belong to a community, that is, either is a member or a stranger. This he wishes to contest by showing how most individuals, indeed, are both. Our point is, however, that this neglects the basis of identification which constitutes membership; it appears noteworthy that Harman fails to recognize how important identification is for identity constituting membership. In this respect, our approach differs from the analysis which Harman presents.

[19] Georg Simmel (1892): *Probleme der Geschichtsphilosophie* (Duncker und Humblot, Leipzig), and idem (1908): *Soziologie*. Untersuchungen über die Formen der Vergesellschaftung (Duncker und Humblot, Leipzig), and Alfred Schütz (1932): *Der sinnhafte Aufbau der sozialen Welt* (Julius Spring, Vienna), transl. (1967): *Phenomenology of the Social World* (Northwestern University Press, Chicago).

[20] Alfred Schütz: "The Stranger: An Essay in Social Psychology," reprinted in Arvid Brodersen: (ed.) (1964): Alfred Schutz, *Collected Papers, II, Studies in Social Theory* (Martinus Nijhoff, The Hague) pp. 91 – 106.

[21] Ibid., p. 96.

[22] Alfred Schütz: "Equality and the Meaning Structure of the Social World," reprinted in Arvid Brodersen, (ed.) (1964): Alfred Schutz, *Collected Papers, II, Studies in Social Theory* (Martinus Nijhoff, The Hague) pp. 226 – 274.

[23] Ibid., p. 246.

[24] Ibid., p. 257.

[25] Ibid.

[26] Georg Simmel (1908): "Exkurs über den Fremden," *Soziologie* (Duncker und Humblot, Leipzig), translated The Stranger (1971): *Georg Simmel on Individuality and Social Forms*, ed. and with an introduction by Donald N. Levine (Chicago University Press, Chicago).

[27] Ibid., p. 143.

[28] Ibid., p. 146.

[29] Ibid., p. 148.

[30] Schütz, *Equality*, op. cit., p. 232.

[31] Uta Gerhardt (1971): *Rollenanalyse als kritische Soziologie*. Ein konzeptueller Rahmen zur empirischen und methodologischen Begründung einer Theorie der Vergesellschaftung (Luchterhand, Neuwied-Berlin) and idem. (1980): "Toward a Critical Analysis of Role," *Social Forces*, Vol. 27, pp. 556 – 569.

[32] Ibid., p. 246.

[33] It is this group with which the present paper mainly will be concerned.

[34] See, for instance Rainer Geissler (1992): *Die Sozialstruktur Deutschlands* (Leske und Budrich, Opladen).

[35] Robert L. Koehl (1957): *RKFDV: Resettlement and Population Policy* 1939-1945, (Harvard University Press, Cambridge).

[36] It may be noted that, in terms of the *Bundesvertriebenengesetz* (Expelle Rights Act), newcomers from regions East of the Oder and Neisse rivers were called expellees. (Only those who arrived from Eastern Germany, i.e. regions West of the Oder and Neisse rivers, were refugees in official terms). However, locals usually labeled all newcomers refugees, and these themselves frequently did the same. Therefore, refugee (Flüchtling) was the category under which both locals and expellees referred to these newcomers in most contexts.

[37] Personal accounts are remarkably similar in these research findings that have been documented for expellees and refugees who arrived in all parts of Western Germany (see, for detailed documentation, Eugen Lemberg/Friedrich Edding (eds.) (1959): *Die Vertriebenen in Westdeutschland* – Ihre

Eingliederung und ihr Einfluß auf Gesellschaft, Politik und Geistesleben, 3 vol. (Ferdinand Hirt, Kiel); Wolfgang Benz (ed.) (1985): *Die Vertreibung der Deutschen aus dem Osten.* Ursachen, Ereignisse, Folgen (Fischer, Frankfurt/Main); Alexander von Plato (1985): "Fremde Heimat. Zur Integration von Flüchtlingen und Einheimischen in die Neue Zeit," Lutz Niethammer/Alexander von Plato (eds.), *'Wir kriegen jetzt andere Zeiten'.* Auf der Suche nach der Erfahrung des Volkes in nachfaschistischen Ländern, vol. 3 (Dietz Nachf. Publ., Berlin-Bonn) pp. 172 – 219; Christiane Grosser/Thomas Grosser/Rita Müller/Sylvia Schraut (1993): *Flüchtlingsfrage – das Zeitproblem.* Amerikanische Besatzungspolitik, deutsche Verwaltung und die Flüchtlinge in Württemberg-Baden 1945 – 1949 (Selbstverlag, Mannheim).

[38] Albrecht Lehmann (1990): *Im Fremden ungewollt zuhaus.* Flüchtlinge und Vertriebene in Westdeutschland 1945 – 1990 (C.H. Beck, München), p. 32, 33. (Our translation).

[39] Ibid., p. 33. (Our translation).

[40] Immo Eberl (1993): *Flucht, Vertreibung, Eingliederung.* Baden-Württemberg als neue Heimat, Begleitband zur Ausstellung, ed. Innenministerium Baden-Württemberg (Thorbecke, Sigmaringen), p. 158. Our translations from contemporaneous texts attempt to preserve the somewhat accusatory but equally matter-of-fact character of these accounts.

[41] The German word used was "Einlieferung" whose literal translation would be admission or delivery.

[42] Mathias Beer (ed.) (1994): *Zur Integration der Flüchtlinge und Vertriebenen im deutschen Südwesten nach 1945.* Bestandsaufnahme und Perspektiven der Forschung. Ergebnisse des Kolloquiums vom 11. bis 12. November 1993 in Tübingen (Thorbecke, Sigmaringen), p. 151. (Our translation).

[43] Ibid.; "Treck" was the word used for the mass exodus when expellees walked or were transported westward, often in freight trains over hundreds/thousands of miles in 1944-1947.

[44] ICD surveys were only carried out in the American zone of occupation, comprising the Laender of Bavaria, Wuerttemberg-Baden, Greater Hesse, Bremen, and the three Western-occupied sectors of Berlin.

[45] Surveys Branch: *Information Control Division,* Surveys Branche, OMGUS (1946): *Report No. 14A,* "German Attitudes Toward the Expulsion of German Nationals from Neighboring Countries," 8 July, p. 3.

[46] Ibid., pp. 3-4.

[47] Ibid., p. 1.

[48] Surveys Branch: *Information Control Division,* Surveys Branche, OMGUS (1946): *Report No. 28,* "An Investigation To Determine Any Changes in Attitudes of Native Germans Toward the Expellees in Wuerttemberg-Baden," 14. November.

[49] Ibid., p. 1.

[50] Ibid., p. 2.

[51] Ibid., p. 3.

[52] Ibid., p. 4. A "no opinion" category was usually provided in the questionnaires but data analysis for this question in the report did not show the proportion of "no opinion"s.

[53] Ibid., p. 4.

[54] Ibid., p. 6.

[55] Ibid., p. 6.

[56] Opinion Surveys Unit, Office of the Director of Information Control, OMGUS (1947): *Report No. 47,* "Opinions on the Expellee Problem," February 20, 1947.

[57] Ibid., p.3.

[58] Ibid., p. 5. PG, for former member of the National Socialist German Workers," Party (NSDAP), was the colloquial expression among Germans at the time for "Parteigenosse" of the Nazi Party.

[59] Ibid., p. 7.

[60] Opinion Surveys Unit, OMGUS: *Report No. 47,* p. 3.

[61] Schütz, Equality, op. cit., p. 257; see also above.

[62] This degrading characterization, which was here used against locals, had been a Nazi label scapegoating persons who were accused of lack of effort to work hard in the service of Nazism.

[63] See above.

[64] Schütz, Equality, op. cit., p. 267.

[65] Ibid., p. 272.

[66] Ibid., p. 246.

[67] See, OMGUS documents in Badisches Generallandesarchiv Karlsruhe, RG 260, 12/63-1/7.

[68] Lucius D. Clay (1950): *Decision in Germany* (Garden City: Doubleday), p. 100.

[69] Ibid., p. 314.

[70] See OMGUS documents in Badisches Generallandesarchiv Karlsruhe, RG 260, 12/22-1/29.

[71] Cf., for details, Hermann-Josef Rupieper (1993): *Die Wurzeln der westdeutschen Nachkriegsdemokratie* 1945 – 1952 (Westdeutscher Verlag, Opladen).

[72] These were: Julius Isaac, an economist and specialist for migration problems who taught at the London School of Economics and Political Science, Carlile A. McCartney, a specialist for Eastern Europe and formerly adviser of the League of Nations, and Jane Carey, a professor of social sciences from New York.

[73] Jane C. Carey (1948): *Assimilation of Expellees and Refugees in Germany*, October 16, p. 20; cf. OMGUS RG 84, POLAD/822/6 (Bibliothek Institut für Zeitgeschichte, Munich).

[74] See also, Christiane Grosser et al., *Flüchtlingsfrage – das Zeitproblem*, op. cit., pp. 32ff.

[75] Careys clarified: "Many newcomers were skilled at various handicrafts previous to their expulsion and flight to Germany. They were used to working in small shops. Thanks to their perseverance, they have set up a number of small industries in western Germany. Thus glass factories have been established by Sudeten Germans long famous for glass manufacture. The writer has seen some of the lace and leather industries which have been developed in various parts of the American occupation zone, together with a number of textile factories, important because of their employment of a large number of women. Some of the artificial flower and handkerchief industries from Czechoslovakia have now appeared in Bavaria, together with glove-making and wood-carving. (...). Further possibilities for loans to such small industries should be explored and the growth of cooperatives should be encouraged. The development of these small expellee workshops and industries must be fitted in with other German manpower needs and should be made part of the economic plan for German and western European industry". (Carey), op. cit., pp. 15, 17.

[76] Marion Frantzioch (1987): *Die Vertriebenen.* Hemmnisse und Wege ihrer Integration (Georg Reimer, Berlin).

[77] Julius Isaac (1948): *The Assimilation of Expellees in Germany*, p. 4; cf. OMGUS RG 84, POLAD/822/6 (Bibliothek Institut für Zeitgeschichte, Munich). In a second report a year later Isaac repeated his recommendation; viz. Julius Isaac, *German Refugees in the U.S. Zone 1948/1949*, e.g. p. 17; cf. OMGUS RG 260, 3/168-2/3 (Bibliothek Institut für Zeitgeschichte, Munich).

[78] Isaac 1948, op. cit., pp. 14-15.

[79] For the tasks of the "Kreis-Residence-Officers," viz. Rupieper, op. cit., pp. 83-109.

[80] Expellees – Cultural Weeks Oct. 1948; Charles M. LaFollette, Director of the Office of Military Government, Wuerttemberg-Baden, at the opening of the Cultural Weeks for New Citizens in Stuttgart-Bad Cannstatt, at 1030 hours, October 16, 1948, cf. OMGUS RG 260, 12/63-1/5 (Badisches Generallandesarchiv Karlsruhe).

[81] For further explication, see Talcott Parsons (1945): "The Problem of Controlled Institutional Change: An Essay in Applied Social Science," reprinted: Uta Gerhardt (ed.) (1993): *Talcott Parsons on National Socialism* (Aldine de Gruyter, New York), pp. 291 – 314.

[82] Kurt Lewin (1943): "Cultural Reconstruction," *Journal of Abnormal and Social Psychology*, Vol. 38, pp. 166 – 173.

[83] See, for a contemporary source, Richard M. Brickner (1943): *Is Germany Incurable?* (Lippincott, Philadelphia).

[84] Uta Gerhardt (1996): "A Hidden Agenda of Recovery: The Psychiatric Conceptualization of Reeducation for Germany in the United States during World War II," *German History*, Vol. 14, pp. 297 – 324.

[85] Talcott Parsons (1945) (see fn. 80). This essay is a social-theoretical analysis of the transformation of Germany at the end of World War II. Parsons relied on his previous analytical approach to Nazi Germany in Weberian terms where he had characterized Hitlerism as charismatic rule in Weberian terms.

[86] Hans Peter Schwartz (1980): *Vom Reich zur Bundesrepublik* (Klett-Cotta, Stuttgart).

[87] See, as an account of West German reconstruction, Axel Schildt/Arnold Sywottek (eds.) (1993): *Modernisierung und Wiederaufbau.* Die westdeutsche Gesellschaft der 50er Jahre (Dietz, Bonn/Berlin).

[88] Talcott Parsons (1969): "The Concept of Society: The Components and their Interrelations," and: " Theoretical Orientations on Modern Societies," both in idem., *Politics and Social Structure* (The Free Press, Collier Macmillan Ltd., New York-London), pp. 5 – 33, pp. 34 – 57; ibid., "Some Theoretical Considerations on the Nature and Trends of Change of Ethnicity," idem. Nathan Glazer/Daniel P. Moynihan (eds.) (1975): *Ethnicity*. Theory and Experience (Harvard University Press, Cambridge/Mass), pp. 53 – 84.

# III The Global and the Local: The Collapse and Reconstruction of Borderlines

CHRISTIE DAVIES, EUGENE TRIVIZAS

# THE COLLAPSE OF THE MORAL BOUNDARIES OF PERIPHERAL COUNTRIES

Until the mid-1970s the Republic of Ireland was a mighty fortress of traditional Roman Catholicism in which church and state were firmly, almost totally locked together.[1] Contraception, divorce and abortion were totally forbidden and there was a more rigorous censorship of all publications than in any other country in Western Europe; foreign newspapers and magazines would regularly have items deleted before they were delivered.[2] Despite the fact that some of Ireland's national heroes such as Roger Casement and Oscar Wilde had been notoriously promiscuous homosexuals, homosexual acts between males even in private were forbidden by law, though in practice prosecutions were no longer brought. Prejudice against and hostility towards homosexuals were strong and widespread.

Such a stance could be maintained because of Ireland's homogeneity and isolation. Almost everyone in the Republic of Ireland was both Irish and Roman Catholic[3]; to be Irish was to be Catholic. There was extensive emigration out of but no immigration into this isolated island on the far periphery of Europe and no foreigners. The Church firmly controlled every aspect of life[4] and moral Ireland seemed as stable as a rock.

However, within the next twenty years a series of dramatic social changes shattered the rock; the most interesting ones came from the outside and penetrated Ireland's moral borders in a way that the Irish political elite could not have foreseen but to which they had to adjust.

One of the most significant changes began in 1983 when Senator Norris of Trinity College, Dublin asked the Irish Supreme Court to strike down the Irish laws prohibiting male homosexual behavior in the light of a finding in the European Court of Human Rights in the Dudgeon case[5] that such laws contravened an individual's right to privacy. The Supreme Court refused to do so and ruled that the laws were still valid[6] even though unenforced in practice. The Irish Supreme Court judges declared that "Homosexuality has always been condemned in Christian teaching as morally wrong. It has equally been regarded by society for many centuries as an offence against nature and a very serious crime".[7]



*G. Preyer, M. Bös (eds.), Borderlines in a Globalized World, 175-188.*

In this way national and religious tradition was strongly affirmed and the moral fortress of Ireland upheld but it led directly to the forceful overthrow of that tradition from outside. Senator Norris went to the European Court of Human Rights in Strasbourg in 1988 and completely derailed the Irish tradition. The European Court of Human Rights ruled that:

> Such justifications as there are for retaining the law in force unamended are outweighed by the detrimental effects which the very existence of the legislative provisions in question can have on the life of a person like the applicant. Although members of the public who regard homosexuality as immoral may be shocked, offended or disturbed by the commission by others of homosexual acts, this cannot on its own warrant the application of penal sanctions when it is consenting adults alone who are involved.[8]

The Irish government was now trapped. It had either to repudiate and withdraw from the European Convention on Human Rights or to decriminalize homosexuality against the wishes of the Irish Roman Catholic Church and Irish public opinion.[9] In June 1993, after a long delay, the Irish Parliament voted that homosexual acts should be legalized despite considerable clerical opposition.[10] The external forces had triumphed over the internal ones and the moral boundary of Ireland had crumbled. Devout Irish Roman Catholics viewed this and other changes "as a frightening decline into the moral quagmire of Europe".[11] The change cannot be described as an aspect of glocalization for it was legal and political in its nature and had nothing to do with trade, economic interdependence with other states or the movement of people. The Irish government had assigned part of its sovereignty to the European Court of Human Rights because it thought it would make Ireland look good internationally. For Ireland to be fully part of the Council of Europe was for the country to appear important, progressive, part of the Western democratic order of things. It had never occurred to Ireland's leaders that the political rights guaranteed by the Convention could be applied to issues such as homosexuality or (worse still in the future) abortion. Also when the Convention had been drafted, many other democratic countries such as Britain and Germany still had laws prohibiting homosexual behavior[12] but by 1988 most other West European countries had abolished these laws. Since in practice the test applied by the European Court of Human Rights when deciding whether a violation of the right to privacy should or should not be permitted is to look at the relevant laws in the majority of the signatory countries, this left Ireland very vulnerable. In the past an Irish government might well have withdrawn from the Convention after this humiliating, indeed degrading, defeat but by 1988 Ireland was too enmeshed with the other European countries. The political elite were more concerned not to lose face in modern liberal Europe than to appease the local Roman Catholic church or to respond to the democratic wishes of its own electorate. The moral borders of Ireland had collapsed and moral power in Ireland had become European not Irish.

The downfall of the laws of Ireland criminalizing male homosexuality has been given prominence here partly because such laws are, as we shall see, strongly and closely tied to the maintenance of national, ethnic and religious borders and partly because Ireland's experience of having its laws regarding male homosexuality forcibly dismantled from the outside has also been similar to that of many other small peripheral nations and autonomous regions based on offshore islands such as Ulster, the Isle of Man, the Channel Islands, Cyprus and Tasmania. They have all in this way experienced a double deborderization as an outside institution has penetrated their moral space and forced them to legalize an activity which they had prohibited because it was perceived as a symbolic threat to the national ethnic and religious boundaries of the community itself. All borders and boundaries were thus suddenly demolished from the outside in a great moral implosion.

Such forms of "deviant" sexual behavior as homosexuality, bestiality and transvestism are more likely to be condemned and severely punished in societies whose leaders wish to maintain strong, clear and rigid social boundaries between their members and people of other nations, ethnic groups or religious persuasions. In such societies holiness consists in maintaining a very clear separation between the sacred and the profane, between the clean and the unclean, and in keeping all things in their correct categories and within their proper boundaries[13] as a perpetual reminder of the need to maintain intact the borders of the group. In such societies homosexuality, bestiality and transvestism, which are forms of sexual behavior that break down the boundaries between two of the most fundamental categories of human experience, viz. 'human' and 'animal,' 'male' and 'female,' are likely to be condemned and punished; and this is especially the case in circumstances where the borders of the group are perceived as under threat.[14] By contrast, in societies which are content to live with weak or ambiguous borders or where the borders are seen as safe, unthreatened, and perhaps unassailable, then the prohibitions against homosexuality, bestiality and transvestism will be much weaker or even absent.[15] People are indifferent to these forms of deviant sexuality in societies which are indifferent to the fate of their borders either because the borders are not a focus of great emotional commitment or because although valued they are not seen as in any kind of danger.[16]

Historically, the strongest taboos against homosexuality, bestiality and transvestism seem to have existed in religious communities such as the Jews or the Parsees, which have an exceptionally strong sense of their separate identity and social boundaries but where their communities lived in exile unprotected by the physical barriers of terrain or distance and survived only because they operated an elaborate code of ritual segregation.[17]

In the case of the Jews the key passages condemning these forms of deviant sexuality are to be found in the law of holiness of the Book of Leviticus:

> You shall not lie with a man as with a woman: that is an abomination. You shall not have sexual intercourse with any beast to make yourself unclean with it, nor shall a woman submit herself to intercourse with a beast: that is a violation of nature. You shall not make yourselves unclean in any of these ways for in these ways the heathen ... made themselves unclean. (Leviticus 18, 22-24)[18]

> If a man has intercourse with a man as with a woman they both commit an abomination. They shall be put to death; their blood shall be on their own heads. (Leviticus 20, 13-14)

> A man who has sexual intercourse with any beast shall be put to death and you shall kill the beast. If a woman approaches any animal to have intercourse with it you shall kill both the woman and the beast. (Leviticus 20, 15-16)

It is clear from the first passage quoted that the taboos are there in order to set apart the Jewish people, the chosen people of God from the heathen, the people outside the socioreligious boundary of the Jews. The taboos are part of an elaborate system of rituals and prohibitions that maintain and reinforce the borders of their group and ensure that the group will continue to maintain its separate identity even under adverse conditions. This is made even more explicit later in the law of holiness in relation to the separation of clean from unclean animals.

> I am the Lord your God: I have made a clear separation between clean beasts and unclean beasts and between unclean and clean birds. You shall not make yourselves vile through beast or bird or anything that creeps on the ground for I have made a clear separation between them and you declaring them unclean. You shall be holy to me because I the Lord am holy. I have made a clear separation between you and the heathen that you may belong to me. (Leviticus 20, 24-27)

The force of these rules lies in their structure, in their emphasis on the keeping apart of separate categories, in the everyday separating out of like from unlike, of clean from unclean as a perpetual reminder of the need to maintain the border between the Jews and the heathen. It is for this reason that homosexuality and bestiality are treated with such harshness; they are forms of sexual behavior that violate the boundaries between basic categories. For the Old Testament Jews homosexuality destroyed the definition of the two sexes who were each defined in relation to the other. The male was by definition complementary to the female and the proper sexual behavior of the male had to relate to the female. Any sexual behavior by a biological male directed towards another male would (at any rate as far as the scriptures are concerned) have placed him in the 'female' category where attraction towards a male is the expected sexual orientation. It is for this reason that sodomy is linked in the Old Testament to bestiality, sexual behavior that breaks down the separate categories of the animal and the human. This link has persisted down to our own time in the use of the English word buggery which can refer to either sodomy or bestiality.

Transvestism similarly breaks down the categories of male and female and in Deuteronomy, one of God's instructions delivered to Moses declares:

> No woman shall wear an article of man's clothing, nor shall a man put on woman's dress; for those who do these things are abominable to the Lord your God. (Deuteronomy 22,5)

All these activities were and are seen by the Jews as unholy, as defiling, together with a large range of other forms of prohibited nonsexual behavior that are in some way destructive of categories and boundaries.

The Jewish model of the punishment of homosexuality is important partly because it feeds into the Christian tradition and provides scriptural support for the legal prohibition of homosexual acts and partly because it shows us why some Christian societies are more censorious of homosexuality than others. In the core countries of Europe there is reasonable security of borders due to the size and influence of the countries concerned and there is a relative lack of concern with border preservation. Borders are weak and in a world where nationalism is in decline governments are willing for borders including moral borders to be left unprotected. In such a world activities such as homosexual acts and bestiality have no capacity to shock since they are no longer a metaphor for the implosion of a society as its moral borders collapse. Where there is no fear of such a disaster, the sexual acts that mimic that disaster no longer excite any great disapproval. Likewise the core countries of Europe are so secular that it is no longer possible to justify the persecution of homosexuals by citing Leviticus, Sodom and Gomorrah, St Paul or St Thomas Acquinas and there are no alternative secular moral authorities that can be used to justify this kind of moral prohibition.

A marked contrast can be seen if we turn to the isolated or beleaguered islands of Europe or Australia. In Ulster and in Cyprus there is strong moral disapproval of homosexual behavior because of the intense ethnic conflicts these peoples have experienced, in Ulster between Protestants and Roman Catholics and in Cyprus between Orthodox Greeks and Muslim Turks. People who live on an island often have a particularly strong sense of separate identity and if there are internal ethnic-religious conflicts these can be especially bitter. Borders are strongly prized, threatened and defended. In consequence homosexual acts, a metaphor of the local people's worst fears, are strictly prohibited; it has nothing to do with family life, for in many other highly familistic societies such as the peoples of the Maghreb there are no such prohibitions of homosexuality.

The liberalization of the law relating to homosexuality in England and Wales in 1967 did not extend to Ulster because the British Parliament knew that it would not be acceptable to either of the two segregated religious communities in the province because of their strong and threatened sense of boundaries and their associated religious fundamentalism. However, in 1981 the European Court of Human Rights ruled in the case of a Mr. Dudgeon that the (unenforced) laws in Northern Ireland penalizing homosexual behavior between adults were an unjustified interference with Mr. Dudgeon's right to respect for his private life and in breach of Article 8 of the European Convention on Human Rights signed by Britain as a member of the Council of Europe. Clause 1 of Article 8 says "Everyone has the right to respect for his private and family life, his home and his correspondence". A majority of the judges by fifteen votes to four refused to accept that such interference in the private lives of homosexuals was justified,[19] even though Clause 2 of Article 8 of the Convention would seem to permit this:

> There shall be no interference by a public authority with the exercise of this right except such as is in accordance with the law and is necessary in a democratic society in the interests of national security, public safety or the economic well-being of the country, for the prevention of disorder and crime, for *the protection of health and morals* and for the protection of the rights and freedoms of others. (Emphasis added)

The Court declared in the Dudgeon case that in a majority of the countries that had signed the Convention, including the rest of the United Kingdom, it was no longer thought necessary or appropriate to use the criminal law to penalize male homosexual acts.[20] It concluded from this that the 'protection of morals' achieved by making adult homosexual behavior a criminal offence could not be important enough to justify such a drastic interference with so intimate an act of private life and infringing the rights of the individual. The right to privacy as laid out in the European Convention and in Article 8 Clause 2 cited above has so many exceptions that it is almost vacuous and meaningless. The Court's ruling is not an assertion of right laid down in the text but is merely based on what has happened in the other Council of Europe countries. The Court in effect ruled that the moral and religious sentiments of any particular individual nation or province can easily be disregarded if these do not conform with the view taken in a majority of the states belonging to the Council of Europe. Thus a supposedly universal right to privacy was upheld in the Dudgeon case because, and only because, the test of what was necessary for the protection of morals was a European one. The "European test" of what was "necessary" now replaced any previous explicit or implicit test based on the particular national moral and religious convictions of the people of the specific nation or province in question (in this case Ulster), even though these local convictions are very strongly held whereas there is no common shared European morality on which all Europeans can agree.

The British government now decriminalized homosexuality in Ulster and brought the law in the province into line with the law in mainland Britain by an Order in

Council.[21] There was very strong opposition to this in Ulster from both Protestants and Roman Catholics; indeed it was about the only thing they have ever agreed about. The staunchly Protestant Democratic Unionist Party ran a campaign against the changes under the slogan 'save Ulster from Sodomy,'[22] and collected a very large number of signatures for a petition against the decriminalization of homosexuality from members of both the Protestant and Roman Catholic communities. However, the British government had no choice but to enforce the ruling of the European Court of Human Rights, regardless of local public opinion.

A very similar sequence of events to that in Ulster later occurred in the case of Cyprus, which country wished to retain its former colonial laws against homosexuality. It might have been thought that the Cypriots would have wanted to abolish this remnant of colonial rule now that they were fully independent. However, the reasons for wishing to keep a law that enforces private morality are often not the same as those for introducing it in the first place. The conflicts in Cyprus between Greeks and Turks that had led to the partition of the island with a great deal of wanton violence, including the widespread rape of Greek women by Turkish soldiers, have made the Greek Cypriots anxious about their identity and boundaries and determined to retain their old laws inflicting penalties on those sexual practices that break boundaries and threaten categories. The Cypriots' anti-homosexual laws were, however, struck down by yet another (eight votes to one) decision in the European Court of Human Rights along the very same lines as the decisions the Court had made earlier in the case of Ulster and the Republic of Ireland.[23]

Cyprus, like Ireland, is a divided island and lies at the very edge of Europe. The defeat of the Cypriots like that of Ulster and the Republic of Ireland was a victory of the center over the periphery. The strength of this point can be shown by looking at an essentially similar conflict in Australia where the state government of the off-shore island of Tasmania sought to retain and uphold its laws making sexual acts between male adults a criminal offence[24] at a time when the other Australian states were getting rid of such laws. By 1988 Tasmania was the only Australian state that still criminalized male homosexual behavior; all the other Australian states together with the Australian federal government had done away with such laws. However, attempts by a minority within Tasmania to bring Tasmania's laws into line with the rest of Australia had failed. In 1988 at the start of the campaign to liberalize the law the Tasmanian Attorney-General John Bennett had responded to the agitation for reform by declaring that "Hell can freeze over before they get homosexual acts legalized in this state".[25] By 1991 it was clear that the would-be reformers had not only lost their case but had annoyed local politicians and people to the point where the editor of a Tasmanian newspaper The Examiner (4 July 1991) could speak of "the beginning of a new era of poofter bashing".[26] Frustrated in Tasmania, the proponents of reform took their case to the United Nations Human Rights Committee. Australia had by now signed the First

Optional Protocol to the International Covenant on Civil and Political Rights, which allows individuals to bring accusations that their human rights have been violated directly to the UN Committee. In December 1991 a Mr Nick Toonan complained to the Committee that his rights had been violated in Tasmania and in 1993 the Australian Federal Government replied to an inquiry by the UN Committee, putting forward both the Tasmanian state government's case and its own point of view (which was totally opposed to that of the Tasmanian) saying:

> The Australian government does not accept that a complete prohibition on sexual activity between men is necessary to sustain the moral fabric of Australian society.[27]

The UN Committee ruled unanimously in April 1994 that the Tasmanian laws punishing homosexual behavior were quite contrary to international standards of human rights to privacy and to equality before the law. The Tasmanian must have known that they were bound to lose, for prior to the UN decision, George Brookes, a member of the Tasmanian Legislative Council, told a visiting British journalist "I would hope that the state government would tell the United Nations to go to buggery".[28] Within months of the UN decision the Australian Federal government had enacted the Human Rights (Sexual Conduct) Act, in effect a Federal privacy act.[29] It was one more clash between the local autonomy and state's rights of a small off-shore island and the might of a central government with a quite different agenda, which was seeking to enforce an international human rights agreement; the situation was almost an exact replica of what had happened in Ireland several years before. In the end the Tasmanian Legislature simply gave way due to the bad publicity the state of Tasmania was receiving and decriminalized homosexuality; once again the liberal center had prevailed over the moral periphery.

The evolution of events in the Isle of Man and the Channel Islands was very similar to that in Tasmania. After the Dudgeon case in Ulster the British government coerced the local parliaments of the Isle of Man and the Channel Islands (self-governing off-shore islands that are affiliated with the United Kingdom but which have their own autonomous legislatures) into abolishing their own local laws penalizing male homosexuality by putting financial and legal pressure on the islands, for example by threatening to withdraw their offshore banking privileges. The British government did not want to have to defend and lose another case in the European Court of Human Rights. The various islands were all small, compact, strongly God-fearing communities with a powerful sense of local identity that they wanted to defend in an increasingly cosmopolitan world; their laws against homosexual behavior were a potent and traditional way of doing this. However, the outside world i.e. the British government and behind the British government, the even more impersonal and unpersuadable European Court of Human Rights forced them to change their laws against their own wishes.

The controversies regarding homosexuality and the law may now be regarded as settled in all these countries but in the case of Ireland abortion, which is totally prohibited in that country, remains a central and controversial moral issue. There is a great deal of concern by anti-abortion forces in the Republic of Ireland that a decision by an external body such as the European Court of Human Rights or one of the organs of the European Community might force Ireland to permit abortion.[30] For this and other reasons the Irish anti-abortionists, a strongly Roman Catholic pressure group, obtained and won with a two-thirds majority a referendum in 1983[31] which made the total prohibition of abortion a part of the Irish constitution. Since abortion was already stringently forbidden by the existing law and liberalization of the law by the Irish Parliament or the Irish Supreme Court was extremely unlikely, it seems likely that this was a way of reinforcing Ireland's moral borders and of securing the Irish moral fortress against external penetration.

Faced with a total ban on abortion at home, Irish women obtained them abroad, usually in Britain. The Irish authorities now tried to stop this traffic first by denying them access to the information that would enable them to locate and contact British abortion clinics[32] and secondly by restricting their right to travel abroad for such a purpose. However, both prohibitions were vulnerable to intervention by the EC, as they violated the freedom of movement of persons, services and information. To forestall any such intervention, the cunning Irish Prime Minister Charles Haughey in 1991 persuaded the European foreign ministers to accept an amendment to the Maastricht treaty saying "Nothing in the Treaty on the European Union or in the treaties establishing the European Communities or in the treaties or acts modifying or supplementing those treaties, shall affect the application in Ireland of Article 40.3.3 (i.e. prohibiting abortion) of the Constitution of Ireland".[33] His crafty mixture of purposes was (a) to reinforce the ban on abortion and to prevent moves to help Irish women to travel abroad to have abortions and thus (b) to ensure Roman Catholic antiabortion support for the Maastricht treaty in the forthcoming referendum. The Irish economy was by now totally dependent on European grants, bribes, subsidies and trade[34] but equally the other European countries were anxious to avoid the embarrassment of an anti-Europe vote in a referendum on Maastricht and were susceptible to blackmail. Once again Ireland's moral borders had been reinforced; the other European countries were primarily concerned with economic and monetary issues and to obtain agreement on these were quite prepared to grant Ireland local moral autonomy. It was a case of the imperatives of economic globalization or at least continentalization being manipulated by a beleaguered country to defend its moral borders.

At about the same time a further crisis arose when a pregnant under-age girl of 14, the victim of unlawful carnal knowledge, who had gone to England with her parents to obtain an abortion was forced to return to Ireland by the Irish Attorney General (the family were threatened that if the abortion went ahead in England severe penalties would be imposed on them when they re-entered Ireland). The Irish Supreme Court later ruled that she be permitted to seek an abortion but on the grounds that she was suicidal and that her life was in danger; they did not say that she had a right to travel.[35] The judges specifically refused to refer the question of a right to travel under European law to the European Court of Justice and said it was a matter for Irish law alone. It would in a sense have been redundant for in 1991 in the case of Spuc vs. Grogan and others, the European Court of Justice had ruled that Irish women have the right to travel within the European Community to obtain abortions.[36] Then in 1992 the European Court of Human Rights awarded damages and costs of 200,000 Irish pounds against the Irish government for having violated human rights in 1988 when the Irish authorities had ordered the Dublin Well-Woman Center and Open Line Counseling to stop giving out abortion information.[37] The European Court of Human Rights declared that Ireland had seriously breached the Convention for the Protection of Human Rights and Fundamental Freedoms. Once again the moral borders of Ireland had been shattered and the universal moral values of Europe had prevailed over the local and particular morality of Ireland. The Irish government now took evasive action by sponsoring a new and complicated referendum on abortion and in November 1992 the Irish voted by a two-thirds majority in each case in favor of the right to travel and the right to have access to information about abortion facilities abroad. It was one more recognition that Ireland's moral borders had collapsed, in part because of hostile decisions made by European institutions to which Ireland was now firmly committed.

Ireland's moral borders were thus destroyed by the institutional imperialism of the European center which forced this tiny isolated country on the periphery to conform to the norms set by the hedonistic, individualistic, rights-obsessed core of Europe. Individuals in Ireland are far more free in consequence but Ireland is now less Irish, less distinctively different from the rest of Europe, a mere suburb of Europe.

One final question remains – why did the Irish political elite not fight harder against the penetration and destruction of Ireland's moral borders? The answer lies in the rapid social and economic changes that took place in Ireland itself in the 1970s and 1980s with the assistance of enormous grants, subsidies and indeed collective bribes from the European Community. This did not constitute glocalization, merely modernization such that a backward peasantry became a highly educated, urban labour force. Traditional morality collapsed and sexual permissiveness triumphed, much as had happened elsewhere in Europe in the 1960s. The proportion of illegitimate births rose from 2% of all births in 1961 to 20% in 1996 and one in three of first births are to unmarried mothers.[38] Divorce is now possible and contraceptive use, which in the past was effectively forbidden, is now legal and widespread. The influence of the Roman Catholic church is crumbling from within and it has lost its moral monopoly.[39] There is nothing odd about these changes[40]; it is just that they have happened much later and much faster in Ireland than elsewhere, but with one exception foreign influence has not been important. The one exception is British television which is important in Ireland because the Irish speak English and most of them live within range of British TV transmitters, designed to cover the UK and which cannot be jammed by the Irish without causing a major conflict with irate viewers in Britain itself. Those who don't, now have illegal boosters or cable. British television undermined Irish morality[41] rather in the way West German television undermined East Germany before unification, not because it was didactic about liberal values but because it portrayed an attractive alternative way of life. British television was permissive, affluent and hedonistic, an alluring, seductive alternative to the stern demands of Irish Roman Catholic morality. However, the other forces classed as 'glocalization' – the rapid movement of people, capital, data – were of no importance; indeed it is doubtful whether glocalization is in any way a significant or a coherent concept.

Glocalization is certainly not a particularly helpful concept for understanding the social and moral changes that have transformed the nature of the Western democratic, capitalist advanced industrial societies in the last half of the twentieth century. The problem is that glocalization as a process is three hundred years old and cumulative if not linear or continuous. Sometimes the globalizing changes have been rapid and sometimes slow but at almost any point in time during this period it would be possible for a contemporary observer to look back and say 'we are more global than we were fifty years ago'. Social, moral and legal changes have not followed a pattern that is anything like this. Crime rates, illegitimacy rates and the incidence of drug and alcohol addiction in Britain, Sweden and several American cities have followed a U-curve pattern, falling in the last half of the nineteenth century, steady in the first half of the twentieth century and rising rapidly since then.[42] Likewise the liberalization of the law in regard to homosexuality, abortion, pornography or the censorship of stage plays is a late twentieth century phenomenon; the nineteenth century Victorians and their European counterparts, though also exposed to the forces of glocalization, did the opposite. They tightened up their moral legislation and made it more restrictive.

There can be no doubt about the marked glocalization experienced by Western Europeans in the nineteenth century with the arrival of the railway and of the steam ship which brought Halifax in what is today Canada closer to London than the North of Scotland had been a hundred years before. The telegraph and the telephone made instant communication at the speed of light possible between opposite ends of the world and the ocean bed was soon covered in cables. The Internet and e-mail are just a minor refinement on this and the twentieth century adoption of travel by aircraft represents a much smaller relative speeding up than that experienced by the generation who moved from horse-drawn vehicles or wind-blown ships to the railway, steam-ship and (later) the automobile. Likewise the nineteenth century saw the rise of free trade and of the limited liability company, the widespread trading in shares and bonds across national frontiers and in many countries a very strong dependence on foreign trade, foreign markets, foreign raw materials and foreign components. Enormous colonial empires were created and there was massive emigration to new countries – to the United States, Canada, Australia, New Zealand, South Africa, Argentina and Brazil. It was a very global world indeed. Already at the beginning of the nineteenth century the Rev Sydney Smith in Britain called the Americans cheats and thieves because the reckless politicians of the state of Pennsylvania had defaulted on the payments due on its bonds raised in the London money market, thus impoverishing European investors.[43] The failure of the potato crop in Ireland in the 1840s resulted in America as well as England, Wales and Scotland being swamped with destitute emigrants. In the 1860s the cutting off of supplies of raw cotton from the American South during the War between the States nearly shut down Britain's largest industry, the cotton textile mills of Lancashire causing immense hardship to ordinary mill-workers. During the high noon of free trade in Britain in the late nineteenth century British farmers rapidly became aware that they could not compete against cheap wheat from Kansas or Saskatchewan or frozen meat from New Zealand or the Argentine. No farmers in contemporary Europe are exposed to anything like that degree of global pressure; they are grossly subsidized and protected.

At the end of the nineteenth and in the early twentieth centuries with the rise of a popular press fed by stories down a wire from the other side of the world, there was a new sense of instant excitement about distant battles and confrontations in Omdurman or Port Arthur, Fashoda or Mafeking, Agadir or Havana. It was a truly global, yet also an intensely national and nationalistic world. At the time it was argued that the enormous scale of economic interaction and interdependence and of foreign travel, migration and communications being experienced had made a future major war impossible. Norman Angell[44] published a book to that effect in 1914, not a good year for making such a prophecy. Unfortunately, the militarist von Bernhardi[45] turned out to be a more accurate prophet, for he could see that for all the interdependence and inter-communications between countries, it was the nation state that gave people their most fundamental identity; they were first and foremost German, French, British, Russian or American, however modern and international their experience might have become. Likewise in the early years of the twentieth century it was taken for granted in progressive circles that the radio and the airplane were bringing nations closer together, not just geographically but in a single moral and political community. As George Orwell pointed out[46], this view was nonsense. Rather these technological advances were a stimulus to nationalism and to national aggression. The growl of the bomber's engine and the blare of the radio broadcast dictator remain two of the most potent noise-based symbols of that era of nationalistic catastrophe.

The crude version of the glocalization thesis is then of very little value in explaining how moral and legal changes cross frontiers. Changes in global patterns of economic life and improvements in travel and communication do not provide an explanation for the breakdown of national moral frontiers; indeed this kind of approach to glocalization is only the old outmoded Marxist model of base and superstructure disguised in modern-sounding high-tech language. There is no such thing as a late capitalism whose inner dynamics shape social change; the key changes that have taken place in law and morality in the late twentieth century are a product of autonomous shifts within legal, political and mass media systems, both national and international, and of changes in the culture of the elites who control these systems. To seek an explanation in economics is a foolish irrelevance.

Ireland was not modernized by the global market-place but by bureaucratically awarded grants, collective bribes and subsidies from the European community. Thus the internal erosion of Irish morality through economic development has a European origin as do the external legal, political and institutional forces which broke through Ireland's moral boundaries. The internal support for these moral boundaries was being eroded at the same time that individual Irish citizens who felt oppressed by the monolithic Irish moral order were calling upon powerful external European legal and political institutions to destroy that moral order from outside. The Irish political and legal elite lost a series of important legal cases and was compelled to dismantle the legal framework enforcing Ireland's moral traditions or to suffer an intolerable loss of face, and to be excluded from being truly part of Europe by the liberal nations at the core of Europe. The periphery 'cannot hold, things fall apart'.[47] In the case of homosexuality the moral borders of Ireland no longer exist and in the case of abortion they are permeable, for information flows in and pregnant Irish women travel out. Nor has this been the experience of Ireland alone, for other small traditional peripheral nations, states and provinces such as Ulster, Cyprus, Tasmania, the Isle of Man and the Channel Islands have also experienced deborderisation and moral implosion.

## NOTES

1 Paul Blanshard (1954): *The Irish and Catholic Power, an American Interpretation,* (Derek Verschoyle London 1954;) Tom Inglis (1998): *Moral Monopoly, The Rise and Fall of the Catholic Church in Modern Ireland,* (University College Dublin Press, Dublin).

2 Paul Blanshard (1954): *The Irish and Catholic Power, an American Interpretation,* (Derek Verschoyle London 1954;) Tom Inglis (1998): *Moral Monopoly, The Rise and Fall of the Catholic Church in Modern Ireland,* (University College Dublin Press, Dublin).

3 Inglis (1998). See also Steve Bruce (1986): *God Save Ulster, the Religion and Politics of Paisleyism,* (Clarendon, Oxford) p. 152.

4 Inglis op. cit.

5 Bruce op. cit. p. 150.

6 European Court of Human Rights, Norris, 1989 Section III paragraphs 21-4.

7 European Court of Human Rights, Norris, 1989 Section III paragraph 24.

8 European Court of Human Rights, Norris, 1989 Section III paragraph 46.

9 Wendy Holden (1994): *Unlawful Carnal Knowledge,* The True Story of the Irish 'X' case (Harper Collins, London) pp. 197-8.

10 Holden op. cit. p 197.

[11] Holden op. cit. p. 198.
[12] Christie Davies (1975): *Permissive Britain*, (Pitman, London 1975).
[13] See Mary Douglas (1966): *Purity and Danger*, (Routledge and Kegan Paul, London 1966).
[14] Christie Davies (1982): "Sexual Taboos and Social Boundaries," *American Journal of Sociology* vol. 87, No 5, March, pp. 1032-63.
[15] Davies (1982) op. cit.
[16] Christie Davies (1983), "Religious Boundaries and Sexual Morality," *Annual Review of the Social Sciences of Religion* vol. 6, Fall, pp. 45-77. See also G. D. Comstock and S. E. Henking (eds) (1997): *Que(e)rying Religion*, (Continuum, New York), pp. 39-60.
[17] Davies (1983) op. cit.
[18] All biblical quotations are from the *New English Bible* (1970), (Oxford and Cambridge University Presses, London).
[19] European Court of Human Rights, Dudgeon Case 1983 para 52.
[20] European Court of Human Rights, Dudgeon Case 1983 para 60.
[21] Bruce op. cit. p. 150.
[22] Bruce op. cit. p. 150.
[23] European Court of Human Rights *Modinos v Cyprus* (Case No 7/1992/352/426). Judgement 20 April 1993.
[24] Miranda Morris, *The Pink Triangle* [University of New South Wales Press, Sydney 1995] pp. 1, 6.
[25] Morris op. cit. p. 41.
[26] Morris op. cit. p. 99.
[27] *Government of Australia submission to the United Nations Human Rights Committee* 27 September 1993.
[28] Morris op. cit. p. 104.
[29] M D Kirby, "Foreword to Morris," op. cit. p. xi.
[30] Tom Hesketh (1990): *The Second Partitioning of Ireland, the Abortion Referendum of 1983* (Brandsma, Dun Laoghaire), pp. 351, 354, 387. Holden op. cit. pp. 48-9.
[31] Hesketh op. cit. p. 52, Holden op. cit.
[32] Holden op. cit. pp. 165, 180-1.
[33] Holden op. cit. p. 185
[34] Holden op. cit. p. 183.
[35] Holden op. cit. pp. 140-3.
[36] Holden op. cit. p. 281.
[37] Holden op. cit. pp. 180-1.
[38] Inglis op. cit. p. 240.
[39] Inglis op. cit.
[40] Davies (1975) op. cit.
[41] Inglis op. cit. p. 246.
[42] Christie Davies (1994): "Does Religion prevent Crime? The Long-Term Inverse Relationship between Crime and Religion in Britain," *Information Theologiae Europae* pp. 76-93.
[43] Rev Sydney Smith (1854): "Letters etc on American Debts," *The Works of the Rev Sydney Smith*, (Longman, Brown, Green and Longmans, London) pp. 672-8.
[44] Norman Angell (1914): *The Great Illusion*, a study of the Relation of Military Power to National Advantage, (Heinemann, London).
[45] General Friedrich von Bernhardi (1914): *Germany and the Next War*, (Edward Arnold, London, 1914).
[46] George Orwell (1968): *The Collected Essays, Letters and Journalism of George Orwell*, (Seeker and Warburg, London 1968).
[47] With apologies to W. B. Yeats.

PETER WAGNER

# BEYOND "EAST" AND "WEST"

## On the European and Global Dimensions of the Fall of Communism

### 1 EUROPE'S BORDERLINES

With the fall of communism across Eastern Europe in 1989 and the official end of the USSR in 1991, the fundamental borderline that divided both Europe and the world after the Second World War, the line that defined "East" and "West," has ceased to exist. Two consequences can be said to have followed from this epochal event, one regional or area-specific, the other general or global.

As a regional or area-specific consequence, the space called "Europe" has opened up again. In the first place, national-states, societies, and peoples were released into (their) history (again). This release has also meant a new beginning for the idea of Europe itself. A common European home and a common European future cannot be envisioned and cannot be constructed anymore without the national-states, societies, and peoples of the former "East".

We can also easily identify a general or global consequence. "East" and "West" were not simply geo-political categories that referred to the *realpolitische* division of the world into two "great power" blocs after the Second World War. "East" and "West" also carried a meaning that was "epochal" in the sense of being constitutive of the identities, indeed the self-descriptions, of the actors within that divided world. "Communism," we remember, presented itself as the organizational alternative to liberal-democratic industrial capitalist market society – and was, in turn, also seen as such. The borderline that ran between "East" and "West" in general and global terms was conceived and accepted to be systemical. In this sense the condition of postcommunism is a truly global one.

Yet it would be highly misleading to present these two consequences as mere matters of fact. Instead, they present the core of postcommunist controversy. The space called "Europe" might have opened up, but it is clearly a pre-structured space, determined by the pre-existence of European integration (as institutionalized today in the EU), by memories of past relations and by expectations for the future. Moreover, the model of a capitalist market economy in conjunction with a liberal-democratic polity might have won the so called competition of the systems, yet its implementation in the



*G. Preyer, M. Bös (eds.), Borderlines in a Globalized World, 189-215.*

former East has proven to be far more difficult and the outcome far more complicated than the term victory tends to imply. What began as a historic moment of liberation has long since led to second thoughts, West and East.

Much of the disappointment, confusion, and resentment that has grown in response to the development of postcommunism and the new global order, I like to suggest, is conceptual in nature. At stake is a kind of discursive (re-) positioning, the appropriation and structuring of new realities. Now that the old demarcations of Europe and the world have fallen, a situation of disorientation exists.

The issue of identity- and boundary-formation(s) associated with the terms "East" and "West" therefore demands careful attention. All the more so, because in order to profit from the new European and global context in a peaceful and forward-looking manner, we need to come to terms with the ways by which and through which we construct and handle our (life-) world(s). Let me begin to develop the European and global dimensions of the fall of communism by reconstructing the borderlines that have defined "East" and "West" in the past (part 2). From the vantage point of such a reconstruction, it will be easier to come to terms with our new, postcommunist condition (part 3).

I will identify the following borderlines or demarcations as having defined "East" and "West" in the past, both as parts and in their relationships:

1. civilization/barbarism with its conceptual twin advanced/backward;
2. capitalism/communism with a further differentiation into 1) the external "Moscow Center" vs. "Washington Center" and 2) internal yet "passive" East/East borderlines between "Moscow Center" and its periphery, as well as between parts of the periphery, and equally internal and equally "passive" West/West borderlines;
3. what came to be known as the three worlds of development: First World, Second World, Third World.

In keeping with these three original delineations of "East" and/versus "West," we can distinguish the following signposts of the new and still emerging European and global post-communist condition:

4. a resurrection of the initial East/West borderline (above: 1);
5. the activation of East/East borderlines (above: 2);
6. the activation of West/West borderlines (above: 2).

While these three signposts demarcate the immediate response to the 1989/1991 changes, I think it is possible to distinguish yet another signpost based on the breakdown of the "three worlds of development" (above: 3), namely, development itself as a global, or better: globalized, issue.

Although in the course of the following discussion there will be plenty of reason to address the hard issues of and debates about political, economic, and social development, the subject of discussion concerns the discoursive formation of borderlines or demarcations as imaginological components of the process of spatial and societal identity-formation. As I will argue, the general line that has divided "East" and "West" *in modern times* is the issue of development, with its political, social, cultural, and economic dimensions transfigured into a spatial representation of its "Other". With the fall of communism, the issue of development has been opened up again in all its dimensions, including its spatial representation.This can be seen as the main characteristic of the European and global condition of postcommunism. In this sense, we all live in postcommunist societies today.

## 2 CHARTING EUROPE'S GREAT DIVIDE

Contrary to a certain contemporary bias, the line that defined "East" and "West" after the Second World War was in fact not the only and *not* the most fundamental border dividing and defining those two entities. Rather, in order to make sense of our contemporary situation of postcommunist reconstruction and invention, we need to appreciate how deep and how significant the division between "East" and "West" in and for Europe has been. And the best way to do this is to begin with the problematic nature of the space called "Europe" itself.

As with all other origins, the origin(s) of why and how the world was first divided and by whom is lost in history. What we do know in our case is that the peoples of the Greater Mediterranean area divided *their* world into three parts called Europe, Asia, and Africa, as early as the $5^{th}$ century B.C. Quite possibly, the term Europe itself is 3000 years old and of Phoenician origin, signifying a direction of travel and trade: "Ouroub," the direction/land of the setting sun, with "Asou," the East, as its opposite. Be that as it may, we also know that this initial division into three parts was not based on something we today would call a European consciousness. If a European consciousness existed at the time, it was formed by the Europe of antiquity, a Mediterranean, even Balcanic, Europe whose borders were by and large defined by its shores. What we today would consider Europe, the entire landmass to the North, no one really knew anything about. This "first Europe," envisioned by "our sea" and constructed by its borders, ended with the rise and expansion of the Roman Empire. The north became known (peopled one might say) and integrated into the European field of vision. Still, however, the focus of this European field of vision remained the Mediterranean. Thus, the initial borderline dividing Europe was a North-South one, with the South setting the discourse, trajectory, and pace of identity-formation and development, while the North did not even possess the status of a periphery.[1]

With the fall of the (original) Roman Empire, a fundamental and foundational shift from the South to the North of Europe sets in. This shift was also accompanied by a re-imagining of the space called Europe. Initially, we should note, this act of reimagining meant that the original South-North border simply moved further north. Until the 18th century, it was quite customary to speak or write about the "North" in reference to Scandinavia, the Baltics, and Russia. Yet this imagined geography also changed. At the end we find the modern consciousness of being European *and* the differentiation into West and East. Both, the modern consciousness of being European and the differentiation into West and East, were in fact mutually dependent, as we shall see. The story begins with Christianity and leads us via modernity to the problematic of communism.

### *2.1 Christianity*

Christianity provided the first imagery of "being European". As with other acts of imagining an identity, this one, too, was based on an act of differentiation as much as one of unification. In this case, a division was made into believers and non-believers, Christians and heathen.[2] Although it had been the barbarians from the North who sacked Rome in 410 AD and again in 455 AD, those barbarians as well as others to the south-east and east came to adopt Christianity as their religion in the course of the centuries that followed. By 1000 AD, a Christian Europe by way of a European Christianity had come into existence (the extreme north, Denmark, Norway, Sweden joined in the twelfth century). Yet this Christian space remained highly contested from its outside, and perhaps more than the common religious and cultural practices and beliefs, the external threat that Islam (first Arabs, later Turks) posed from the seventh century onwards led to a certain unified, European conception or self-awareness.[3] The crusades are here a case in point. It is with some ironic pleasure that I quote at this point the 20th century historian of the Byzantine state:

> ... the significance of the Byzantine victory of 678 cannot be overestimated. ... In the defense of Europe against the Arab onslaught this triumph of Constantine IV was a turning point of world-wide historical importance, like the later victory of Leo III in 718, or Charles Martel's defeat of the Muslims in 732 at Poitiers at the other end of Christendom. Of these three victories which saved Europe from being overwhelmed by the Muslim flood, that of Constantine IV was the first and also the most important. ... The fact that it [Constantinople] held saved not only the Byzantine Empire, but the whole of European civilization.[4]

In the above passage, Ostrogorsky, steeped as he was in the chronicles of yore and passionate about his subject to the point of racism, almost succeeds in making us forget one historical fact, namely, that Christianity itself was split. There was Rome and there was Constantinople, both claiming to be capitals of Christian faith. And while the Pope in Rome had to admonish, instruct, influence, or simply deal with worldly rulers, the Emperor in Constantinople was the direct inheritor of the Christianized Roman Empire who stood at the head of a bureaucratic (later theocratic) state and whose authority was directly given by God.

The split between a Catholic and an Orthodox Christianity, expressing the split between a Western and an Eastern Roman Empire, is highly significant. For this split inaugurates the first European East-West divide. At the beginning, it was in fact the East who set the discourse of identity-formation. The West was almost completely overrun by the Germanic tribes. During those truly "dark ages," Constantinople saw itself as the New Rome, preserving and protecting Christianity, as well as keeping the idea of the (formerly Roman) Empire alive. However, Constantinople and its Empire, too, were almost continually threatened by invasions, due for the most part to the geographical location spanning southeastern Europe and Asia Minor. From this geographical location, the Eastern Roman Empire also inherited its unique political-cultural make-up of Roman institutions cast into a Greek-Hellenic form. Over the course of the Byzantine Empire's existence or development, the Greek-Hellenic form molded and took-over the Roman heritage.[5] Greek replaced Latin as the official language and the theocratic form of rule began to dominate; the latter clearly a different path of development than the one followed (or enforced) in the Catholic part of Europe where the separation of church and state became one of the characteristic elements of the West. In this context we also encounter the missions to Christianize the barbarians in the southeast and east (for Byzanz: the North), based on the Greek alphabet (Cyrillic) and the Eastern rite.

With the final fall of Constantinople to the forces of Sultan Muhammad II ("the Conqueror") in 1453, the Byzantine Empire ended. But Orthodox Christianity lived on. The Ottoman Empire that ruled in the southeast for over four hundred years tolerated different religions in its realm. Orthodox Christianity, thus, also became a focal point for the identity-formation of the southeastern Slavs under Ottoman rule. The center of Orthodoxy, however, shifted to the east. Under Ivan III, who had married the niece of the last Byzantine Emperor, the Grand Duchy of Muscovy was proclaimed the "Third Rome". From this time onwards, Russian princely leaders claimed the title of "tsar" (Emperor).[6]

Christianity, thus, can be said to have provided an initial vision of a common – European – space based on a shared identity. At the same time, it was also the first source for the recognition of a European "West-East" axis, a recognition already tied to *qualitative* assumptions about the respective identities involved. Indeed, the Christian East/West divide is a powerful undercurrent in the process of European identity-formation, always present, always there to be re-discovered.[7]

*2.2 Modernity*

The explicit construction of a European identity by way of a West-East differentiation and imaginology became the theme of modernity. Between the fifteenth and the eighteenth century, a massive and unique transformation occurred that completely restructured European politics, society, and the economy.[8] It is this "great transformation," of which Polanyi's market society is a distinct part, that in its creation of a European consciousness simultaneously implants the first specifically West-East axis: civilization/barbarism with its conceptual twin advanced/backward.

As with the earlier conceptions of "Europe," the modern one came about by travel, trade, and war. Of course, we tend to think first of the great voyages of discovery that brought Europe together by providing a new Other to fuel the imagination and fill the royal treasuries.[9] We thereby tend to forget that Europe did not only discover the outside – it also began to discover itself. Renaissance and Humanism engendered a common European republic of letters, the wars that followed in the wake of the Reformation ended with the Peace of Westphalia (1648) and the creation of the modern European state system. From this consolidated position, the new Europeans, the British, French, Germans, etc. began to discover in the 18th century their European neighbors in the east and southeast:

> [I]t was on the way to Constantinople, and on the way to St. Petersburg, that eighteenth-century travelers discovered Eastern Europe. [...] These were the great destinations, the capital of the Orient and the capital of the North, but travelers inevitably observed the lands and peoples along the routes.[10]

The Ottoman Empire's presence in the southeast of Europe after the fall of Constantinople had set somewhat of a precedent for this discovery. In the eyes of political thinkers from Machiavelli to Bacon and Harrington, the Turkish political and economic order became a key case for the comparison of different political and economic orders. This process of comparison certainly led the way to a first conscious identification of "Europe" in rational-secular terms.[11]

What the eighteenth century travelers – diplomats and their spouses on the way to their assignments, young aristocrats, and (aristocratic) teachers and their aristocratic pupils on a European "Grand Tour" – discovered "along the routes" and brought back to captivated audiences in the form of travel memoirs, differed significantly from what others had noticed before. For what really vexed the traveler to those unknown places and undoubtedly titillated his/her readers at home were the living conditions the traveler discovered. This is what William Coxe, tutor to the teenage nephew of the Duke of Marlborough, had to tell his readers about traveling *and* living conditions in Poland in the late 1770s:

> Our only bed was straw thrown upon the ground, and we thought ourselves happy when we could procure it clean. Even we, who were by no means deli-

> cate, and who had long been accustomed to put up with all inconveniences, found ourselves distressed in this land of desolation. Though in most countries we made a point of suspending our journey during night, in order that no scene might escape our observation; yet we here even preferred continuing our route without intermission to the penance we endured in these receptacles of filth and penury: and we have reason to believe that the darkness of the night deprived us of nothing but the sight of gloomy forests, indifferent crops of corn, and objects of human misery. The natives were poorer, humbler, and more miserable than any people we had yet observed in the course of our travels: wherever we stopped, they flocked around us in crowds; and, asking for charity, used the most abject gestures.[12]

Coxe's above account was *news* to his readers at the time of its publication. Indeed, a neat distinction between scientific description and travel account only developed much later – diaries of travels or "voyages" were an accepted and popular form of communicating "facts" about hitherto unknown places and peoples, flora and fauna. One should also note that the communicated astonishment about the living conditions works by comparison: other parts of Europe Cox's travel party visited were *not* like that. A quick comparison with England as travel destination for other Europeans is here instructive. French and German travelers who came to England at around the same time that Coxe's party traveled in the other direction came away with decidedly different impressions. Count Kielmansegge, visiting from Hanover in 1761, could only marvel at the "'well-kept garden'" that was Essex, while Abbé Le Blanc already in 1747 duly noted the industriousness of the English and the general prosperity that characterized the entire country.[13]

The differences in material development between parts of Europe, and especially between a Western and an Eastern half, that were beginning to be thematized in the travel literature of the 18$^{th}$ century found their correlate in the new theme of despotism in the political (philosophical) literature. The initial occupation with the Ottoman Empire as Europe's Other had a political dimension – comparing forms of government and rule – *without* being necessarily evaluative in the sense of extolling the virtues of "Europe" against the vices of the "Orient". Exactly this shift – the comparison between the Ottoman Empire and the rest of Europe in which the former is found inferior and evil – occurred from the late 17$^{th}$ century onward. The age of Enlightenment created with critique and emancipation two neologism that became the method and the standard, respectively, of political judgment. Although Louis XIV was able to proclaim "l'état, c'est moi," the principle of absolute rule by a Monarch was giving way to the principles of the separation of powers and democratic representation as cornerstones of a legitimate government. Despotism became the neologism to describe and judge the political rule not only in the Ottoman Empire, but in all parts considered to be Asiatic or Oriental – that is, *not* European.[14] It was the perplexing situation of an "in-betweenness" that led to the invention of "Eastern Europe" and the "Balkans" as distinct spaces, European and Eastern (Asiatic or Oriental, depending if the determining relation was Russia or the Ottoman Empire) at the same time.

All this imagining had a serious and all-too-real background. With the modern matrix brought forth by Renaissance and Reformation, the discovery of the new world, the Copernican and Newtonian revolutions in science, the Enlightenment, and the beginnings of industrialization, a new definition of Europe ensued that articulated differences as differences of conditions and levels of development. It should be clear that from the point of general cultural development, a "West"/"East" divide did not exist the way it was seen. The great cultural-intellectual movements such as Renaissance and Enligthenment were European-wide phenomena, even for the Russian Empire (under the reform tsars Peter the Great and Catherine the Great) and the lands under Ottoman rule (by the 18th century, Ottoman power in the Balkans had passed its peak and outside influences were felt again). An intellectual-cultural unity of experience existed above the "East"/"West" divide, differentiated by historical-political divisions shaped by the process of European state and Empire building.[15] Moreover, the developmental divide that was drawn between "West" and "East" did not reflect the realities within the "West" itself. Rather, the self-conception with which "Western" observers began to operate, and the contrast that was produced, was also an act of self-delusion: a spatial displacement as much as a representation of developmental problems that were rather familiar to the outside observer: the poverty of the peasantry (or: "the people") and the indifference of the aristocracy. Nevertheless, *in comparison*, Europe had begun to differentiate itself along a west/east axis of movement in terms of infrastructure, general living conditions, and general political circumstances by the 18th century. And with that, it became possible to articulate those differences in terms of a spatial representation, an imaginological short-cut, if you will: "West" and "East".

The 19th century, in essence, only completed in deed and thought the division between "West" and "East" that had been recognized and set in motion by its predecessor. The process of industrialization heightened the economic and material differences between a "Western" and an "Eastern" half of Europe. Although, once again, the real development was more differentiated than that. Comparing solely the development on the Continent, industrialization proceeded quite apace in the Czech lands of the Habsburg Empire, while in Hungary, the industrial revolution never quite took off. Poland, in turn, can not be simply assessed as such because what we today consider Poland was since the Congress of Vienna (1815) part of the Habsburg, Wilhelminian German, and Russian Empires. The southeast remained in terms of industrialization the most backward part of the "East," once again with the significant exception of the regions within the Habsburg realm which fared comparatively better. As for the Russian Empire, its sheer seize almost defies any generalization; nevertheless, it is clear that in the course of the nineteenth century, industrialization fared better in some select, "western" (and historical) centers than even in (European) Russia as a whole.[16] All those necessary differentiations not withstanding, the process of industrialization completed the general developmental difference between "West" and "East," indeed, it brought the matter of developmental difference to what one might call a *paradigmatic* point. With the process of industrialization, an ideal of what it means to be and become "modern" was finally formulated: urbanized, mechanized, rationalized, educated, and oriented towards economic growth.

For our purposes, it is important to stress that this economic and material development also had an ideational component. The ideal of what it means to be and become modern, embedded in the process of industrialization, was also expressed in the belief in civilization and progress which characterized the "Western" imagination in the second half of the nineteenth century. The price of that belief was the equally powerful sensation of *ambiguity*. Reason may have triumphed, the passions tamed, yet as the nineteenth century was drawing to a close, the sciences themselves began to undermine common notions of certainty and social scientists began to be concerned with the seemingly irrational aspects of modern life, such as subjectivity, mass behavior, and sexuality (and one of them, Freud, discovered the unconscious in the process). Doubts about civilization and progress were therefore beginning to be felt and it was quite convenient to be able to externalize those doubts, to have them displaced and represented by a wild, barbaric Other *against* which civilization and progress could still triumph (in the British case by virtue of the proverbial gatlin gun; in the German case, partial to the notion of a Kulturnation, Karl May's Kara Ben Nemsi or Old Shatterhand could stand for both, Kultur in the form of Christian religion, and civilization in the form of Bärentöter and Henrystutzen, the guns of the hero[17]). In the European context, the Balkans became the place/space where the nightmares of European civilization where deposited: at the crossroads of the "Eastern" world: Asiatic and Oriental at the same time.

When Count Dracula advised Jonathan Harker upon the latter's arrival at the castle that "[w]e are in Transylvania; and Transylvania is not England. Our ways are not your ways, and there shall be to you many strange things' author Bram Stoker could already count on his readership's familiarity with the Count's assessment and, more importantly, on his readership's readiness to believe the Count.[18] By the end of the nineteenth century, the gap between the western half and the eastern half of Europe in terms of industrial-economic development had become obvious and the imaginology of Europe's "East" as a place of barbaric brutality and savage beauty (barbarity in all its erotic and sexual variants) had been firmly implanted on the cognitive map of industrial and Imperial Europe. Therein lies the disturbing effect that communism in the East exerted on the European, and ultimately global, imagination.

*2.3 Communism*

As Ivan T. Berend has recently reminded us, communism can be seen as a revolt of the periphery.[19] This interpretation makes sense if we consider the *initial* development of communism, its *later* attraction to what came to be called the Third World, and its *combined* impact on what came to be called the First World. Let me first present communism as "revolt of the periphery" – and then make some vital differentiations and qualifications.

A good way to start thinking about the relation between communism and the East of Europe is to remind ourselves of the logic of the argument presented thus far. In tracking the elements and the development of a West/East schism, the "East" or the periphery itself has remained silent. This silence of course has an objective reason. The structuration of the discourse on "Europe" was based – intellectually and spatially – on a sequence of European centers from Athens to Paris and London, temporally expressed in the sequence "antiquity," "middle ages," "modern times". The power of definition and the corresponding silence of the defined are part of that story. Yet it would be all-too simple (not to use the word mechanistic) if one were to insist on the silence of the periphery as a realist expression of what happened. For the comparison that we saw emerging in the 18th century worked both ways. The East also began to look West. Two responses initially emerged out of this other comparison: a state-centered, state-induced, and state-controlled imitationism, on the one hand, and in response an inward-looking authochtonism, on the other.

As the West discovered its power in comparison with the East, so did the East discover its weakness in comparison with the West. The transnational clan of the European aristocracy proved to be a transmission belt of standards and tastes; of anything considered to be modern or just de rigeur. Imitation became the means by which Monarchs and nobles in the self-discovered East wished not only to share in the development of the Other, but also to counter the power that this Other projected if not exerted in their interactions.

With the significant exception of Russia, the importation of Western institutions, politics, and policies became also a highly important element in the struggles for national liberation and national recognition throughout the nineteenth and into the twentieth century. Becoming western meant becoming European which meant liberating oneself from the yoke of the East, Asiatic or Oriental, Russian or Turkish. Yet the West itself was also an ambiguous mirror. For those lands and peoples caught inside the four-center force-field made up of Russia, Ottoman Empire, Austria, and Germany, *modern* European history had not been very kind and liberation also meant the constitution of a people against powerful Imperial interests which were part of a system of "Great Powers". Furthermore, liberation and oppression were themselves ambiguous terms: national liberation in a multi-ethnic context could not help but raise the question of the titular nation and the specter of the suppression of other ethnic groups as minorities within the framework of a nation-state [sic]. At any rate, the logic of the nation-state, the congruence of nationhood and stateness, became the revolutionary principle in the East. Undoubtedly, the success that romantic notions about the distinctiveness of peoples, such as Herder's, enjoyed in this revolutionary context was in no small measure due to the "backwardness" that was acutely felt. The West had successfully claimed the lead in political and economic development, and had embedded its own self-understanding in a West-East imaginology. For the East, that is: for all those considered to be barbaric and backward, culture became a rallying point against civilization; or, to put it differently, the original unity of the people as *Volk against* the political unity imposed by *Empire*. That the people *as* "Volk" were in fact the product of an elite imagination should be duly noted and kept in mind.

One question has remained open thus far. Was Eastern Europe Western Europe's "periphery"? As the preceding discussion has made clear, conceptually or imaginologically this was indeed the case, with important repercussions for the self-understanding of both parts. Imaginology by way of the ideological structuration of politics and policies clearly influenced both sides. The *direct* economic *dependence* of the East on the West of Europe is a different issue. Here the available evidence is rather mixed. Yet even if dependency in the by now classical meaning of the term is questionable in the case of East/West during the period of industrialization and Empire, the difference in development lends itself to a broader understanding of the term periphery. At any rate, it was such a broader understanding of "backwardness" in comparison with the wealth, comfort, and power of the West that animated the desire to be modern in the East.

The strategy chosen to "catch-up" with the West, to modernize as it came to be called much later, was, as already noted, development from above: state centered, state induced, and state controlled. Educational system, the military, and industry were all to be stomped out of nothing, molding the forms in an attempt to force the currents of modernity to follow. As Reinhard Bendix noted about one of the earliest such attempts, the creation of the Academy of Sciences in Russia under tsar Peter the Great:

> Under these [i. e. the given] conditions, foreign scientists as well as students had to come to Russia since there was no Russian university from which Russian scientists could be recruited, and Russian secondary education in the early eighteenth century did not prepare students for advanced work. Vasilii Tatishehev, one of Peter's emissaries to Sweden, suggested to the tsar that an academy without educational institutions on which to build would be a waste of money. Peter replied that he knew 'a Russian academy would resemble a watermill without water, but that [this] beginning would compel his successors to complete the work by digging a canal that would bring in the water.[20]

Reality remained obstinate, to say the least. For all the modernity that was desired or willed into existence, the key problematic, namely the transformation of an agrarian into an industrial society, remained unresolved. Thus, if the "social question" became the key metaphor of the agrarian-industrial transformation in the West, the "agrarian question" became the key metaphor of the compromise transformation in the East. I am using the word "compromise" here advisedly. For the desire to be "modern," to share in the wealth and power of the "West," was balanced by the wish on part of the (mostly aristocratic-agrarian) elites to retain the existing political and social relations. The transformation that ensued was therefore a "compromise" transformation in the double meaning of the word. It was not allowed to touch the socio-economic and political institutions and relations in the service of agrarian-aristocratic societies, remained concentrated in the major urban areas, and as such presented a compromise between modernizing and traditionalist interests. Luxury consumption, so to speak, was the actual goal of development, and as for that, democracy was a luxury item.

Thus, the earliest critical response that the top-down modernization elicited from within the respective modernizing societies took aim at the surface effects and their lack of deep-structural involvement. Importation of western institutions and fashions appeared only to serve a select view who wallowed in their newly-rich status while the rest of the country was being underdeveloped. The positive vision of development offered by this strand of criticism was itself rather problematic. Against the "westernizers," the "Easterners" or "autochthonists" championed the peasantry and the village community as the original sources for and models of development. This nationalistic response (against foreign influences – the German "Überfremdung" – no less) more often than not was based on a blend of romantic conceptions of the "Volk" and conservative ideals of a natural order.[21]

In this context, communism – or better: Bolshevism – promised nothing less than cutting through the Gordian knot of the Eastern Transformation. There was only one minor problem:

Communism in the East was not supposed to happen. And this was a position taken by the international labor movement itself. Tsarist Russia was considered to be *the* center of reaction in Europe. Already during the Revolution of 1848, Marx and Engels advocated "the war with Russia" as the only war "made by [a] revolutionary Germany". What was then an assessment based on revolutionary tactics and strategies with a nationalistic bend, turned thereafter into a historical-structural assessment. Russia, it seems, was always on the verge of *a* revolution, but its intolerable conditions were also not ripe for *the* revolution. This made the revolution that would ensue organically out of the Russian conditions into a somewhat murky affair. Nevertheless, for the later Engels, the importance of such a revolution for the rest of Europe, when (or if) it happened, could not be denied "if only because it will destroy at one blow the last, so far intact, reserve of the entire European reaction".[22]

In this sense, Communism as Bolshevism *was* a revolt of the periphery; an attempt not only to join the "developed" world, but even to surpass its most cherished achievements and circumvent its most dreaded problems. Thus, when the Bolshevik Revolution occurred in Russia, it shook-up the entire framework in which European politics had been cast *including its accepted "West"/"East" divide* – and as such radiated outward into the rest of the world.

With the end of the Second World War, the most institutionalized, closed, and brutal borderline was created in Europe: the borderline of the East-West conflict predicated on two opposing and competing systems of societal organization.[23] Interestingly enough, the new borderline, which ran in geographical terms along the Elbe river and along the Leitha river, combined the old borderline with the equally historical borderline between a German "East" and "West". Furthermore, what had been an internal European borderline, as discussed above, now became a borderline of global significance.

The division between "East" and "West" thereby reached a totally different level, as did its imaginology.[24] The difference was cast into systems, localized, and internationalized. Following an interpretative suggestion made by Kenneth Jowitt, we can identify the post-Second World War order as a "centered regime world" revolving around the two "centres" of Moscow and Washington.[25] First World, Second World, Third World became the terms designating that order. For our purposes, an important shift and re-imagining occurred with that designation. The developmental division that had defined the imaginology of "East" and "West" in modern times now was seen between First and Third World, or between "North" and "South" as the difference was spatially expressed. The Second World enjoyed an entirely different status. Development was not anymore the category that divided the parts and accounted for their difference. On the contrary, development came to be seen as that which united "East" and "West" in a common problematic of modernization.[26] The systemic difference, in turn, was now a *political* one. From the formulation of totalitarianism to that of Soviet-type societies, the capacity of the party- or even leader-led state apparatus to command and control virtually every aspect of society and the absence of individual rights and freedoms were considered to be the hallmark of difference that distinguished "East" from "West". To this, one needs to add the arsenal of destruction that the two sides accumulated, refined, and brought in position against each other. Under the shadow of the atomic bomb, the new division between "East" and "West" appeared to be well-nigh forever.[27] Of course, we now know how long or rather short "forever" can be. This leads us to some important qualifications that have to be made.

In the first place, a revolt of the periphery *in Europe* did not really take place. Instead, in Europe, the post-Second World War creation of the "East" was the result of Soviet occupation and influence. With the significant exception of Yugoslavia, the state socialist or "real-existing" socialist regimes in what was dubbed "Eastern Europe" by the "West" were erected in a tortuous and brutal process of double-dealings, purges, and fraudulent elections. That state socialism was initially imposed remained a source of friction and rebellion for all societies. Also, "real-existing" socialism was hardly uniform across the region of "Eastern Europe" and in its specific settings developed over time. As seen from their ex post facto final form, real-existing socialist regimes came to vary from the more reformist, flexible, and open regimes in Yugoslavia and Hungary, to the more nationalist, rigid, and closed regimes in Romania and Albania. "Eastern Europe" in this sense became another, if different, imaginological straightjacket for a pluriverse of countries, peoples, cultures, languages.

It is tempting to view the variance of real-existing socialism across the region as a result of long-standing determinants. Thus, all countries or regions that had earlier partaken in some way in the process of development of the "West" retained a certain independence (if only of mind), while all those countries or regions that had been more closed off prior to the imposition of real-existing socialism simply continued along their "closed" path. There is, I think, some truth to that. The variance within the region will occupy us again in the context of postcommunist identity-formation. Suffice it so say at this point that while real-existing socialism was certainly imposed by the Soviet Union on its "satellite states," real-existing socialism for better and for worse did not encounter a tabula rasa in each case.

Nevertheless the above qualifications should not deter us from making the following two general points about the post-Second World War order. First, from the point of view of the West, the new borderline that divided "East" and "West" in terms of two competing systems of societal organization was supposed to be "eternal". Although the issue of reform in the Soviet Union and its "satellite states" was clearly considered important and clear signs of a major crisis were discussed by the late nineteen-seventies, the specter of the Soviet Union as a military superpower always brought up the issue of the Soviet Union's collapse as an actual threat to the rest of the world. In the meantime, the existence of the "West" remained fundamentally secure as well. As long as the Second World existed, the unity of the First World could never be in doubt. Second, for the East, forty-five years of state socialism in its various guises made a profound impact on those societies. Perhaps the greatest impact those forty-five years had was at the "soft" level of political culture and social (also individual) psychology. That this impact was not uniform across the entire region does not minimize the importance of the impact as such.

I have traced in the above part the imaginological relationships that developed around the categories "East" and/versus "West," highlighted their origins, and noted some of their political (i.e. real-world) implications. What began as a simple directional device in the service of travel, trade, and war became an imaginological relationship based, in fact, on the displacement and spatial representation of developmental problems that accrued in the process of modernization. Finally, communism provided an alternative and global divide: a second world between the first and the third world of development; a second world based on a fundamentally political distinction and with an *ambiguous* developmental status. It is now high-time to return to the present and the condition of postcommunism.

## 3 POST COMMUNIST BORDERLINES AND BEYOND

The fall of communism, the so called "annus mirabilis" of 1989, was clearly an epochal event: the end of Europe and the world that the Second World War had created. Where do Europe's internal borders lie at present?[28] And what happened to the great global divide between the two competing systems of societal organization?

Three modes of answering the above questions have developed in the past decade: historical, structural, and global. All three modes are predicated on the fall of communism as their defining element and basis for theorizing. This explains the resurrection of the traditional "East/West" borderline, the activation of the East/East borderline, and the search for global alternatives in the context of an activated West/West borderline. "East" and "West" are very much alive, indeed, they appear to have been reinvigorated by the fall of communism. The unfolding story, its logic of development, leads us from the problematic of return and integration to the problematic of globalization. In lieu of a conclusion, I will present a global perspective that is predicated on the condition of postcommunism as a common problematic of transformation at the end of the twentieth century, north, south, east, west.

### *3.1 the Problematic of Return*

Perhaps the single most important consequence of the fall of communism has been the (re-) opening of the borders that characterized and determined "Europe" and the world since the end of the Second World War. For the space called "Europe" this (re-) opening has meant *concretely* the loss of a separate spatial and societal category, "Eastern Europe". At the same time, this loss also and equally *concretely* has meant the problematization of the spatial and societal category of "Europe" itself. A huge question-mark has been placed behind "Europe," and there is considerable uncertainty as to what a possible new answer might be. The *historical answer* that has been offered in the former "East" and that has also been picked up in the former "West" can be summarized as: return to Europe. Its origins can be traced to the division of the Cold War and presents another veritable "revolt of the periphery" – only this time, the target was the world that the allied powers had created.

As discussed in part 2.3, the Second World of real-existing socialism was more pluralist than the Western terms "satellite states" or "Eastern Europe" were meant to denote. Indeed, what those Western terms actually were belittling was the imposition of real-existing socialism on the area east of the Elbe and southeast of the Leitha by Soviet occupation and intervention in the aftermath of the Second World War. It should therefore not be surprising that the "order of Yalta" became the focal point of dissident discourse and radical opposition. From the Polish October in 1956 to the battlecry of the Hungarian revolution, "for Hungary and for Europe," in the same year and onward, the rejection of "real-existing socialism" was always coupled with a rejection of *foreign* domination and an insistence on a common European past in the expectation of a common European future.

Of major importance for the dissident discourse in this regard became from the late nineteen-seventies onward the idea of Central Europe. As Lonnie R. Johnson aptly put it, "Central Europe was a means searching for alternatives to the Iron Curtain, the Cold War, and the partition of Europe".[29] The idea of Central Europe, of course, had existed before, infamous as an enlarged political and economic zone under German tutelage, as put forth by Friedrich Naumann during the First World War. What made "Central Europe" special and usable within Eastern dissident discourse was that its political and economic meaning was transformed into a cultural-historical one. It was the unity of a cultural-historical experience, from Christianization to the great struggles for freedom, that defined the region: an experience whose spatial setting was neither "West" nor "East". The autonomy of Central Europe as a unique space was stressed and the European "West" was criticized for its acceptance of capitalist commodity culture. Nevertheless, there was no question that Central Europe was Europe: communism had "kidnaped" the region, its original and lasting destiny was therefore "West" and not "East.[30]

The discoursive reconstruction of Central Europe also involved an act of differentiation – based, in fact, on a combination of pre-1914 and post-1945 elements.[31] Christianity was defined as Latin Christianity, that is, Catholicism, and Orthodox Christianity was viewed as thoroughly Eastern, that is, Russian. The initial East-West divide we have encountered in part 2.1 thereby reemerged as a powerful element in the discourse of an *alternative* "Eastern" identity-formation. Communism, in turn, was identified as Eastern, that is, Russian, precisely because it was a choice against freedom and freedom was viewed as a key European value.[32] Of course, the act of differentiation posed the interesting problem of the borders of Central Europe itself. Clearly, Southeastern Europe was thereby excluded as was Northeastern Europe, the former because it was predominantly Orthodox, the latter because it had ceased to exist as a region of independent national states. Nevertheless, both modes of exclusion were highly contestable and were contested by "Central European" writers themselves. Furthermore, the future remained necessarily open, even if a complete break-down of communism across the entire region, including Russia, was not foreseen or theorized. Despite the possible and articulated differences, there remained an underlying unity provided by the larger context of the struggle for "Europe" and against communism. As Neumann has pointed out, the discourse on Central Europe had one "Other" and enemy: the East, defined by Russia and all it stood for (anti-European, communist, etc.).

With the fall of communism, it might appear as if the idea of Central Europe had "arrived at its moment of truth".[33] That moment, however, proved to be highly predetermined and the truth turned out to be rather relative. The discourse of Central Europe was quickly "kidnaped" (pardon the pun) by the Realpolitik guiding the process of European integration. It became a discoursive device or signpost to distinguish those who always had been a part of Europe from those who had never been really part of it. The regional differences that we have noted are now in danger of being cast into a new European imaginology that feeds off the Eastern, that is, Central European, imagination while at the same time subverting its cultural-political aspirations. The "adventure" of the eastern enlargement of the EU has already led to a re-positioning of the major candidates in terms of their "readiness" and the debate itself is being waged about costs and standards.[34] For all those who do not belong to the select circle of possible EU members, the claim of a "return to Europe" has become solely a moral one and an exceedingly difficult one to make.

### *3.2 The Problematic of Integration*

For the Eastern desire to "return to Europe," the Western response to the fall of communism has been vital – and disillusionary. To be fair, nothing has influenced the former West's attitude towards the former East more than the West's own disillusionment in the face of the Eastern transformation following the fall of communism. That disillusionment has only heightened the uncertainty about the demarcations and societal identities that the fall of communism has wrought. Perhaps nothing illustrates this better than the structural answer that has dominated Western scholarship and politics vis-a-vis the Eastern transformation.

Integration became the key term of the "annus mirabilis" and its aftermath. Already Jürgen Habermas, writing under the spell of the moment, called the revolutions of 1989 a "revolution of recuperation". What those revolutions were supposed to recuperate was the creation of liberal-democratic, capitalist-market societies. Beyond and above the unexpectedness of the events, the goal (or should I say "telos"?) appeared to be clear. The people had (finally) spoken – *against* communism *and for* the open society.[35]

In the years that have since passed, it has become progressively less clear "what the people are turning away from" and even less clearer still "to where their eyes are turned".[36] Nevertheless, the perspective (or should I say "paradigm"?) of integration still predominates discussion and scholarship *in the West.* In this perspective, the societies of the former Eastern Europe have no choice but to integrate themselves into Western – European and global – structures of norms and action. The transformation process that ensues because of this integration has come to be viewed as a "double transformation". Politically, it is about the transformation of the communist party-led (even party-leader led) state-bureaucracies into some variant of a pluralist, representative democracy with a clear separation of powers and governed by the rule of law. Economically, it is about the transformation of the former Soviet-type command economies into some variant of a market economy based on private property and managerial prerogative.

From this "double transformation," political and social scientists have inferred a "dilemma of syncronicity". The necessary economic reforms, especially the privatization of state enterprises, lead to problems such as high unemployment and a large portion of the people will therefore have to defer its dream of a better life for at least some time to come. At the same time, the necessary political reforms, especially the introduction of free elections, provides the people with legitimate means by which to voice their grievances and disappointment. Hence, a "dilemma of syncronicity" ensues because the two necessary reform processes can cancel each other out: people may vote *against* the economic reforms by voting *for* nationalist, retrograde political parties and candidates, thereby democratically stopping both, the economic and the political reforms.[37]

The vagaries of the new Eastern transformation appear to support the general integration perspective sketched out above. Especially the specter of nationalism that has come to haunt the political landscape of the former "Eastern Europe" appears to fit the logic of the dilemma well. Missing from the integration perspective, as historians and area specialists have pointed out, are a genuine appreciation of the complexities and specificities of the societies themselves, their own histories, traditions, cultures.[38] But this could be a small price to pay for formal clarity and explanatory power. After all, do not most – and predictably not all! – political actors and forces in the former Eastern Europe wish to integrate themselves, to return to Europe?

In a recent essay on the European context of the new global order, Michael Zürn defines the new Europe as "comprising the European Economic Area (the EC countries plus the former EFTA [European Free Trade Association] countries) and those countries of Eastern Europe that have the best chances of integrating into this region, that is, Poland, Hungary, the former Czechoslovakia, and parts of the former Yugoslavia". The map that accompanies the text, entitled "Europe," includes the countries of the former Yugoslavia, yet leaves the rest of Southeastern Europe, as well as Northeastern Europe, *blank* and simply breaks-off further east. There is some telling irony involved in all this that Zürn certainly is not aware of. He begins his essay by stating that "Europe is arguably the one region in the world that has changed the most since the mid-1980s' acknowledges that "there are different notions of what Europe is," and concludes by writing that "academics ought to be prepared to concede that the realist notion of international politics ... is no longer sufficient to describe the fundamentals of world politics at the end of our century". All the same, Zürn himself has opted for one of the most restricted *and realist* notions of Europe and European politics.[39] The result is a clear juxtaposition of a new global condition and the maintenance of the West-East divide based on a new *Realpolitik* of integration.

The tension that is evident in Zürn's essay reflects the opening of the old, that is *modern*, West-East divide within a new reality. The fall of communism here spells the end to what used to be called the "competition of the systems". Capitalism, broadly conceived, won, while socialism, narrowly conceived, lost.[40] Thus, the East is again relegated to the status of Europe's "periphery" whence it had been placed in the West-East imaginology of modern times. Moreover, the old line of demarcation now nicely complements the new. Stripped of its Second World special status, "the East has become the South".

It seems rather paradoxical that the perspective of integration should in fact be predicated on a "renaissance" of modernization theory.[41] For the original reception of modernization theory, in its classical more or less Parsonian garb, in East European studies had been a reaction to the stagnant totalitarianism-paradigm and the staleness of Cold War scholarship. Although modernization studies did circumvent the issue of the political (a major problem, indeed!), they contributed some rich and more often than not unflattering studies of the realities behind the "iron curtain," and preserved the issue of the political as a huge question-mark behind the data.[42]

The present "renaissance" of modernization theory follows its own logic as a response to the fall of communism – and *not* in response to the condition of post-communism as one might assume. In the absence of an organizational alternative to liberal-democratic, industrial capitalist market society, the model of the "West" has re-emerged. Adam Przeworski recently summed up the key point of that "renaissance" quite effectively, "[t]oday, modernization means liberal democracy, consumption-oriented culture, and capitalism".[43] The question, however, is if the "West" as such can still fill the void that the fall of communism left behind and define modernity and modernization in a single image and as a single model.

For the countries of the former "Eastern Europe," the issue of integration poses itself in a double fashion: as an integration into already existing institutional arrangements, as exemplified for example by the EU, *and* as an exiting into history. In the former instance, the logic of integration is set by the former "West" and therefore leaves the former "East European" countries no choice but to plead their case from the position of Europe's periphery. In the latter instance, the countries of the former "East" are confronting their respective selves, their own histories, traditions, and cultures, and the legacy that real-existing socialism left behind in each case. The internal or domestic problematic of the new Eastern transformation, I like to argue, is linked to a general European and global transformation.

### *3.3 The Globalization of Europe*

We have arrived full-circle at this point. The past is still present precisely because more is at stake in the transformation process of "Eastern Europe," the extension towards the "East," and the globality of post-communism than the clear-cut integration-paradigm suggests. The historical and structural closure posited by the integration perspective in fact needs to be broken-up. In its stead, we need to integrate the new Eastern transformation into a European and global process of transformation. At the same time, history is not important because of past developments, it is important because of the present context; here, the integral dynamic (Eigendynamik) of postcommunism as a process of societal identity-formation can take the explanatory lead. Out of this general complex of transformation, the issue of borderlines or demarcations as sources of identity-formation is clearly one of the most important.

We can begin by pointing towards a veritable modernization of modernization theory that has been carried out in the political and social sciences in the (now former) West in the past twenty-some years. Since the late nineteen-sixties, early nineteen-seventies, political and social science research in the – former – West has successively come to abandon a universalistic and unilinear conception of modernity and modernization. Several developments have brought about this abandonment and revision. To begin with, modernization theory had to face the seeming failure of the western model of development and the persistence of underdevelopment in the Third World (Middle and South America, virtually all of Africa, and countries/regions in the Middle and Far East). Somewhat later, the special case of Japan and the rise of the Southeast Asian "little tigers" sent a shock-wave through the entire West because Japan and Southeast Asia seemed to demonstrate that "failure" and "success" of development could not be conceived in terms of a linear, ready-made "catching-up" with the western model by way of a standardized and unified "diffusion". Thus, the idea of a golden path of development and of a "grand theory" to account for its failure and/or success was virtually abandoned in the literature. Instead, a differentiated view of development has been called for: still aware of the global North-South divide, yet emphasizing the internal, indigenous conditions for development. Especially the relationship between capitalist development, prosperity, and democracy has come to be considered highly problematic. To this one needs to add a new global dimension brought about by the realization that the western path of development, predicated as it is on economic growth, creates severe ecological problems.[44]

As already noted above, the revision, if indeed not abandonment, of the classical framework of modernization theory has recently been countered by a revitalization of the "West" as model in response to the fall of communism. The recent crisis in Southeast Asia appears to have had a similar impact, if (still) less pronounced because that crisis cannot simply be compared to the fall of communism and should the crisis not deepen (and lead to a collapse, which would also severely impact the West), Southeast Asia will remain a major economic player in the world economy. To leave the ground of polemics aside, let me quote a recent assessment by Wolfgang Zapf, written after the fall of communism (but prior to the Southeast Asian crisis):

> ... modern societies are those societies that have realized a competitive democracy in their political sphere, a market economy in their economic sphere, and mass consumption and a welfare state in their societal sphere. Modernization is the developmental path leading to those basic institutions and at the same time refers to the extension and modification of those institutions.[45]

What Zapf in his definition at least acknowledges (and Przeworski in his definition, see above, misses), is the fact that modernity and modernization did not stop with the creation or realization of liberal-democratic, industrial capitalist market societies. For this reason, the modernization of modern, i. e. "western" societies has in fact become a central theme in political and social science research. The process of transformation that is being debated in this case ranges from changes in the industrial-economic organization of these societies and changes in the social structure to changes in the political system including electoral behavior and the social bases and programs of old and new political parties and movements. Regardless of whether these changes are summed up as "reflexive modernization," as "consequences of" or a "second modernity," as "postmodernization," or even as a new phase in the process of "globalization": at issue is a process that changes the foundational structures of the western societies themselves and thereby tears open the teleological self-understanding (*Endzeitverständnis*) of modernity, pace Fukuyama, from within its very center.[46]

One characteristic of this process of transformation on a global scale should at this point be especially noted: the opening and closing of society/-ies as part of the general process. The shock-waves and disturbances that are caused by this transformation process, akin to the transformation from agrarian to industrial society, pose fundamental problems to the norms and institutions, that is, to the regulatory mechanisms of all nationally-constituted societies.[47] Thus, the challenge of the new transformation process has brought the creation and stabilization of societal identity, the foundational theme of the modern social sciences, once again to the fore. Here, scientific research and public discourse meet in the concern about the state and future of democracy in changing societies within a global context.[48]

The end of the East-West conflict presents in this and for this process clearly another qualitative censure. With it, the "North/West" is confronting itself. Already existing differences and tendencies in development have come to the fore. The variations within the development of the developed "West" now present the bases for new, national (domestic), supra-national, international and global, conflicts and searches for solutions. At the same time, the "South" has lost its special position within the East-

West conflict and now has to compete for attention and funds against the former "East".

Modernity and modernization are not anymore, if they ever truly had been, the self-understood answers to the questions of the whereto and wherewithal of development. They themselves have become problematic, not the least for the former West itself. Thus, we need to understand the integration of the East into Western structures of norms and action quite differently from what the renaissance of modernization theory suggests to us. An integration is taking place, but it concerns both sides of the process; the countries of the former East have to integrate themselves into a formally Western context which is undergoing a fundamental transformation itself; the necessary transformation of the former in order to integrate into the latter thus resembles a high-wire act without securing strings and security net. In this sense, we can speak of the combined process of integration/transformation as a *crisis* with *identity* as its arena of conflict.

The process of transformation in the East characterizes nothing less than a total overhaul at the level of society itself.[49] Thus, the politics of reform, the very complex of policy making, amounts to a societal project. To formulate this differently: reform is a matter of *Gesellschaftspolitik.*[50] Politics," thus, do come "first". Yet for better and for worse, "politics" are not exhausted by the creation of institutions in the narrow sense of the term, nor can politics be simply reduced to a particular set of economic measures and their implementation.[51] Instead, the politics of reform in the new Eastern transformation concern the creation and stabilization of new, in the sense of *postcommunist*, societal identities.

Several layers specific to the Eastern context ought to be distinguished in this regard. First and foremost, is the specificity of the national. Historically, the area of Europe's East is multi-ethnic, and for the most part of modern history it was divided among the Russian, Habsburg, German (Prussian, later Wilhelminian), and Ottoman Empires. National liberation and the creation of national states came rather late, and when it did, it came about through a virtual storm of wars (First and Second World War) and forced migrations. Most contemporary national states in the East are still not ethnically homogeneous and the memory of injustices that were perpetrated in the course of the creation of each "nation" still linger on – as does the logic of the nation as a homogeneous unit, which is diffused by the titular nation through the educational system and the mass media.

To this, we certainly need to add the impact of communism. Here, I think, we need to distinguish between the international and the domestic level and relativize the "proletarian internationalism" of communism. There was always a relationship of power involved between the Soviet Union and its "brother states," noted even in such slogans as "To learn from the Soviet Union means to learn how to win!" ("Von der Sowjetunion lernen heißt, siegen lernen!"). This, of course, was most evident in those instances when the Soviet Union (and some brother-states) intervened in national developments (Hungary, Czechoslovakia). Poland and Romania are good examples of the two poles of my point: in the former, nationalism preserved itself as one of the sources of a counter-communist position, in the latter, communism was in fact wedded to nationalism and nationalism began to determine the domestic communist regime. Thus, nationalism is a powerful political option and presence after the fall of communism. It has enjoyed an already well-established presence in the past, and the new democratic institutions coupled with a weak democratic political culture do not offer much by way of resistance to nationalistic tendencies.[52]

We certainly know what price the politics of identity-formation can exact in the context of the new Eastern transformation. In the light of the conflicts that we have witnessed and the potentiality for conflicts yet to come, it may seem that the "price of freedom" (P. Wandycz) for the East was and remains its utter dependence on, even subservience to, the West. But the knowledge of the civil war that tore Yugoslavia apart, the present civil war in the Kosovo, and other, "lesser" conflicts in the area of the former Soviet Union should not blind us to the fact that "East" and "West" today share a common space and problematic of transformation, European and global. If modernity as a general condition has raised borderlines or demarcations to a conscious, i. e. "reflexive," level, globalization is providing the question marks behind them.

Perhaps here the "West" can and does have something to learn from the "East". The ideas of "Central Europe" and the "return to Europe" that have guided oppositional discourse in the East in the past and continue to be important are not exhausted by the *Realpolitik* of European integration. Instead, they point beyond the categories of "East" and "West" into which first European and later global history had been cast. For once, the "West" could discover itself through the "East's" discoursive evocation. At issue in this discovery would be the very meaning of "Europe" itself, its traditions and cultures, and its position in a new, globalized world.[53]

Although we still do not know what mix of long-standing determinants and new possibilities will finally emerge in and for Europe and the world, there is (still) reason to hope that this mix will be the product of a conscious decision for a common, shared and peaceful future.

## NOTES

1 For the above paragraph, see the classic study by Denys Hay (1957): *Europe: The Emergence of an Idea* (Edinburgh: Edinburgh University Press); and Pim den Boer (1995): "Europe to 1914: the making of an idea," Kevin Wilson and Jan van der Dussen, eds., *The History of the Idea of Europe* (London and New York: Routledge), pp. 13-82; as well as, Traian Stoianovich (1994): *Balkan Worlds: The First and Last Europe* (Armonk, NY and London: M. E. Sharpe).

2 St. Augustin, *Concerning the City of God against the Pagans*, trans. by Henry Bettenson (1984), (London: Penguin), esp. Book I, pp. 5-47.

3 Self-awareness in contrast to self-confidence, as stressed by Pim den Boer, "Europe to 1914," p. 29.

[4] George Ostrogorsky (1969): *History of the Byzantine State*, rev. ed., trans. by Joan Hussey (New Brunswick, NJ: Rutgers UP), p. 125.

[5] I am here partial to Ostrogorsky's authoritative insistence that the Byzantine Empire did in fact develop over the course of its existence. However, I wish to distance myself from Ostrogorsky's metaphysical interpretation that the Empire ended because its "mission" of preserving "the heritage of the ancient world" was fulfilled; Ostrogorsky, *History of the Byzantine* State, p. 572.

[6] Derived and shortened from "caesar". Ostrogorsky, *History of the Byzantine State*, p. 572; Perry Anderson (1974): *Passages from Antiquity to Feudalism* (London: NLB), p. 231; Perry Anderson (1974): *Lineages of the Absolutist State* (London: NLB), p. 201.

[7] For the formulation of a "primordial Iron Curtain," Lonnie R. Johnson (1996), *Central Europe: Enemies, Neighbors, Friends*, (New York and Oxford: Oxford University Press), p. 24.

[8] The story has been told many times before, its causes and dynamic has occupied some of the most eminent scholars in the social sciences and humanities, and we are still unsure about the exact whys and hows. Good synthesizing discussions can be found in David S. Landes' (1969) introduction to his classic *The Unbound Prometheus: Technological Change and Industrial Development in Western Europe from 1750 to the Present* (Cambridge, etc.: Cambridge University Press), and in Daniel Chirot (1985): "The Rise of the West," *American Sociological Review*, vol. 50, pp. 181-195.

[9] Gerard Delanty (1995): *Inventing Europe: Idea, Identity, Reality* (Houndmills and London, etc.: Macmillan), pp. 44-47.

[10] Larry Wolf (1994): *Inventing Eastern Europe: The Map of Civilization on the Mind of the Enlightenment*, (Stanford, CA: Stanford University Press), pp. 43-44.

[11] Perry Anderson in following Frederico Chabod, calls Machiavelli's comparison between "the Turk" and "the king of France" "one of the first implicit approaches to a self-definition of 'Europe'". I think it is *very* "implicit". The actual comparison is embedded in a general discussion about how to hold a state after conquest, a discussion which ranges from Alexander the Great to "our times" and the forms are not tied to a spatial recognition (safe for Asia in the case of Alexander the Great and not mentioned in conjunction with "the Turk"). Perry Anderson, *Lineages of the Absolutist State*, p. 398; Nicollò Machiavelli (1985): *The Prince*, a new translation with an introduction by Harvey C. Mansfield, Jr., (Chicago and London: University of Chicago Press), 16-19 (ch. IV).

[12] William Coxe (1785): *Travels into Poland, Russia, Sweden, and Denmark*: Interspersed with Historical Relations and Political Inquiries (London), as cited in Larry Wolff, *Imagining Eastern Europe*, p. 27. Coxe's account became a best-seller and served as a reference for many travelers who came after him.

[13] As cited and presented in Eric J. Hobsbawm (1969): *Industry and Empire: From 1750 to the Present Day* (Harmondsworth: Penguin Books), pp. 23-27.

[14] Reinhart Koselleck (1973): *Kritik und Krise: Eine Studie zur Pathogenese der bürgerlichen Welt*, (Frankfurt/M.: Suhrkamp), pp. 81-103; Perry Anderson, *Lineages of the Absolutist State*, p. 398 n. 4, pp. 399-401.

[15] Making a strong case for East Central Europe in this regard, Piotr S. Wandycz (1992): *The Price of Freedom: A History of East Central Europe from the Middle Ages to the Present* (London, etc.: Routledge).

[16] Iván T. Berend and György Ranki (1982): *The European Periphery and Industrialization, 1780-1914*, trans. by Éva Pálmai (Cambridge: Cambridge University Press;) Piotr S. Wandycz, *The Price of Freedom*, pp. 166-180.

[17] Eric J. Hobsbawm, *The Age of Empire*, 1875-1914 (New York: Vintage, 1989); H. Stuart Hughes, *Consciousness and Society: The Reorientation of European Social Thought, 1890-1930* (New York: Vintage, 1977).

[18] Bram Stoker (1979): *Dracula* (Harmondsworth: Penguin (orig. 1897)), p. 32.

[19] Ivan T. Berend (1996): *Central and Eastern Europe, 1944-1993: Detour from the Periphery to the Periphery*, (Cambridge, etc.: Cambridge University Press), xi-xiii and passim.

[20] Reinhard Bendix (1978): *Kings or People: Power and the Mandate to Rule*, (Berkeley, CA: University of California Press), p. 499.

[21] Iver B. Neumann (1996): *Russia and the Idea of Europe: A study in Identity and International Relations* (London and New York: Routledge), pp. 28-39; Lucian Boia (1997): *Istorie si Mit in Constiinta Româneasca* (Bucharest: Humanitas), pp. 38-55.

[22] Friedrich Engels (1978): "On Social Relations in Russia," (1874), *The Marx-Engels Reader*, ed. by Robert C. Tucker (New York: Norton), pp. 665-675.

[23] It is interesting to note the power of wording at this point. In using "East-West" conflict we are already putting the blame on the Eastern part of the conflict (the East is in conflict with the West, but not necessarily the other way around). As proof, try switching the words around: West-East conflict.

[24] Michael Paul Rogin (1987): *Ronald Reagan, the Movie, and Other Episodes in Political Demonology*, (Berkeley, CA: University of California Press), ch. 1 (the title essay), pp. 1-43, and ch. 8, "Kiss Me Deadly: Communism, Motherhood, and Cold War Movies," pp. 236-271.

[25] Ken Jowitt (1992): *New World Disorder: The Leninist Extinction*, (Berkeley, CA: University of California Press), esp. ch. 5. I should note that Jowitt rejects the inference of a "Washington Center" on the grounds that Washington was never able to exercise the kind of symbolic and direct power over a pluriverse of Western partner-states. I agree as far as Jowitt's objection goes. For in the last instance, the logic of Cold War confrontation also worked in unifying the West and placing it under the undisputed leadership of Washington. As to the symbolic power – perhaps now that the Cold War is over we are beginning to realize how much power the myth of "America" has and continues to exercise.

[26] Charles Gati, ed. (1974): *The Politics of Modernization in Eastern Europe: Testing the Soviet Model*, (New York, etc.: Praeger Publishers;) Walter D. Connor(1979): *Socialism, Politics, and Equality: Hierarchy and Change in Eastern Europe and the USSR*, (New York: Columbia University Press).

[27] Werner Link (1980): *Der Ost-West Konflikt: Die Organisation der internationalen Beziehungen im 20. Jahrhundert* (Stuttgart: Kohlhammer), esp. pp. 216-226.

[28] "Where do Europe's internal borders lie?" The opening sentence of Jenö Szücs (1990): *Die drei historischen Regionen Europas*, transl. by Béla Rásky (Frankfurt/M.: Verlag Neue Kritik).

[29] Lonnie R. Johnson, *Central Europe: Enemies, Neighbors, Friends*, p. 252.

[30] I am referring here to the most famous essay on the idea of Central Europe as a "kidnaped West" (written, as its author maintains, for a Western audience), Milan Kundera (1984): "The Tragedy of Central Europe," *The New York Review of Books*, April, pp. 33, 36, 38. For critical discussions: Krishan Kumar (1992): "The 1989 Revolutions and the Idea of Europe," *Political Studies*, vol. XL, no. 3 (September), pp. 439-461; Iver B. Neumann (1993): "Russia as Central Europe's Constituting Other," *East European Politics and Societies*, vol. 7, no. 2 (Spring), pp. 349-369.

[31] Thus the famous definition by Timothy Garton Ash (1989) of "East Central Europe" *The Uses of Adversity: Essays on the Fate of Central Europe* (New York: Random House), p. 250 n. 10.

[32] Mihály Vajda (1989): "Who excluded Russia from Europe? (A Reply to Šimeèka)," George Schöpflin and Nancy Wood, eds., *In Search of Central Europe* (Cambridge: Polity Press), pp. 168-175.

[33] Krishan Kumar, "The 1989 Revolutions and the Idea of Europe," p. 442.

[34] Barbara Lippert (1998): "Der Gipfel von Luxemburg: Startschuß für das Abenteuer Erweiterung," *Integration*, vol. 21, no. 1 (January), pp. 12-31; Christian Meier (1997): "Transformation der Außenwirtschaftspolitik: Zur Wechselbeziehung von EU-Integration und regionaler Kooperation der Staaten Ostmitteleuropas," Bundesinstitut für ostwissenschaftliche und internationale Studien (ed.), *Der Osten im Prozeß der Differenzierung: Fortschritte und Mißerfolge der Transformation* (München: Hanser); (1998): "Europa: Auf der Kippe," *Der Spiegel*, nr. 27, p. 128.

[35] Jürgen Habermas (1990): "What Does Socialism Mean Today? The Revolutions of Recuperation and the Need for New Thinking," Robin Blackburn ed., *After the Fall: The Failure of Communism and the Future of Socialism* (London and New York: Verso), pp. 25-46; Ralf Dahrendorf (1990): *Betrachtungen über die Revolution in Europa* in einem Brief, der an einen Herrn in Warschau gerichtet ist (Stuttgart: DVA, 1990).

[36] Ralf Dahrendorf: *Betrachtungen über die Revolution in Europa*, p. 93.

[37] Claus Offe, besides Adam Przeworski, has developed the conception of the "double transformation" and the "dilemma of syncronicity;" Claus Offe (1994): *Der Tunnel am Ende des Lichts: Erkundungen der politischen Transformation im Neuen Osten* (Frankfurt/M.: Campus).

[38] I should note at this point that the Western reception of the idea of Central Europe was predictably not so much guided by the idea of a "return to Europe" as it was by the idea of a "return to history".

[39] Michael Zürn (1995): "The Challenge of Globalization and Individualization: A View from Europe," Hans-Henrik Holm and Georg Sorensen, eds., *Whose World Order?* Uneven Globalization and the End of the Cold War (Boulder, CO: Westview Press), pp. 137-163, quotes pp. 137, 139, 163.

[40] Joschka Fischer (1989): *Der Umbau der Industriegesellschaft: Plädoyer wider die herrschende Umweltlüge* (Frankfurt/M.: Eichborn), esp. 58-59; Klaus von Beyme (1994): *Systemwechsel in Osteuropa* (Frankfurt/M.: Suhrkamp).

[41] See Klaus Müller (1991): "Nachholende Modernisierung? Die Konjunkturen der Modernisierungstheorie und ihre Anwendung auf die Transformation der osteuropäischen Gesellschaften," *Leviathan*, vol. 19, no. 2, pp. 261-291; also: Klaus Müller (1992): "'Modernising' Eastern Europe. Theoretical Problems and Political Dilemma," *European Journal of Sociology*, vol. 33, pp. 109-150.

[42] For a recent discussion: Thomas Bremer, Wim van Meurs, Klaus Müller (1998): "Vorwärts in die Vergangenheit? Zur Zukunft der Osteuropaforschung," *Osteuropa*, vol. 48, no. 4 (April), pp. 406-408.

[43] Adam Przeworski et al. (1995): *Sustainable Democracy* (Cambridge, etc.: Cambridge University Press), p. 4.

[44] David Apter (1987): *Rethinking Development: Modernization, Dependency, and Postmodern Politics* (Newbury Park: Sage;) S. N. Eisenstadt: *Tradition, Wandel und Modernität*, trans. by Suzanne Heintz (Frankfurt/M.: Suhrkamp, 1979;) Dieter Nohlen and Franz Nuscheler (eds.) (1993): *Handbuch der Dritten Welt*, vol. 1: Grundprobleme, Theorien, Strategien (Bonn: J.H.W. Dietz).

[45] Wolfgang Zapf (1994): "Wohlfahrtsentwicklung und Modernisierung (1993)," Wolfgang Zapf, *Modernisierung, Wohlfahrtsentwicklung und Transformation:* Soziologische Aufsätze 1987 bis 1994 (Berlin: edition Sigma, 1994), pp. 175-186, quote p. 181.

[46] Wolfgang Zapf (ed.) (1990): *Die Modernisierung moderner Gesellschaften: Verhandlungen des 25. Deutschen Soziologentages in Frankfurt am Main* (Frankfurt/M.: Campus); Roland Robertson (1992): *Globalization: Social Theory and Global Culture* (London: Sage;) Ulrich Beck (1993): *Die Erfindung des Politischen: Zu einer Theorie reflexiver Modernisierung* (Frankfurt/M.: Suhrkamp;) Anthony Giddens (1990): *The Consequences of Modernity* (Stanford, CA: Stanford University Press).

[47] On the special issue of migration in this context, see Mathias Bös (1997): *Migration als Problem offener Gesellschaften: Globalisierung und sozialer Wandel in Westeuropa und Nordamerika* (Opladen: Leske und Budrich).

[48] One of the better treatments spanning scientific and general discussion (despite its title), Benjamin R. Barber (1996): *Jihad vs. McWorld*: How Globalism and Tribalism are Reshaping the World (New York: Ballantine Books).

[49] Jadwiga Staniszkis (1991): "Dilemmata der Demokratie in Osteuropa," Rainer Deppe, Helmut Dubiel, and Ulrich Rödel (eds.), *Demokratischer Umbruch in Osteuropa* (Frankfurt/M.: Suhrkamp), pp. 326-347. In this early, important discussion of the "dilemmas of democracy" in Eastern Europe, Staniszkis distinguishes five such dilemmas which can be summarized as follows: 1) demobilization: the process of transformation was initialized by a process of mobilization, yet for the transformation to continue, for the necessary consolidation to set in, mobilization has to be taken back from above; 2) the ambiguous importance of the state: the state takes on a renewed importance as sole representative of the common interest and initializer of the entire reform process, which also makes new abuses of state power possible; 3) the Russian problem: the process of transformation in Eastern Europe remains within the orbit and within the influence of a new Russian colonial state; 4) the ambiguous solution of the presidency: as an attempt to fill the power vacuum left behind by the communist party, the presidency as institution is rather ill-defined; 5) the restrictive context of reform activity: both internal economic crisis and external economic dependence reduce the options available to the political actors. Obviously, this classification was meant to pertain to the "transition" period immediately following the events of 1989. It is also important to realize that her empirical reference point is the case of Poland, or more generally, the cases of the "velvet revolution" (V. Havel). In our context, the reader should also note the concern about Russia and the emphasis on the responsibility of western politicians for the caution of western investors in her discussion. Both points are powerful Leitmotifs of the Eastern reform discourse; the latter now slightly

tampered by the realization that capitalist investment is not something that western politicians can command. Of course, there is also an added problem here which already brings us around to the point of our argument: in the present context, western politicians have a hard time making the case for investments abroad as something beneficial to their respective constituents; in some cases, such as Germany's, more investments at home (no matter what the source) are sought after. In the German context, the entire debate on investment is further complicated by the domestic West-East divide: it is still the case that investment in the East of Germany (again: no matter what the source!) is not seen as investment in Germany, period, but rather as "aid" (which, in the perverse logic of "public investment," it is).

50 As with so many German terms, is, too, is virtually untranslatable. "Social politics" is rather awkward. I have borrowed the term from the social reporting (social indicators, social structure) literature, although even there the term leads a rather underground existence. See for example Roland Habich and Heinz-Herbert Noll with Wolfgang Zapf (1994): *Soziale Indikatoren und Sozialberichterstattung: Internationale Erfahrungen und gegenwärtiger Forschungsstand* (Bern: Bundesamt für Statistik der Schweiz).

51 Wolfgang Merkel (1996): "Institutionalisierung und Konsolidierung der Demokratie in Ostmitteleuropa," Wolfgang Merkel, Eberhard Sandschneider and Dieter Segert (eds.), *Systemwechsel 2: Die Institutionalisierung der Demokratie*, (Opladen: Leske und Budrich, 1996), pp. 73-112; Olivier Blanchard, Kenneth A. Froot, and Jeffrey D. Sachs (eds.) (1994): *The Transition in Eastern Europe*, vol. 2: Restructuring (Chicago: University of Chicago Press).

52 However, as Catherine Durandin has pointed out, in the light of the region's multi-ethnic past, the exclusivism of nationalism can (should) be seen as "a betrayal of tradition"; Catherine Durandin (1994): "Occidentalistes et Nationalistes en Europe Central et Orientale: De la Guerre Froide à la Guerre Chaude," *L'autre Europe*, nos. 28-29, pp. 105-114.

53 George Schöpflin, "Central Europe: Definitions Old and New," George Schöpflin and Nancy Wood (eds.), *In Search of Central Europe*, pp. 7-29. That such a discovery has to include Russia should not even deserve a special mention.

FRANCISCO ENTRENA

# SOCIO-ECONOMIC RESTRUCTURINGS OF THE LOCAL SETTINGS IN THE ERA OF GLOBALIZATION

## 1 INTRODUCTION: FROM LOCALISM TO THE GLOBALIZATION OF LOCAL SPACE

In every society and every era, socio-economic practices are continually under way to organize, manage or restructure the territorial space as a place for people to live and for production. In other words, this space is the result of social processes of construction, deconstruction and reconstruction.[1] Localism was a common feature of such processes in all traditional societies. These were a heterogenous mosaic of more or less isolated, highly diversified and plural socio-spatial units, with virtually independent economies untouched by exogenous influences. Each one of these units was characterized by cultural homogeneity and by ways of life inextricably linked to a space, closed as it was to outside influences, all of which nurtured autarchy, conservatism, traditionalism, ethnocentrism and, altogether, narrow localist visions of socio-economic problems and processes. This gave rise to a cyclical and unfaltering concept of time, life and the course of cosmic phenomena, whose stability was seen in the transformations of the natural world with each coming of the seasons and in the everyday sequence of birth, growth, death and regeneration of all living material.[2] In its turn, this meant that the processes of formation and reproduction of society usually occurred within its own specific territory and people's everyday life ran its course in a local spatial scenario. In this space there developed the socialization process which molded people's ways of thinking, attitudes or behavior patterns; their habitus, indeed, which placed and identified them socially in relation to self and others.[3] There was usually a clear correspondence between the spatial field, in which the socio-vital activity of the population was enacted, and the symbolic-cultural framework which determined people's behaviourial habitus, as the latter usually developed within the former. This explains the localist character usually manifested by this habitus.

Stability, conservatism and isolation, so typical of local spaces in the past, contrast sharply with the instability, the high degree of bonding with the rest of society and the usual socio-economic restructuring processes of the spaces of today. At the present time, people's everyday socio-vital activity still takes place in spatially or socially



*G. Preyer, M. Bös (eds.), Borderlines in a Globalized World, 217-228.*

localizable settings (for instance, even those who travel extensively usually have a fairly restricted and identifiable circle of family and acquaintances). Even so, the genesis of their habitus is ever more conditioned by socio-economic, politico-institutional and cultural processes alien to their immediate setting and beyond their control, as their everyday spatial and personal setting tends to lose its traditional localist character and is swept into the whirl of globalization. In this context, as we shall discuss in the following pages, we are seeing socio-economic restructurings of local settings which manifest themselves in processes which are heading towards their deterritorialization or deborderization and attempts at their reterritorialization or reborderization.

## 2 APPROACH TO GLOBALIZATION: FROM THE DECLINE OF THE ETHNOCENTRIC IDEA OF PROGRESS TO THE RISK SOCIETY

The term globalization has become very popular over the present decade. Here we use this term to refer to the fact that the whole of the world's population is now immersed in a single global society.[4]

In fact, globalization is not so very recent, for it may be said of the process set in motion during the Renaissance by Western European society which began to spread its socio-productive and organizational patterns all over the world. These were considered ethnocentrically as a paragon of civilization and progress. Globalization was under way when Columbus set out on his voyage which would lead him to America, or, less Eurocentrically, when the Chinese carried out their explorations and commercial expansion in the tenth century.[5] The conquest and colonization of South America by Spain and Portugal and of North America by Britain and France were also examples of the gradual propagation of Western economic, institutional and socio-economic paradigms all over the world, that is, globalization. Later, several colonizations at the end of the XIX and the beginning of the XX centuries, by a handful of European powers, of virtually the whole of the African continent, as well as huge areas of Asia, Latin America and Oceania were all part of the globalization process.

Decolonizations after the Second World War saw the emergence of numerous new independent countries, together with great expectations for their economic and socio-political development.[6] Modernization theories provided the sociological framework with which to explain and promote this development. As is well known, these theories as well as several criticisms of them (the most outstanding of which are the theories of dependence, unequal exchange and center-periphery),[7] retained a conception of development as a tacit continuation of the globalization processes which had begun almost five centuries before with the gradual worldwide expansion of the Western economic, institutional and socio-cultural model. Today, however, when we refer to globalization, we do not mean Westernization, but a completely new situation in which we are seen a worldwide spreading in all directions of processes and economic flows, at the same time as groupings of interests and networks of social or institutional relations of a transnational character are tending to consolidate.

All this gives rise to global interconnections which create meshes of political decisions and effects interwoven between states and their citizens, which affect the nature and action of national political systems.[8] We have moved from a society which operated largely at a nation-state level to one which acts economically, institutionally and socio-culturally on a planetary scale.

As a consequence of present globalization processes, we are coming to a time when it is not single states, but groups of states, that is to say, humanity as a whole, that will constitute the determining social unit, the model of what we understand by society, and therefore, the point of reference for many scientific studies. Humanity is immersed in a process of global integration. Societies are becoming more and more interdependent and interconnected. Humanity is no longer simply a set of statistical data or a philosophical category; it has become a real social unit in itself, a whole integrating all the world's population.[9]

The gradual transition towards more complex, global relations and institutional and socio-economic organization, is gradually eroding from above the sovereignty of states as well as their capacity for action. In this new transnational scenario, we now can speak of the existence of an unique world system[10], something that has not happened even in the most recent past, for, as Peter Worsley points out, a single human society has never existed until our time.[11] The social unit which serves as a point of reference for many phenomena of development and structural change is no longer particular states, but humanity divided into states.[12]

This situation comes hand in hand with the gradual decline in the ethnocentric idea of progress which inspired previous globalization processes such as Westernization, and in it, according to Lipovetsky[13], the sense of historical continuity has been lost. For some authors, such as Vattimo[14] or Lipovetsky himself, this has laid the foundations of a new age which is breaking away completely from modernity and which they call postmodernity. This society lives in and for the present. In it:

> confidence and faith in the future dissolve, no-one believes in the future of the Revolution and progress, people want to live in the "here" and "now," striving after quality of life and personalized culture. In the social sense, attention is turned towards the self, and individual and corporative narcissism is rife. The individual only has eyes for him/herself or his/her group.[15]

The truth is that postmodern theorists have not succeeded in leaving modernity behind. Rather they have defined their position in relation to it. Here I agree with Albrow[16] in that the much-heralded end of history has not come. The only thing that has happened is that modernity has been replaced by globality. Nor does Beck, Giddens and Lash's reflexive modernization concept[17] share the apocalyptic vision of history put forward by those authors who embrace the postmodern point of view. For these authors, the present world situation is not a crisis, but shows the victory of capitalism which has evolved and produced new social forms. These are the result of modernity's tradition of criticism and rupture, which has given way to its radicalization, casting off the mores and premises on which industrial society was based and paving the way towards another modernity.[18]

In this new modernity, which is to be found in the present era of globalization and is the result and cause of it at one and the same time, the Western version of the modern urban-industrial paradigm is no longer the almost universally sought-after goal. It is no longer that target on the horizon of change on a worldwide scale that was so characteristic of the idea of progress inherent in Eurocentric unilinear evolutionism which inspired and legitimized past forms of globalization. At the present time, the idea that there are many routes and targets possible in the change towards modernization has become widespread. Today, social evolution is explained from multilinear viewpoints.[19] So we may speak of multiple modernities in this era of globalization.[20] This opens the doors to pluralism and tolerance but also to relativism and uncertainty.

Giddens has called our time an age of manufactured uncertainty[21], as to a large extent it is the result of human action. For his part, Beck has referred to ours as a risk society.[22] As opposed to the "classical" dangers and risks (natural catastrophes, managerial or financial bankruptcies, wars, and so on) which are reasonably easy to foresee, there are now new risks that are difficult to predict, that virtually no-one is answerable to and which open scenarios of irreparable damage (a case in point is the nuclear accident at Chernobyl). It is not just that we do not know how to get things right any more: we cannot even forecast with any precision how far we will get them wrong.

Little wonder, then, that there are feelings of helplessness, uncertainty and lack of confidence both individually and collectively, made even more intense by the hectic pace of socio-economic changes and the high degree of reflexivity in today's world. In fact, all societies are reflexive, for they are made up of human subjects, be they individuals or groups, whose very nature is to continually discuss, reflect upon, react to and rethink the social situation in which they find themselves.[23] In traditional local societies, social reflexivity had relatively little impact, however, and economic, social and institutional processes were fairly easy to manage and predict because they were carried out in a local, regional or nation-state spatial setting. This setting knit society together, and it was perceived as a unified entity, like a fabric or a web.[24]

However, the constant mobility of people, ideas and commodities all around the world that present-day globalization entails, means that society's self-image, as well as the preferences and expectations of individuals or different local populations, greatly diversify and become ever more unstable, unpredictable and often contradictory and conflicting. In this situation, the capacity of intense social reflexivity to bring about unforeseen effects on social actions, increases so much that social, economic and institutional processes become highly erratic and volatile and, consequently, very difficult to control. It is responsible for the never-ending rearticulation and reformulation of all attempts at regulating these processes. One of the results all this is that people are gradually losing control over the far-reaching socio-economic processes which determine the organization and running of the local spatial settings in which they live from day to day. So there emerges a deborderization of directives governing the local, and, as we shall see in the next session, this could be conceived as deterritorialization.

## 3 THE DETERRITORIALIZATION OF THE LOCAL

In contrast to the localism of traditional societies, in our globalized ones, ease of communication tends to make us forget what is happening on our doorstep and turns our attention to what is going on thousands of kilometers away. We are becoming more and more linked to what is distant and alien, and more and more detached from what is near and familiar.[25] In this way, society is undergoing increasing deborderization or deterritorialization of symbolic-cultural points of reference in collective and individual identity. This, in turn, gives rise to feeling of anomie, of apparent involvement with things distant and a sense of not belonging to one's own local setting.

The present-day globalized situation makes it necessary to find a new way of addressing existing sociological models, using the nation-state as an analytical framework, as well as taking into account social spaces and actors above and below this framework.[26] This is because globalization produces, among others, two opposite effects, which nonetheless mutually influence and reinforce each other. These are two tendencies which are society's growing homogenization and integration into the world arena, on the one hand, and the unending quest for local identities, traditions and idiosyncrasies, on the other. If we look towards the first of these trends, globalization could be conceived as the set of processes which lead to a single world.[27] In this way, a kind of world unification comes to the fore, threatening to empty the contents of the contexts of action of specific local or regional spatial settings, whose problems and socio-economic processes are ever more bound up in the unpredictable global skein. Globalization's deterritorializing effects on these settings is shown in people's continuing loss of control over their own destiny, and in the fact that their social and historical significance (what could be conceived as their autochthony) tends to become disassociated from the economic role and function which they generally play in the present global context.[28] In this way, both the socio-productive dynamics and the organization and running of the local develop in line with worldwide interests and decisions taken at extra local level.[29]

As a consequence of all this, many local communities are undergoing a profound crisis. To a large extent the social relations and socio-economic processes which occur in them are determined less and less by social actions and strategies springing from relations among autochthonous classes and are more and more influenced or decided by socio-economic interests or world-reaching arrangements coming from well outside their territorial borderlines. In this way, local places have become a sort of spatial heteropies[30] or heteronomous settings with regard to the very varied and barely predictable rules governing the organization and running of spaces on a worldwide scale.

The gradual deterritorialization or deborderization of the local is also due to the fact that globalization brings with it production and distribution systems which go beyond the local, regional or state-national levels[31] . As a consequence, international economy is no longer the sum of the economies of many nations, but a process interconnecting national economies and involving them in a permanent search for increased efficiency and advantage over competitors. Whereas in times past, the production, processing and consuming of a certain commodity occurred in relatively restricted local, regional or state-national spaces, today this process is tending to become ever more complex, and at the same time, large multinational corporations are casting their nets over the whole planet.

This split between production and territory means that the former often loses its autochthonous character because goods can be imported from afar or marketed far afield, and consequently they are no longer an essential part of the organization or distribution system of the territory from which they spring. This is mainly because increasingly industrialized production processes usually necessitate the involvement of many nations, regions and local communities, whose productive activities are ever more globally homogenized and deterritorialized as far as their organization, running and extension are concerned.

## 4 ATTEMPTS AT RETERRITORIALIZATION: TRENDS TOWARDS THE ASSERTION OF LOCAL PARTICULARISMS

Globalization processes bring about a great variety of consequences and reactions depending on the peculiarities of each specific local context[32] . Even so, at the present time we are seeing certain similar trends which are gathering momentum: these are collective demands and projects aimed at the social rearticulation, economic development or recovery of the socio-demographic vitality of many specific local regions or territories. A variety of attempts at reterritorializing or reborderizing the local are taking place, in the form socio-economic restructuring processes.

As a result of these processes, the sovereignty and manouverability of the state is usually eroded from below. This is because local and regional governments, in an adaptive and reflexive reaction to globalization, are often demanding greater powers of the central government to apply policies to attract investment and increase development and employment, as well as more autonomy in the socio-economic organization and running of their respective territories. This explains the frequent demands on the part of these local governments to negotiate directly with large transnational corporations.

Another expression of these attempts at reterritorialization is the present trend towards fragmentation, diversification and the search for or stressing of local or regional particularisms. To this end, we are seeing the emergence or revival and restructuring of political or sociocultural singularities peculiar to certain territories.

Without doubt, these tendencies towards the reinforcement of the local are due to growing disenchantment with the urban-industrial paradigms of modernity. This often leads to a nostalgia which creates or fans the flames of phenomena such as local nationalism or xenophobia.[33] The considerable spread of these phenomena and the radicalism they sometimes manifest can be interpreted as the expression of reflexive attitudes of particularism and "gut" rejection of the universalizing tendencies of globalization. As Robertson has pointed out, we are now witnessing a kind of "universalism of particularism".[34] This contradicts Parsons[35] for whom societies evolved from particularism to universalism on their way to modernity.

### *4.1 The Local Community as a Development Unit*

Today's tendencies to consider the local community as a development unit may also be interpreted as attempts at reborderization. In this perspective, the pursuit of development may be understood as a local response to the challenges afforded by globalization processes.[36] One of the basic objectives of this response is to avoid the negative effects deriving from these processes: environmental damage, socio-economic disintegration and deterritorialization of local areas. So, often, one of the purposes of development is to contribute to the creation or reinforcement of meshes of social relations in these areas.[37] This, while helping to fortify the local associative fabric, can also have favorable repercussions in the reterritorialization of its space, for it is likely to increase the degree to which its inhabitants take upon themselves the management of the socio-economic and cultural resources of the territory – the territory they feel they belong to, for on it they build their means of socio-economic production and reproduction, their daily lives, their culture and their collective identity.

Behind the present swing towards considering the local community as a development unit, we may give the following reasons:

a) In the face of the present homogenizing and universalizing tendencies of globalization, the above-mentioned attempts at reterritorialization may be understood as strategies, on the part of different social groups, which, although immersed to a smaller or larger extent in the world society, live in specific settings and in this way are trying to find more advantageous roles for themselves in their insertion into the global.

b) Having considerably reduced the socio-economic power margin of the state, globalization has caused the virtual breakdown of the welfare policies, in which governments are hurrying to "throw old commitments overboard".[38] As a result of this, we are witnessing the crumbling of institutionalized social protection systems and the socio-economic conditions which have formed the structural foundations on which people, more or less autonomously, have reached fulfilment as individuals. In these circumstances, macrosocial projects which used to be the mainstay of state policies are now virtually impossible to get off the ground or maintain. This would explain why so many people needing socio-economic and/or existential support, look nostalgically back at the small or medium-sized local community or why we are in the presence of increasing tendencies towards the creation or development of different social movements or other forms of microsolidarity of a primary or group nature. One of the basic aims behind this is to find microsocial territorial settings that are easier to manage and regulate in solving the most immediate socio-economic problems facing the population.

c) The necessity of devising local responses to such phenomena as insecurity felt by the population caused by high levels of unemployment, socio-vital precariousness and uncertainty about the short- and long-term future. The fairly high levels of development we have achieved save us from some traditional insecurities about the world around us, but make us depend on other new ones.[39] Variables such as climate, quantity and/or quality in harvests from one year to the next, drought, illness and local or regional epidemics, which have shaped people's daily life over the millennia have given way to other variables which are the result of ways of action and social relations whose influence are becoming ever more globalized. This is happening in a context in which science is often being used for material gain, and natural resources are being exploited to such an extent that the productive and socio-institutional bases on which social order and human identity are founded are beginning to fall apart. The enormity of the consequences which may ensue from this model of exploitation of natural and human resources has not been fully contemplated. This explains to a large extent why this model is still extant in spite of bringing in its wake social imbalances and inequalities, as well as putting at risk the environment and the human race itself.

Within this risk society, the development options open to local communities could be understood as attempts, put forward by public administrations or cropping up more or less spontaneously, in an effort to find alternative ways to employment and a socio-economic place, as well as create social spaces more conducive to individual and collective fulfilment, based on that sense of vital self-confidence and assurance which comes of knowing that in some measure we can control the variables which will decide our destiny.

## 5 AS A CONCLUSION: SOME PARADIGMATIC CASES OF TRENDS TOWARDS THE LOCAL TERRITORIALIZATION OF SOLIDARITIES

In the face of the growing insolidarity, imbalances, aggravation of socio-economic problems and deterritorialization effects brought about by globalization, then, we are witnessing different attempts at reterritorialization. Regardless of their degree of radicalism or success, these attempts are reflexive adaptive reactions of the local to the global, which consciously or not, are striving towards the reterritorialization or reborderization of many local settings, and therefore trying to regain their social revival, their socio-economic development as a community or even the recovery or buttressing of their local community independence or identity. On occasion, the latter takes on a markedly nationalist character which strengthens group social bonds, which are heavily territorialized or localized in certain spaces. Paradoxically, in this global age, we are experiencing a reversal of what was considered up to now as progress. In this way, universalist individualism, one of the distinctive traits of modern society, is losing ground to community or group social forms, based on particularist and localist solidarities, occupying or orbiting a specific territorial setting, which, as is well known, were prevalent in traditional societies.

These social forms are more or less conscious responses to the growing demands for resuscitating certain aspects of community life – especially the concern for the common good. However, this resuscitation cannot be carried out without falling back on that normative criterion of self-realization and fulfilment which symbolize modernity's individualism.[40]

The present re-emergence of community or group territorialized solidarities is often shown in common social phenomena such as tribes. These may be seen as a reflection of social fragmentation in our times of uncertainty and crisis. As Michel Maffesoli points out[41] , tribes are organized around set phrases, trade names and catchy consumer slogans.

This social tribalism often comes to the surface in the form of youth groups or gangs, whose actions, which are often violent, are usually centered on a specific neighborhood or local or regional community. This is the territory that irrationally they feel they must defend or liberate – it is a substratum on which they build and project their identity as a social group. Indeed, the re-emergence of these tribalisms could be interpreted as one expression of the trends towards the reterritorialization of social bonds and solidarities. In Spain, one example of this is the violence of gangs of youths belonging to the most extreme nationalist sectors in the Basque Country.

Although not tribal in character, other paradigmatic cases of social solidarities, in which territorial bondings stand out over and above class links, are those which sometimes develop in the whole population of certain local or regional communities. The reinforcement of these bondings is usually a response on the part of these communities as a defense against environmental dangers or socio-economic problems affecting their territory which have resulted from directives generally taken far away and having far-reaching effects. In these cases in which the effects of globalization are felt by the whole of the inhabitants of a specific local community, old class differences or animosities tend to be left to one side. In their stead emerge new forms of solidarity in which interclass social protest movements are articulated.

One example of the confluence into a common front of traditionally antagonistic social sectors and classes is to be found in Andalusia. This is an extensive agricultural region covering the whole of the south of Spain, which has great inequalities in the distribution of land-ownership (especially in the west). Although notable modernization, economic growth and development have taken place over the last few decades, the progressive globalization of its socio-economic structure is threatening its agricultural production capacity (there is a crisis of overproduction and tendencies of European agricultural policies to discourage production) and profoundly affecting old local power structures. Globalization is also bringing about polarization and spatial segregations which are modifying traditional relationships between classes and giving rise to new social inequalities. As a consequence, this region is suffering from chronic and worsening unemployment (especially in the agrarian sector), with high levels of illegal employment, poverty and other forms of social exclusion. This explains the concern of the intense social mobilizations experienced during 1998 in Andalusia about the negative effects which may be incurred by the European Agricultural Policies' proposal for modifying the Common Organization of Markets, with its plans to intervene in the olive sector in order to subsidize the number of trees planted to the detriment of production obtained from them. On this occasion, important landowners and their representative organizations joined forces with salaried farmworkers and their unions. The fact that olive oil production is a crucial activity over much of the region, as well as the growing dependence of its whole economy on decisions taken in Brussels, the capital of the relatively global European setting, are obviously the reasons behind this interclass and territorialized unity of social forces in the same struggle.

## NOTES

[1] Nigel Thrift (1996): *Spatial Formations* (Sage Publications / Theory, Culture and Society); see especially: On the Determination of Social Action in Space and Time.

[2] Francisco Entrena (1992): "Cambios en la concepción y en la organización del espacio rural," *Revista de Estudios Regionales* 34: pp. 147-162, pp. 154-155.

[3] Pierre Bourdieu (1989): "Social Space and symbolic power," *Sociological Theory* 7: pp. 14-25.

[4] Martin Albrow (1996): "Introduction,"Martin Albrow and Elizabeth King, eds., *Globalization, Knowledge and Society* (Sage Publications / ISA, London), pp. 3-13, at p. 9.

[5] Alessandro Bonanno (1994): "Globalización de sector agrícola y alimentario: crisis de convergencia contradictoria," Bonanno, Alessandro, ed., *La globalización del sector agroalimentario* (Ministerio de Agricultura Pesca y Alimentación, Serie Estudios, Madrid), pp. 15-49, at p. 17 and following.

[6] Francisco Entrena (1998): "From the credibility crisis of formal organizations to the re-emergence of the group: an ecosystemic approach," *Free Inquiry in Creative Sociology* 26 (1), in press.

[7] Wider approaches to these theories are to be found in Francisco Entrena (1994): "Las nuevas funciones del agro y el desarrollo rural: del productivismo al énfasis en la calidad," *Rivista di Economia Agraria* XLIX (2): pp. 318-337, pp. 323-325. See also Johann Graaff (1996): "Changing ideas in Marxist thought in Southern Africa," Jan K. Coetzee and Johann Graaff, eds., *Reconstruction, Development and People* (International Thomson Publishing, Durban, Southern Africa), pp. 83-105.

[8] David Held (1991): "A Democracia, o Estado-Nacao e o Sistema Global," *Lua Nova* 23: pp. 145-194, p. 179.

[9] Piotr Sztompka (1995): *Sociología del cambio social* (Alianza Editorial, Madrid), p. 111.

[10] For an insight into the dynamic and disruptive nature of this world system, Immanuel Wallerstein's definition is very useful in, El moderno sistema mundial. La agricultura capitalista y los orígenes de la economía-mundo europea en el Siglo XVI, Volume I (Siglo XXI editores, Madrid, 1984.) This author conceives the world system as a social system, a system which has limits, structures, groups, members, rules for legitimation and coherence. Its life springs from of conflicting forces which keep it together by tension and pull it apart inasmuch as each one of the groups strives ceaselessly to model it for its own benefit (p. 489.)

[11] Peter Worsley (1984): *The Three Worlds*: Culture and World Development (Weidenfeld and Nicolson, Londres), p. 1.

[12] Norbert Elias (1990): *La sociedad y los individuos* (Península, Barcelona), p. 188 and following.

[13] Gilles Lipovetsky (1990): *La era del vacío*. Ensayos sobre el individualismo contemporáneo (Anagrama, Barcelona), p. 51.

[14] Gianni Vattimo (1986): *El fin de la modernidad*, Nihilismo y hermenéutica en la cultura posmoderna (Gedisa, Barcelona), see especially the Introduction and the first session "El nihilismo como destino."

[15] Josep Picó (1988): *Modernidad y posmodernidad* (Alianza Editorial, Madrid), p. 37.

[16] Martin Albrow (1996): *The Global Age*. State and Society Beyond Modernity (Polity Press / Blackwell Publishers Ltd., Great Britain), see especially the Introduction and chapter 9.

[17] Ulrich Beck, in Ulrich Beck, Anthony Giddens and Scott Lash (1995): *Reflexive modernization* (Polity Press, Cambridge); especially chapters 1 and 4.

[18] Ulrich Beck, in Ulrich Beck, Anthony Giddens and Scott Lash (1995): *Reflexive modernization* (Polity Press, Cambridge) p. 3.

[19] See Julian Steward (1979): *Theory of culture change* (Urbana: University of Illinois Press). For this author, XX century research has gleaned overwhelming evidence to suggest that particular cultures diverge significantly from one another and do not pass through unilinear stages (p. 28.)

[20] Here I am using the very appropriate title of the 34th International Congress to be held at the International Institute of Sociology, University of Tel-Aviv (Israel), from 11th to 15th of July, 1999.

[21] Anthony Giddens (1996): *Más allá de la izquierda y la derecha*. El Futuro de las políticas radicales (Ediciones Cátedra, Madrid), pp. 13 and 85.

[22] Ulrich Beck (1992): *Risk Society*. Towards a New Modernity (Sage Publications, London.) As is well known, the crux of Beck's argument is that risk has become a central and defining element of today's society, in such a way that "while in classical industrial society the 'logic' of wealth production dominates the 'logic' of risk production, in the risk society this relationship is reversed" (p. 12.)

[23] See Emilio Lamo de Espinosa (1990): *La sociedad reflexiva.* Sujeto y objeto del conocimiento sociológico (Centro de Investigaciones Sociológicas / Siglo XXI editores, Madrid.) According to this author, "human beings... have the double capacity to think about themselves and their situation (i.e. to produce/create ethnoscience) and to learn what others say about them and their situations (i.e., to speak and to read)" (p. 166.)

[24] Daniel Bell (1977): *Las contradicciones culturales del capitalismo* (Alianza Universidad, Madrid). This author points out (pp. 21-22) that this vision of society as a fabric or spider's web, as a more or less closed system, was deeply embedded in the XIX century imagination. It has also been implicit in some of the theoretical sociological developments of this century, for example in the writings of such outstanding authors as Parsons.

[25] Emilio Lamo de Espinosa (1996): *Sociedades de Cultura y Sociedades de Ciencia.* Ensayos sobre la condición moderna (Ediciones Nobel, Oviedo), pp. 136-138.

[26] Rafael Pardo (1992): "Globalización, cambio disciplinar y teoría sociológica: Notas metodológicas para una Sociología del Sistema Mundial," Carlos Moya, Alfonso Pérez-Agote, Juan Salcedo y José Felix Tezanos, eds., *Escritos de Teoría Sociológica.* En Homenaje a Luis Rodríguez Zúñiga (Centro de Investigaciones Sociológicas, Madrid), pp. 865-914, at p. 911.

[27] Roland Robertson (1992): "Globality, global culture and images of world order," Haferkamp y Smelser, eds., *Social Change and Modernity* (Berkeley, University of California Press), pp. 395-411, at p. 396.

[28] Manuel Castell (1987): "Technological change, economic restructuring and the spacial division of labour," H. Muegge, Walter B. Stöhr, P. Hesp and B. Stuckey, eds., *International Economic Restructuring and the Regional Community* (Avebury, Great Britain), pp. 45-63, at p. 58.

[29] Alessandro Bonanno and Karen Bradley (1994): "Spatial Relations in the Global Socio-Economic System and the Implications for Development Planning," David Symes and Anton J. Jansen, eds., *Agricultural Restructuring and Rural Change in Europe* (Agricultural University Wageningen, Netherlands), pp. 49-64, at p. 63.

[30] Here I take, though not literally, Henri Lefebvre's (1976) terminology in, *La revolución urbana* (Alianza Editorial, Madrid). Lefebvre uses the term heterotopy of space to express his conception of the other place, as against the same place, which he considers to be isotopy (p. 45.)

[31] William H. Friedland (1994): "Globalization, the State and the Labor Process," *International Journal of Agriculture and Food* 4: pp. 30-46, p. 30.

[32] Juan Pablo Pérez Sáinz, "Entre lo global y lo local. Economías comunitarias en Centroamérica," *Sociología del Trabajo* 30: pp. 3-19, p. 3.

[33] Anthony Giddens (1996): *Más allá de la izquierda y la derecha.* El Futuro de las políticas radicales (Ediciones Cátedra, Madrid), p. 88.

[34] Roland Robertson (1993): *Globalization.* Social Theory and Global Culture (Sage Publications, London), chapter 6.

[35] Talcott Parsons (1976): *El sistema social* (Revista de Occidente, Madrid), see especially chapter 11.

[36] alter B. Stöhr, ed. (1990): *Global Challenge and Local Response.* Initiatives for Economic Regeneration in Contemporary Europe (London / New York: The United Nations University), see especially the "Synthesis" and the "Introduction."

[37] Manuel Pérez Yruela y Mª del Mar Giménez (1994): "Desarrollo local y desarrollo rural: el contexto del programa 'Leader'," *Papeles de Economía Española* 60-61: pp. 219-233, p. 225.

[38] Xan Bouzada (1995): "Elementos teóricos relativos al desarrollo comunitario local y a su práctica en la comunidad autónoma de Galicia," *Papers Revista de Sociología* 45: pp. 81-100, p. 83.

[39] Emilio Lamo de Espinosa (1996): *Sociedades de Cultura y Sociedades de Ciencia.* Ensayos sobre la condición moderna (Ediciones Nobel, Oviedo), p. 137.

[40] Alessandro Ferrara (1997): "The paradox of Community," *International Sociology* 12 (4): pp. 395-408, pp. 400, 404 and 405.

[41] Michel Maffesoli (1995): *The Time of the Tribes*: The Decline of Individualism in Mass Society (Sage Publications / Theory, Culture and Society), see especially: Foreword by Rob Shields, "Masses or Tribes, The Emotional Community: Research Arguments and Sociality versus the Social, and Tribalism."

# INDEX





*G. Preyer, M. Bös (eds.), Borderlines in a Globalized World, 229-238.*

# CONTRIBUTORS

Axford, Barrie, Prof. ; Department of Politics; Oxford Brookes University; Headington Hill Hall; Oxford OX3 OBP; United Kingdom.

Bös, Mathias, Dr.; Institut für Soziologie; Lehrstuhl für Soziologie II; Ruprecht Karls-Universität Heidelberg; Sandgasse 7-9; 69117 Heidelberg; Germany.

Chase-Dunn, Christopher, Prof.; Department of Sociology; Johns Hopkins University; Baltimore; MD 21218; USA.

Davies, Christie, Prof.; Dept of Sociology, ; University of Reading, ; Whiteknights, ; Reading RG6 6AA, Great Britain.

Eisenstadt, Shmuel, Prof.; Van Leer Jerusalem Institut; The Hebrew University of Jerusalem; Faculty of Social Sciences; PO 4070; Jerusalem 91040, Israel

Entrena, Francisco, Dr.; Departamento de Sociología; Universidad de Granada; 18071 - Granada; Spain.

Gerhardt, Uta, Prof.; Institut für Soziologie; Lehrstuhl für Soziologie II; Ruprecht Karls-Universität Heidelberg; Sandgasse 7-9; 69117 Heidelberg; Germany.

Hall, Thomas D., Prof. ; Department of Sociology; DePauw University; 100 Center Street; Greencastle, IN 46135, USA.

(Hohenester, former) Soultanian, Birgitta, Dr.; Pädagogische Hochschule Heidelberg, Keplerstraße 87, D-69120 Heidelberg.

Lee, Richard E., Ph. D.; Fernand Braudel Center; SUNY-Binghamton; Binghamton, NY 13902-6000; USA.

Preyer, Gerhard, Dr. habil.; Fachbereich Gesellschaftswissenschaften; Johann Wolfgang Goethe – Universität; Frankfurt am Main; Germany.

Trivizas, Eugene, Dr.; Dept of Sociology; University of Reading; Whiteknights; Reading RG6 6AA, Great Britain.

Wagner, F. Peter, Ph. D.; Institut für Politikwissenschaft; Karl-Glöckner-Str. 21/E; Justus-Liebig Universität Gießen; 35394 Gießen; Germany.

# Social Indicators Research Series

1. V. Møller (ed.): *Quality of Life in South Africa.* 1997 ISBN 0-7923-4797-8
2. G. Baechler: *Violence Through Environmental Discrimination.* Causes, Rwanda Arena, and Conflict Model. 1999 ISBN 0-7923-5495-8
3. P. Bowles and L.T. Woods (eds.): *Japan after the Economic Miracle.* In Search of New Directories. 1999 ISBN 0-7923-6031-1
4. E. Diener and D.R. Rahtz (eds.): *Advances in Quality of Life Theory and Research.* Volume I. 1999 ISBN 0-7923-6060-5
5. Kwong-leung Tang (ed.): *Social Development in Asia.* 2000 ISBN 0-7923-6256-X
6. M.M. Beyerlein (ed.): *Work Teams: Past, Present and Future.* 2000 ISBN 0-7923-6699-9
7. A. Ben-Arieh, N.H. Kaufman, A.B. Andrews, R. Goerge, B.J. Lee, J.L. Aber (eds.): *Measuring and Monitoring Children's Well-Being.* 2001 ISBN 0-7923-6789-8
8. M.J. Sirgy: *Handbook of Quality-of-Life Research. An Ethical Marketing Perspective.* 2001 ISBN 1-4020-0172-X
9. G. Preyer and M. Bös (eds.): *Borderlines in a Globalized World.* New Perspectives in a Sociology of the World-System. 2002 ISBN 1-4020-0515-6

KLUWER ACADEMIC PUBLISHERS – DORDRECHT / LONDON / BOSTON

MIX
Papier aus verantwortungsvollen Quellen
Paper from responsible sources
FSC® C105338

If you have any concerns about our products,
you can contact us on
**ProductSafety@springernature.com**

In case Publisher is established outside the EU,
the EU authorized representative is:
**Springer Nature Customer Service Center GmbH**
**Europaplatz 3, 69115 Heidelberg, Germany**

Printed by Libri Plureos GmbH
in Hamburg, Germany